ORLANDO

RICHARD GRULA
JIM & CYNTHIA TUNSTALL

EYEWITNESS TRAVEL

Left **Mennello Museum** Center **Drag queen diva** Right **Merritt Island National Wildlife Refuge**

917,5924
or 71 2
2014

Produced by Departure Lounge, London
Printed and bound by South China Printing Co. Ltd
First American Edition, 2002
14 15 16 17 10 9 8 7 6 5 4 3 2 1
Published in the United States by
Dorling Kindersley Limited, 80 Strand, London
WC2R 0RL, UK
Reprinted with revisions
2004, 2006, 2008, 2010, 2012, 2014
Copyright 2002, 2014
© Dorling Kindersley Limited

A catalog record for this book is available from
the Library of congress.

ISSN 1479 344X
ISBN 978-1-46540-277-6

Within each Top 10 list in this book, no
hierarchy of quality or popularity is
implied. All 10 are, in the editor's
opinion, of roughly equal merit.

MIX
Paper from
responsible sources
FSC
www.fsc.org   FSC™ C018179

Contents

Orlando's Top 10

The Magic Kingdom® Park   8

Epcot®   12

Disney Hollywood Studios®   16

Disney's Animal Kingdom®
Park   18

Islands of Adventure®   20

Universal Studios
Florida®   24

SeaWorld® Orlando   28

Wet 'n Wild®   34

Merritt Island   36

Kennedy Space Center   38

Thrill Rides   42

Smaller Attractions   44

Ways to Have Fun on
the Cheap   46

Places to Cool Off   48

Parks & Preserves   52

The information in this DK Eyewitness Top 10 Travel Guide is checked regularly.
Every effort has been made to ensure that this book is as up-to-date as possible at the time of
going to press. Some details, however, such as telephone numbers, opening hours, prices,
gallery hanging arrangements and travel information are liable to change. The publishers
cannot accept responsibility for any consequences arising from the use of this book, nor for
any material on third party websites, and cannot guarantee that any website address in this
book will be a suitable source of travel information. We value the views and suggestions of
our readers very highly. Please write to: Publisher, DK Eyewitness Travel Guides,
Dorling Kindersley, 80 Strand, London WC2R 0RL, UK, or email travelguides@dk.com.

COVER: Front - Alamy Images: Greg Balfour Evans, Main; **Dorling Kindersley**: Stephen Whitehorn clb.
Spine - **Alamy Images**: Ian Dagnall b. Back - **Alamy Images**: Dennis MacDonald ca; **Dorling Kindersley**:
Stephen Whitehorn cra; **Getty Images**: Stone / Doug Armand cla.

Left **One Ocean™ show at SeaWorld®** Center **Universal Studios®** Right **Gatorland**

Golf Courses	54	Day Trips West	82
Sports & Outdoor Activities	56	Day Trips North & East	84
Spas	58		
Museums	60	**Around Orlando**	
Cultural Venues & Organizations	62	Walt Disney World® Resort & Lake Buena Vista	88
Festivals & Events	64	International Drive Area	96
Places to Shop	66	Kissimmee	106
High-End Restaurants	68	Downtown Orlando	112
Family Restaurants	70	Winter Park, Maitland, & Eatonville	118
Places to Have a Drink	72		
Live Music Venues	74	**Streetsmart**	
Hip Clubs	76	Practical Information	126
Gay & Lesbian Hangouts	78	Places to Stay	142
		General Index	150
Dinner Shows	80	Street Index	160

Left **SeaWorld® Orlando** Right **Kennedy Space Center**

Key to abbreviations
Adm admission charge payable, **DA** disabled access

3

ORLANDO TOP 10

Orlando Highlights
6–7

The Magic Kingdom®
Park 8–11

Epcot®
12–15

Disney Hollywood
Studios®
16–17

Disney's Animal
Kingdom® Park
18–19

Islands of Adventure®
20–23

Universal Studios
Florida®
24–27

SeaWorld® Orlando
28–33

Wet 'n Wild®
34–35

Merritt Island
36–37

Kennedy Space Center
38–41

ORLANDO'S TOP 10

🔟 Orlando's Highlights

One word describes Orlando's transformation in the last three decades: stunning. The city and its suburbs have gone through a Cinderella-like metamorphosis, where plain Jane has become a worldly beauty. Millions of tourists are seduced every year by sophisticated resorts, a wide range of theme parks, must-see attractions, happening nightclubs, and winning restaurants. Here are the Top 10 Orlando sights – Orlando's best of the best.

1 The Magic Kingdom® Park
The park that started Disney's Florida empire combines fantasy, adventure, and the future in a package of rides and shows that focuses on Disney movies and TV programs. *See pp8–11.*

2 Epcot®
Inquiring minds love this Disney park, which features technology in Future World and the culture, architecture and enticing food of 11 nations in World Showcase. *See pp12–15.*

3 Disney Hollywood Studios®
Lights, camera, action! Movies, TV shows and stomach-churning thrill rides come together in a theme park that sometimes also serves as a working studio. *See pp16–17.*

4 Disney's Animal Kingdom® Park
Visitors are brought face to face with the wild world of animals, but this kingdom's spacious environmental design doesn't always offer a front-row seat. *See pp18–19.*

5 Islands of Adventure®
Universal's star theme parks recreate the exciting worlds of Harry Potter, Transformers, and the Simpsons' Springfield. Be warned that 9 of its 13 rides have height or health restrictions, so it's not for the young, weak of stomach, or squeamish. *See pp20–23.*

Previous pages **Incredible Hulk Ride, Islands of Adventure®**

6 Universal Studios Florida®
What Disney can do, Universal can equal. The movie and TV themes here can make people's wildest dreams come true or worst nightmares (special effects) a reality. From Transformers to Terminator, the silver screen comes to life. *See pp24–7.*

7 SeaWorld® Orlando
Its laid-back pace, educational angle, and animal actors make this a popular stop for those wanting a break from the lines and stifling crowds at other parks. *See pp28–31.*

8 Wet 'n Wild®
Some say it's hard to beat Disney's water parks, but this rival has the most thrills money can buy on the city's water scene. *See pp34–5.*

9 Merritt Island
Located at the Kennedy Space Center, this wildlife refuge is great for learning about local and migrating animals, while also enjoying a bit of fishing or hiking. *See pp36–7.*

10 Kennedy Space Center
The appeal of man in space has turned America's No. 1 space center into a stellar attraction complete with live rocket launches and exhibits. *See pp38–41.*

For more on the Top 10 sights in Orlando **See pp42–85**

The Magic Kingdom® Park

Walt Disney's first Florida theme park opened in 1971, envisaged as a place where dreams could come true, even if only for a little while. It took six years and $400 million to create "Disneyland East," which has surpassed Walt's own dream: instead of being a spin-off of California's Disneyland® Park, it has become the USA's most popular theme park, attracting more than 17 million visitors every year (some 40,000 each day). Although little has changed in 40 years, with more than 40 major attractions and countless minor ones, this is a true fantasy land for the young and young at heart.

○ A smoked turkey leg at Tomorrowland's Lunching Pad makes a good quick bite, but it's cheaper to bring your own snacks and water (bottles can be filled at the park's numerous fountains).

◑ FastPass *(see p132)* cuts the amount of time spent standing in line for the park's most popular rides and shows.

Guests of Disney resorts get extra time in the parks with the "Extra Magic Hour" program: each day one park opens an hour earlier or closes 3 hours later.

Visit midweek, as the park is at its busiest on weekends and early in the week.

Smoking is only allowed in designated outside areas.

◉ World Drive • Map F1 • 407-824-4321 • www. disneyworld.com • Open at least 9am–7pm daily, call for seasonal hours. • Adm (1-day ticket): adults $101.18, children (3–9) $89.47 (including tax). Children under 3 go free.

Top 10 Attractions

1. Splash Mountain®
2. Big Thunder Mountain Railroad
3. Peter Pan's Flight
4. Space Mountain®
5. Stitch's Great Escape™
6. Buzz Lightyear's Space Ranger Spin
7. The Many Adventures of Winnie the Pooh
8. Prince Charming Regal Carousel
9. Seven Dwarfs Mine Train
10. Pirates of the Caribbean®

Splash Mountain®
Disney's 1946 film *Song of the South* inspires this wildly popular flume ride, with Brer Rabbit leading the way through swamps, caves, and "the Laughing Place." Expect twists, turns, and a 52-ft (16-m), 45-degree, 40-mph (64-kmph) climax.

Big Thunder Mountain Railroad
Not the raciest of coasters, but the turns and dips, and realistic scenery, combine to make this an exciting trip on a runaway train through gold-rush country *(above)*.

Peter Pan's Flight
A flying pirate galleon soars over the sights of London and arrives in Never Land, where Peter Pan battles Captain Hook to save Wendy and her brothers.

Space Mountain®
Orlando's first in-the-dark roller coaster is a ride on a rocket that shoots through hairpin turns and drops at what feels like breakneck speed, although top speed is only 28 mph (45 kmph). The cosmic effects and detail enhance this thrilling ride.

Stitch's Great Escape™
This family-friendly adventure is based on the mayhem of Stitch's experiment in outer space. The ride uses sophisticated technology, with sights, sounds, and smells to add to the pandemonium.

6 Buzz Lightyear's Space Ranger Spin

Use the laser cannons on the dashboard to set off sight-and-sound effects as you hurtle through the sky and help *Toy Story's* most famous hero save the world.

7 The Many Adventures of Winnie the Pooh

Pooh, Eeyore, and a whole host of A. A. Milne's lovable characters come to life in this tranquil ride through the Hundred Acre Wood.

Magic Kingdom® Park Plan

8 Prince Charming Regal Carousel

This wonderfully refurbished 1917 carousel is a real beauty. It has handsome wooden horses and an organ that plays Disney classics. Kids love it, and adults love reminiscing about the rides of yesteryear.

9 Seven Dwarfs Mine Train

An exciting addition to Fantasyland®, Seven Dwarfs Mine Train is a twisty, high-speed rollercoaster trundling through the Enchanted Forest and the dwarves' deep diamond mines.

10 Pirates of the Caribbean®

Timbers are a-shiver as your boat cruises past a town under siege from a band of rum-soaked, Audio-Animatronic buccaneers. Dank dungeons, yo-ho-ho's, and brazen wenches – all scurvy pirate life is here.

Park Guide

Due to the crowds and distance involved, it takes around 20 minutes to get from the parking lots (via tram, boat, or monorail) to the park's attractions. Once inside, the Tip Board at the end of Main Street USA has the latest information on the length of lines and times of shows. Park maps are available from Guest Services to the left of the entrance. You'll need at least a day or parts of several to get the most out of the Magic Kingdom®.

Attraction number		1	2	3	4	5	6	7	8	9	10
Minimum height:	(inches)	40	40	–	40	40	–	–	–	–	–
	(cm)	102	102	–	102	102	–	–	–	–	–
Recommended age group		8+	9+	all	9+	9+	all	all	all	3+	3+
Duration (minutes)		10	4	3	3	15	5	4	2	3	8

For information on Disney's tour options See p129

It's a Small World

🔟 Shows & Next Best Rides

Wishes Nighttime Spectacular

This explosive show runs nightly during summer and holidays (occasionally at other times of the year). Liberty Square, the main gates, and Frontierland® are the best areas in the park to take in the fabulous display. If you want to view from outside the Magic Kingdom®, Disney's Grand Floridian, Polynesian, Contemporary, and Wilderness Lodge resorts all have good views from upper floors.

Walt Disney World® Railroad

The antique steam-driven trains that travel this 1.5-mile (2-km) perimeter track offer a good overview of the park's sights, but more importantly allow you to get from A to B without the legwork. The 20-minute ride stops at City Hall, Main Street USA®, and Frontierland®.

Cinderella Castle

Standing 185 ft (56 m) high, this park icon is a sight to behold. Complete with Gothic spires, it's the quintessential fairytale castle, reminiscent of Neuschwanstein, mad King Ludwig of Bavaria's creation. Inside, there's only one thing of interest to visitors, the Cinderella's Royal Table restaurant, where guests can partake of a character breakfast (see p71).

The Magic Carpets of Aladdin

This four-passenger carpet ride lets the rider glide gently up and down and from side to side around a giant genie's bottle. Watch out for the sneaky, water-spitting camels.

It's a Small World

The insidious theme song will eat at your brain for months

after you visit, but small kids adore this slow-boat cruise through "lands" where small, Audio-Animatronic, costumed characters sing *It's a Small World After All* in their Munchkin-like voices.

Hall of Presidents
6 Every US president has an Audio-Animatronic likeness in this fascinating educational show that really highlights the wizardry of Walt Disney Imagineers (designers). The presidents nod and wave, and Abe Lincoln is the keynote speaker.

Mickey's PhilharMagic
7 Disney magic meets Disney music in a 3-D film spectacular starring Mickey Mouse, Donald Duck, and other favorite Disney characters animated in a way never seen before. Set in the PhilharMagic concert hall in Fantasyland®.

Haunted Mansion
8 A corny yet fun special-effects show with a cult following. It's a slow-moving, slightly scary ride-in-the-dark that passes a ghostly ball, graveyard band, and weird flying objects.

Monsters Inc. Laugh Floor
9 "Monster of Ceremonies" Mike Wazowski brings his furry comedian friends to the digital stage in this kid-friendly comedy club. Audience members help power the city of Monstropolis with their laughter.

Magic Kingdom® Park Plan

Country Bear Jamboree
10 Audio-Animatronic bears croon and bellow songs in this knee-slapping revue. The finale has the audience hooting and clapping for an encore.

Magic Kingdom® Parades
During summer (and occasionally at other times of the year) a key park event is the evening parade (times vary). The original show was the Main Street Electrical Parade, which was christened at California's Disneyland® Park before moving to the Magic Kingdom® in 1977. Its replacement is the bigger, better, and brighter SpectroMagic. This electrifying, 20-minute extravaganza brings fountains, creatures, and floats filled with Disney characters to "light". It has no less than 204 speakers cranking out 72,000 watts, uses 75 tons of batteries (enough to power 90 houses for the duration), and 100 miles (160 km) of fiber-optic cable. The whole show is powered by 30 mini-computers. Arrive early and try to find a spot in front of the castle. If you can't stay until dark falls, there's a 15-minute Share the Dream Come True Parade (3pm daily) where guests can see their favorite Disney characters in a procession that leaves from Frontierland® to finish off down Main Street USA®.

Attraction number	1	2	3	4	5	6	7	8	9	10
Recommended age group	all	all	all	3+	3+	8+	all	8+	all	all
Duration (minutes)	20	20	–	3	11	30	15	8	–	17

10 Epcot®

Walt Disney imagined Epcot® (Experimental Prototype Community of Tomorrow) as a futuristic township where people could live, work, and play in technologically enhanced splendor. After his death in 1966, the idea changed dramatically, and Epcot® opened in 1982 as a park of two halves: Future World focuses on science, technology, and the environment, while World Showcase spotlights the cultures of several nations. The pairing works because both sections are educational and appeal to curious adults and kids alike. Be warned, the park is vast, a fact that has led some to joke that its name is an acronym for "Every Person Comes Out Tired."

🐠 Future World: the Coral Reef in the Living Seas Pavilion is way better than most in-park restaurants *(see p95)*. Book ahead. World Showcase: Try fresh pastries at the Patisserie in the French Pavilion.

🎢 Use FastPass *(see p132)*, a ride reservation system.

Save time and energy by using the shuttle boats to cross from Future World to the World Showcase.

This theme park is best toured in two days, if not more.

✪ Epcot Center Dr, Walt Disney World® Resort • Map G2
• 407-824-4321
• www.disneyworld.com
• Future World: Opens 10am–7pm daily; World Showcase: Opens 11am–9pm daily. Hours are often extended during holidays and in summer months.
• Adm: adults $95.85, children (3–9) $89.46 (including tax). Children under 3 go free.

Top 10 Future World Exhibits

1. Test Track
2. Innoventions East
3. Innoventions West
4. The Seas with Nemo & Friends
5. Ellen's Energy Adventure
6. Journey into Imagination with Figment
7. Soarin'
8. Mission: SPACE®
9. Spaceship Earth
10. Living with the Land

Test Track
This ride takes you through the tests carried out on automobile prototypes before they hit the consumer market. Riders get to experience brake tests, S-curves, and a 12-second, 65-mph (104-kmph) burst of speed. You must be at least 40 inches (102 cm) tall.

Innoventions East
A refrigerator that can compile a grocery list and a toilet seat with a built-in warmer are among the "smart" furnishings in the House of Innoventions exhibit. Kids like this pavilion's Internet Zone with games such as virtual tag.

Innoventions West
Few can resist Video Games of Tomorrow, a Sega presentation that lets visitors try out next generation games. In the same pavilion, Medicine's New Vision is an exhibit that offers video games along a medical theme.

The Seas with Nemo & Friends
Board a "clamobile" and join your undersea pals to find Nemo. In the same pavilion is the interactive show "Turtle Talk with Crush," also inspired by the same Pixar film.

Ellen's Energy Adventure
A show-and-ride focusing on themes from "fossil fuel" dinosaurs to future energy concerns.

6 Journey into Imagination with Figment

An open house at Dr. Channing's Imagination Institute is turned inside out by Figment, a playful purple dragon who causes chaos and leads the tour through his upside-down house.

7 Soarin'

Feel the exhilarating rush of this free-flying hang-gliding adventure over the magnificent landscapes of California *(below)* . You must be 40 inches (102 cm) tall to take this ride.

Epcot® Park Plan (Future World)

8 Mission: SPACE®

This popular thrill ride takes you on a journey to space with a crash landing on Mars. It is intense and not for anyone prone to motion sickness, or sensitive to tight spaces, loud noises or spinning. If you don't go on the "Mission" you can enjoy interactive games at the "Advance Training Lab."

Park Guide

The main entrance is convenient for Future World, where nine pavilions encircle Spaceship Earth. Getting to World Showcase Lagoon and the 11 nations beyond requires a longer trek, though handy boat shuttles run from Showcase Plaza to the pavilions of Germany and Morocco. A second entrance, at International Gateway, is accessible from Disney's Yacht Club, Beach Club, and BoardWalk Inn resorts. Maps that give up-to-date show information are available at both entrances.

9 Spaceship Earth

The ride inside is nothing to write home about. But this giant golf ball – actually a 180-ft (55-m) geosphere– is an engineering marvel, made of 11,324 triangular aluminum panels that absorb the rain rather than letting it run off.

10 Living with the Land

The best of the vast Land Pavilion's exhibits involves a boat ride through rain forest, desert, and prairie biomes. It's followed by a look at agricultural experiments including hydroponics and growing plants in simulated Martian soil.

Attraction number	1	2	3	4	5	6	7	8	9	10
Recommended age group	8+	8+	8+	all	all	all	8+	12+	all	all
Duration (minutes)	5	–	–	30	32	6	5	45	17	13

For science on a smaller scale at the Orlando Science Center See p60 &p113

Overview of World Showcase Pavilions

World Showcase Pavilions

Canada

1 The star attraction here is the inspirational 360-degree CircleVision film, *O Canada!*, which reveals some of the country's scenic wonders. You also get to experience traveling by dogsled. Outside, Canada's rugged terrain is convincingly re-created. Gardens that are based on Victoria's Butchart gardens, a replica of an Indian village, and the Northwest Mercantile store, selling items such as tribal crafts and Canadian maple syrup, can be explored.

China

2 The CircleVision movie, *Reflections of China*, is a fascinating journey through China's natural and man-made riches. The pavilion features a 15th-century Ming dynasty temple, a ceremonial gate, and tranquil gardens. The Yong Feng Shangdian Department Store *(see p92)* is a wonderful treasure trove of Asian goodies. Try not to miss the dynamic Dragon Legend Acrobats who perform several times each day.

Morocco

3 Look for the Koutoubia minaret, a copy of the tower from a 12th-century mosque in Marrakesh, and you've found this exotic pavilion. Inside, the typical souk architecture is embellished by beautiful carvings and mosaics. The Casbah marketplace *(see p92)* is bursting with hard-to-resist crafts sold by "merchants," and you can see carpets being woven on looms. "Local" cuisine such as couscous is available in the Pavilion's restaurant *(see p95)*.

American Adventure

4 Enhance your knowledge of US history in a 30-minute dramatization featuring Audio-Animatronic actors. Mark Twain and Benjamin Franklin are the narrators who explain key events, including the writing of the Declaration of Independence, and Susan B. Anthony speaks out for women's rights. The Voices of Liberty singers perform in the main hall of the pavilion, which is modeled on Philadelphia's Liberty Hall.

Japan
A breathtaking five-story pagoda, based on Nara's 8th-century Horyuji temple, forms the centerpiece of this architecturally amazing pavilion. The traditional Japanese gardens are pretty impressive, too, and a perfect spot to escape the throngs. The peace and quiet is only occasionally broken by the beat of drums: go investigate: the Matsuriza troupe is one of the best shows in Epcot®.

Norway
Norway's Maelstrom ride takes you on a 10-minute journey through fiords and fairy-tale forests in a dragon-headed vessel. You land in a 10th-century Viking village, where a short film portrays Norway's natural treasures. The realistic replica of Oslo's 14th-century Akershus Castle houses the restaurant *(see p95)*.

United Kingdom
Examples of typical British architecture through the ages line the quaint cobblestone streets here. Apart from shops selling quintessential British merchandise

Future World

Epcot® Park Plan (World Showcase)

(teas, china, crystal, and more), there's also a park with a bandstand and a roaming improv troupe providing entertainment.

Mexico
El Rio del Tiempo (River of Time) is an eight-minute multimedia boat ride that explores Mexico's past and present, from the Yucatan's Mayan pyramids (the pavilion is housed in a replica of one) to the urban bustle of Mexico City life. Mariachis entertain, and there's a *plaza* with stalls selling colorful souvenirs such as sombreros, *piñatas*, and leather goods.

France
This pavilion sports scale replicas, including the Eiffel Tower, and shops selling French products. The 18-minute, five-screen film, which sweeps through glorious landscapes accompanied by the music of French composers is a highlight.

Germany
In this cartoon-like, archetypal German village, you'll find a miniature model railroad, including a wonderfully detailed Bavarian Village. The Biergarten restaurant (complete with brass band) serves traditional food, and shops sell everything from Hummel figurines to wines and cuckoo clocks.

IllumiNations
Created to celebrate the millennium, Epcot®'s stunning fireworks and laser show is still thrilling visitors every night at 9pm. It is a grand half-hour, sound-and-vision nightcap which also brings the World Showcase Lagoon fountains into the act. There are scores of good viewing places all around the edge of the Lagoon.

Disney Hollywood Studios®

Like Universal Studios®, Disney Hollywood Studios® underscores Orlando's standing as a small, but growing, film production center and offers an up-close look at the world of "Lights! Camera! Action!". The park cost $300 million to create and the result is an effective fusion of fun and information; the attractions tend to be complex, involving rides, shows, and educational commentary, so there really is something for everyone. Nostalgic references to Hollywood's heyday are balanced by high-tech trickery, making this a must for anyone with even a remote interest in the movies.

A hand-dipped ice-cream cone at Hollywood Scoops slides down a treat, but for more substantial refreshment, try the Sci-Fi Dine-In Theater, serving diner fare in a 1950s retro setting, where guests can watch B-movie clips.

Use FastPass *(see p132)*, a ride reservation system, to cut the amount of time spent standing in line for the most popular rides and shows.

As in all Disney parks, smoking is only allowed in designated outdoor areas.

Backstage Magic Tour, a 6–8-hour tour behind the scenes at Disney Hollywood Studios®, Epcot®, and Disney World®, is available by calling 407-939-8687.

⊛ Epcot Resorts Blvd
• Map G2
• 407-824-4321
• www.disneyworld.com
• Open at least 9am–7pm, sometimes later
• Adm: adults $95.85, children (3–9) $89.46 (including tax), children under 3 go free.

Top 10 Attractions

1 Rock 'n' Roller Coaster® Starring Aerosmith
2 Twilight Zone Tower of Terror™
3 Fantasmic!
4 Indiana Jones™ Epic Stunt Spectacular
5 Muppet™ Vision 3-D
6 Studio Backlot Tour
7 The Legend of Captain Jack Sparrow
8 Star Tours
9 Beauty and the Beast Live on Stage
10 Voyage of the Little Mermaid

1 Rock 'n' Roller Coaster® Starring Aerosmith

A sign warns, "prepare to merge as you've never merged before," but by then it's far too late. Your limo zooms from 0 to 60 mph (97 kmph) in 2.8 seconds and into multiple inversions as Aerosmith blares at 32,000 watts *(above)*.

2 Twilight Zone Tower of Terror™

The spooky surroundings are a facade in front of the real terror, a gut-tightening, 13-story fall. To many, it's Disney's best thrill ride.

3 Fantasmic!

Lasers, fireworks, waterborne images, and a sorcerer mouse are the stars of this end-of-day extravaganza that pits the forces of good against Disney villains such as Cruella De Ville and Maleficent. Performance times vary seasonally.

4 Indiana Jones™ Epic Stunt Spectacular

Indy's action-packed day is full of thrills and spills, and near-death encounters. A stunt co-ordinator explains how it's all done.

5 Muppet™ Vision 3-D

Miss Piggy, Kermit, and the rest of the crew star in a show celebrating both Henson's legacy and Disney's special-effects wizardry and audio-animatronics.

For another movie-flavored theme park See pp24–7

Studio Backlot Tour
What begins as a tram tour through movie sets and the prop department ends at Catastrophe Canyon. Here, explosions, floods, and fire give riders a bit of a shake-up before getting to see behind the Canyon's scenes.

The Legend of Captain Jack Sparrow
Tour Davey Jones' Locker, the deck of the Black Pearl, and other highlights from all four *Pirates of the Caribbean* movies with animatronic characters and a disembodied pirate skull as a guide.

Entrance

Disney Hollywood Studios® Park Plan

Star Tours
Climb in and swallow hard: your 40-seat spacecraft is going on a journey riddled with dips, bumps, and laser fire. The *Star Wars*–inspired show is presented in digital 3-D video with a flight-motion simulator.

Park Guide

Pick up a map from Guest Services, to the left of the entrance. Staff are on hand to help you find your way around and provide information. The tip board at Sunset and Hollywood boulevards lists up-to-the-minute information on show schedules, wait times, visiting celebrities, and ride or show closures. This park tends to be less busy at the beginning of the week, when many visitors hit the Magic Kingdom® or Epcot®, and it can easily be tackled in one day.

Beauty and the Beast Live on Stage!
The music from the animated film alone is enough to sell this Broadway-style show. The sets, costumes, and production numbers are pretty spectacular, too.

Voyage of the Little Mermaid
This show uses cartoons, live characters and Audio-Animatronics, as well as special effects with lasers and water to create an underwater grotto. Young children may find the lightning storm scary.

Attraction number		1	2	3	4	5	6	7	8	9	10
Minimum height:	(inches)	48	40	–	–	–	–	–	40	–	–
	(cm)	122	101						101		
Recommended age group		9+	9+	all	all	all	all	all	8+	all	all
Duration (minutes)		3.5	4.5	30	40	25	35	15	10	30	17

🔟 Disney's Animal Kingdom® Park

As the name implies, wildlife rules at the latest addition to Disney's empire of fun, which is home to over 1,700 animals and around 250 species spread across 500 acres (200 hectares) of lush landscape. Here, the serious issue of conservation is combined with the playfulness of a theme park, though critics complain that the landscaping makes it hard to see the animals, especially in the hottest parts of the day. There's compensation in the fact that the park has some enthralling shows, rides, and attractions reflecting conservation and nature at Disney.

🍴 Restaurantosaurus (*see p71*) serves up kid-friendly fast food for lunch and dinner.

🐾 The best times to see the animals are as soon as the park opens and within an hour of it closing, especially during the hot months (May–Sep).

Use FastPass (*see p132*), a ride reservation system that helps cut the amount of time spent standing in line for the most popular rides and shows.

As in all Disney parks, smoking is allowed only in designated outdoor areas.

🚩 Savannah Circle, Walt Disney World Resort
• Map G1
• 407-824-4321
• www.disneyworld.com
• Open at least 8am–6pm, sometimes 7am–7pm. Call for seasonal hours.
• Adm: adults $95.85, children (3–9) $89.46 including tax. Children under 3 go free.

Top 10 Attractions

1. Kilimanjaro Safaris®
2. Pangani Forest Exploration Trail®
3. Festival of The Lion King
4. Kali River Rapids®
5. Maharajah Jungle Trek®
6. The Tree of Life
7. It's Tough to Be a Bug!®
8. Finding Nemo – The Musical
9. DINOSAUR
10. The Boneyard®

1 Kilimanjaro Safaris®

The park's most popular ride *(right)* puts you on a large safari jeep to bump along dirt tracks looking for black rhinos, lions, zebras, and more. You're reminded that it's a theme park, though, as a staged adventure unfolds – guests have to save the elephants from "poachers". The animals are real, but that baobab tree was made by Disney's Imagineers.

2 Pangani Forest Exploration Trail®

As you're surrounded by thick vegetation, it's sometimes hard to see the animals on this walk-in-the-woods with a difference. The gorillas are the main attraction, but if the stars of the show prove shy, there are also hippos, exotic birds, and weird-looking mole-rats.

3 Festival of The Lion King

One of Orlando's best shows won't fail to throw you into the spirit of things when it gets going. This production uses singers, dancers, and *The Lion King*'s popular score to emphasize nature's diversity.

4 Kali River Rapids®

The park's conservation message is evident on this exciting raft ride, which passes from a lush landscape to one in the process of being scorched for logging. You need to be 38 inches (96 cm) tall or more to ride, and like to get wet!

For other Disney sights and attractions **See pp88–91**

Maharajah Jungle Trek®
The giant Old World fruit bats, some with man-sized wingspans, are easily spotted, but the Bengal tigers are elusive when it's hot. You might also see Komodo dragons, tapirs, and deer on this atmospheric Asian stroll.

The Tree of Life
The park's symbol is this 145-ft (44-m) tall tree created by Walt Disney Imagineers. Look carefully: there are 325 mammals, reptiles, amphibians, insects, birds, dinosaurs, and Mickeys carved into its trunk, limbs, and roots.

Disney's Animal Kingdom® Park Plan

It's Tough to Be a Bug!®
Located inside the Tree of Life's 50-ft (15-m) base, this 3-D, effect-filled show offers a view of the world from an insect's perspective. The climax is sure to make an impression.

Finding Nemo – The Musical
The Theater in the Wild is transformed into an enchanted undersea world for this original stage show, which merges puppetry with live performances. The show lasts for 30 minutes.

DINOSAUR
Expect to be shaken up on this wild ride, which takes you back 65 million years. Convincing animatronic dinosaurs lurk in the darkness. There's a 40-inch (102-cm) minimum height requirement.

The Boneyard®
Possibly the best of its kind in any of the Disney parks, this playground is a perfect place for kids to burn off surplus energy. The play area is built around the "remains" of dinosaurs. It's both educational and fun.

Park Guide

The park, which is Walt Disney World® Resort's largest, is divided into six zones: Oasis (the entrance area); Discovery Island (with the Tree of Life at its center); and the lands of Camp Minnie-Mickey (the main children's zone), Africa, Asia, and Dinoland USA® radiating out from it. Maps are available at Guest Relations, at the entrance to the park.

Attraction number	1	2	3	4	5	6	7	8	9	10
Recommended age group	all	all	all	8+	all	all	all	all	9+	3 to 12
Duration (minutes)	14	–	28	5	–	–	7	30	4	–

For another conservation-oriented park See pp28–31

Islands of Adventure®

Orlando didn't have a lot to offer adrenalin junkies until Universal unveiled its second Central Florida park in 1999. Billed as the "world's most technologically advanced theme park," no local rivals can touch Islands of Adventure®'s (IOA) thrill power and innovation (although Tampa's Busch Gardens [see p82] is also highly rated by thrill-seekers). With terrifying roller coasters, three heart-stopping water attractions, and stunningly creative rides, it is the place to head for those who like to live dangerously.

Green Eggs and Ham Café

● Go on. Try a green eggs and ham sandwich at the Green Eggs and Ham Café.

◐ The Universal Express system (see p132) cuts the amount of time spent standing in line for the most popular rides and shows.

Some of the park's rides have shorter lines for single guests and couples willing to split up.

During thunderstorms, the park's plentiful outdoor rides close.

◉ Hollywood Way • Map T1 • 407-363-8000 • www.universalorlando.com
• Open at least 9am–7pm, call for seasonal hours.
• Adm: adults $97.98, children (3–9) $91.59 (including tax), children under 3 go free.
• One-day tickets can be upgraded to a two-day pass if you find you want to spend another day in the park.

Top 10 Attractions

1. Incredible Hulk Coaster®
2. The Amazing Adventures of Spider-Man®
3. Doctor Doom's Fearfall®
4. Pteranodon Flyers®
5. Jurassic Park River Adventure®
6. Flight of the Hippogriff™
7. Harry Potter and the Forbidden Journey™
8. Dragon Challenge®
9. Poseidon's Fury®
10. The Cat in the Hat™

The Amazing Adventures of Spider-Man®
Slap on 3-D glasses and battle the baddies while fireballs and other high-definition objects fly at you. The experience is amazing *(below)*.

Doctor Doom's Fearfall®
This ride climbs 200 ft (61 m), before dropping and pausing at several levels to maximum thrilling effect.

Pteranodon Flyers®
Eye-catching metal gondolas swing from side to side on this prehistoric bird's-eye tour around the park's Jurassic Park zone.

Incredible Hulk Coaster®
You blast out of the darkness at 40 mph (64 kmph), go weightless, and endure seven inversions and two drops during this white-knuckle ride *(below)*.

Jurassic Park River Adventure®
This ride starts slowly but quickly picks up speed as some raptors get loose *(below)*. To escape you will have to take an 85-ft (26-m), flume-style plunge.

Flight of the Hippogriff™
This family-friendly Harry Potter-themed coaster introduces you to the Hippogriff and takes you on a training flight over the Forbidden Forest, Hagrid's Hut, and Hogwarts grounds.

Harry Potter and the Forbidden Journey™
Walk through the gates of Hogwarts to board this ride and encounter a horde of Dementors and a quidditch match.

Islands of Adventure® Park Plan

Park Guide

Despite the elevators and moving sidewalks, it can still take 20 minutes to get to the attractions from the parking lot. Try to arrive early; if you are staying in a Universal Resort, you can get in before other visitors and enjoy the benefits of free Universal Express access, which allows you to skip long lines by showing your room key. Other visitors can buy a Universal Express Plus Pass from as little as $20 plus tax.

Dragon Challenge™
These two floorless coasters do five rollovers and come within 1 ft (30 cm) of each other no less than three times. If you are really coura-geous, go for seats in the front row.

Poseidon's Fury®
Visitors tour the ruins of the ancient Temple of Poseidon before passing through a swirling vortex of water and looking on as all hell breaks loose when Poseidon and Zeus have an almighty battle.

The Cat in the Hat™
Hold on as your couch spins and turns through 18 Seussian scenes. The Cat, Thing One, and Thing Two join you on a ride through a day that's anything but ordinary.

Attraction number		1	2	3	4	5	6	7	8	9	10
Minimum height:	(inches)	54	40	52	36	42	36	48	54	–	–
	(cm)	137	102	132	91	107	92	122	137	–	–
Recommended age group		9+	8+	10+	7+	9+	9+	9+	9+	all	8+
Duration (minutes)		2	4	0.5	1.5	6.5	2	5.5	2.5	6	5

Left **One Fish, Two Fish....** Center **Dudley Do-Right** Right **Jurassic Park® Discovery Center**

🔟 Gentler Attractions

1 One Fish, Two Fish, Red Fish, Blue Fish™
Fly your fish up, down, and all around on an aerial carousel ride just 15 ft (4 m) off the ground. If you don't do what the song says, you'll get sprayed with water.

2 Caro-Seuss-El™
This merry-go-round replaces the traditional horses with interactive versions of Dr. Seuss's cowfish, elephant birds, and mulligatawnies. Regular carousels will never seem the same again.

3 If I Ran the Zoo
The 19 interactive stations in this Seussian playground use features such as flying water snakes, caves, and water cannons, and include a place to tickle the toes of a Seussian critter.

4 Jurassic Park® Discovery Center
See through a dinosaur's eyes, match your DNA to theirs, and watch an animatronic velociraptor "hatch" in the laboratory. There are several interactive stations, where kids can brush up on their dinosaur facts.

5 The Mystic Fountain
Make a wish at this fountain in Sinbad's Village. This wonderful fountain is interactive and is surprisngly playful, asking questions of and teasing guests. Watch out that it doesn't spray you, so don't stand too close.

6 Camp Jurassic
Burn off energy in an adventure playground full of places to explore, including dark caves where "spitters" (small dinosaurs) lurk. See if you can find out how to make dinosaurs roar.

Triceratops Discovery Trail

7 Me Ship, The Olive
The play area here is full of interactive fun, while Cargo Crane offers an alternative hands-on experience: a chance to fire water cannons at riders on Popeye & Bluto's Bilge-Rat Barges *(see p21)*.

8 High in the Sky Seuss Trolley Train Ride!™
Follow the story of the Sneetches™ on this gentle ride above the attractions of Seuss Landing.

9 The Eighth Voyage of Sinbad Stunt Show
This show is filled with stunts, giant flames, and explosions, as Sinbad hunts for lost treasure.

10 Storm Force Accelatron®
Dizziness is the name of the game as you and X-Men superhero Storm spin your vehicle fast enough to create electrical energy that will send the evil Magneto to the great beyond.

Top 10 Facts

1. Steven Spielberg produced the 3-D films shown in Spider-Man.
2. Spider-Man's screens are up to 90 ft (27 m) wide.
3. The 15-Hz square audio wave shock used in Spider-Man is a frequency low enough to make humans sick.
4. Each "Scoop" on the Spider-Man ride actually only moves 12 inches (30 cm) up or down.
5. Dragon Challenge™'s two dragons travel at up to 60 mph (96 kmph) and 55 mph (88 kmph) respectively.
7. Dragon Challenge™'s structure is 3,200 ft (975 m) long and can handle 3,264 riders per hour.
8. At 3,180 ft (969 m), the Dragon Challenge™ line is the longest in the world.
9. The Hulk is 3,700 ft (1.1 km) long and can handle 1,920 riders per hour.
10. The Hulk's G-force is the same as that experienced in a F-16 fighter jet attack.

IOA's "State-of-the-Future" Rides

Guests at Islands of Adventure® (IOA) get a first-hand demonstration of some of the most technologically advanced coasters and attractions ever created. At the top of the list is The Amazing Adventures of Spider-Man® (see p20), which took half a decade and more than $100 million to develop and was then upgraded in 2012. New digital film technologies had to be invented for the convincing floor-to-ceiling 3-D images that are projected to a moving audience. The "Scoop" motion simulator, wind cannons, and pyrotechnics are precision-synchronized by a vast computer network. Computers also play a big part in the Dragon Challenge™ (see p21). They calculate the weight of every passenger load, then adjust the speed and departure sequence in order to maximize thrills on this dual coaster. Unique to the Incredible Hulk Coaster® (see p20) is a thrust system that blasts cars out of a tunnel instead of the usual long, slow haul to the top of an incline. But even with all these high-tech innovations, some low-tech touches can't be avoided. Just below the Hulk stretches a huge net designed to catch personal belongings that fall from screaming riders.

The Incredible Hulk

Riders experience zero-gravity inversions as they are spun upside down at 110 ft (33 m) above the ground before dropping 105 ft (32 m) at more than 60 mph (96 kmph).

The Amazing Adventures of Spider-Man®

Universal Studios Florida®

Universal's first park in Florida opened in 1990, with movie-themed rides and shows, and a mission to steal some of Disney Hollywood's limelight. But it is only since a revamp that the park has really taken off, due largely to the runaway success of the hugely popular Men in Black™ Alien Attack, Terminator 2®: 3-D, and the child-friendly Woody Woodpecker's KidZone.

The Universal globe

🔵 Don your movie star shades and grab a pastry and a cappuccino at the Beverly Hills Boulangerie.

🔵 The Universal Express ticket *(see p132)* lets you cut the amount of time spent in lines for the most popular rides and shows.

VIP tours *(see p129)* help beat the crowds during peak periods.

Note that some rides don't open until around 11am.

🔵 *1000 Universal Studios Plaza*
• *Map T1*
• *407-363-8000*
• *www.universalorlando.com*
• *Open at least 9am–7pm but call to check seasonal hours.*
• *Adm: adults $97.98, children (3–9) $89.46 (including tax), children under 3 go free.*

Top 10 Attractions

1. Terminator 2®: 3-D
2. The Simpsons Ride™
3. Men in Black™ Alien Attack
4. Twister – Ride It Out®
5. Shrek 4-D™
6. Transformers: The Ride-3D
7. Disaster!
8. Despicable Me
9. Hollywood Rip Ride Rockit®
10. Revenge of The Mummy®

Men in Black™ Alien Attack

You and your "alienator" must keep the intergalactic bad guys from taking over the world as you spin through the streets, looking to shoot the monstrous bugs *(below)*.

Twister – Ride It Out®

The special effects make you feel as if a tornado is sucking the air out of the room as a 5-story funnel cloud really does make cows fly. Rated PG-13.

Terminator 2®: 3-D

Live stage action, six 8-ft (2.4-m) robots, and an amazing three-screen, 3-D film *(below)* combine for a stunning, action-packed show (PG-13).

The Simpsons Ride™

Swoop, soar, and smash your way through Krustyland on a motion simulator ride with Bart and the rest of the US's favorite cartoon family.

Shrek 4-D™

See, hear, and feel the action in "OgreVision" as Shrek and Donkey set off to rescue Princess Fiona from Lord Farquaad.

For Universal's sister park, Islands of Adventure, See pp20–23

Despicable Me
6 Explore the lair and secret lab of super-villain Gru in this interactive 3-D digital adventure. Laugh as riders are transformed into minions and taken to a minion-inspired dance party.

Universal Studios Florida® Park Plan

Disaster!
7 This interactive ride gives visitors a walk-on role in some of the world's worst disasters, from fires and floods to earthquakes and subway accidents.

Park Guide

It takes about 20 minutes to get from the parking lot to the attractions. Once inside, if you feel disoriented, park hosts can advise you on how best to get from A to B. If you are staying at a Universal hotel, make use of the early admission perk; if you haven't got that option, try to arrive an hour before the park opens and hit the major rides first. The park tends to be quietest midweek, and the crowds seem to evaporate when it rains, so this park is a good bet in bad weather. While it's mostly a built up mix of soundstages, backlots, sets, and shops, there are some green areas in which to take time out.

Transformers: The Ride-3D
8 Be a part of the smashing, explosive action of this thrilling ride, based on the popular Transformers movies, which includes 60-ft (18-m) tall high-definition 3D robots.

Hollywood Rip Ride Rockit®
9 Riders choose their own music soundtrack for this 65-mph (105 km/h) coaster, Orlando's tallest, towering 17 stories above Universal, and can buy a dvd of their ride to take home.

Revenge of The Mummy®
10 This high-speed roller-coaster propels guests through Egyptian tombs to face their fears. "Dark ride" scenes and a revolutionary induction track ensures its popularity.

Attraction number		1	2	3	4	5	6	7	8	9	10
Minimum height:	(inches)	–	40	42	–	–	40	–	–	51	48
	(cm)		102	107			102			130	120
Recommended age group		all	8+	8+	8+	8+	8+	8+	8+	13+	8+
Duration (minutes)		23	4	4	18	20	5	5	4	2	4

For more attractions in the International Drive area See pp96–9

Left **A Day in the Park with Barney™** Right **Beetlejuice's Graveyard Revue™**

TOP 10 Shows & Kids' Stuff

1 Fear Factor Live
Do you have the nerve to participate in this extreme audience participation show? Perform all kinds of stunts as you compete against other guests. Unscripted and unpredictable.

2 Beetlejuice's Graveyard Revue™
Dracula, Wolfman, Frankenstein, and Beetlejuice rock the house with music and pyrotechnic special effects in an 18-minute show. Rated PG-13.

3 Curious George Goes To Town
Follow in the footsteps of that mischievous monkey Curious George at this interactive playground, which offers water-based fun and an arena with thousands of soft sponge balls.

4 Blues Brothers
Non-purist fans of this film, who don't need to see John Belushi and Dan Ackroyd in the key roles, will enjoy this foot-stomping 20-minute revue.

5 Animal Actors on Location
This creative animal show features wild, wacky, and occasionally weird live and video animal action. Expect plenty of audience participation.

6 Woody Woodpecker's Nuthouse Coaster®
Very similar to the Barnstormer ride in Disney's Magic Kingdom® *(see p8)*, this 55-second ride for the young (and timid adults) has just one corkscrew curve.

7 E. T. Adventure®
Everyone's favorite extra-terrestrial takes guests on a bike ride to save his planet. Peddle through strange landscapes to meet Tickli Moot Moot and other characters that Steven Spielberg created for this ride.

8 A Day in the Park with Barney™
The puffy purple dinosaur is adored by preschool kids, so this 25-minute sing-along show is guaranteed to get small fans into a frenzy. Everyone else should probably steer clear.

9 Fievel's Playground®
This partially hidden water playground has a house for kids to explore and a mini water slide, for which the line is often painfully slow.

Fievel's Playground®

10 Universal Orlando®'s Horror Makeup Show
A hilarious and educational look at special effects makeup used in the movies. Explore the secrets with movie-clips, props, and demonstrations.

For Orlando's best dinner shows See pp80–81

Top 10 TV Shows and Films made at Universal Studios Florida®

1. Family Feud
2. Ace Ventura Jr: Pet Detective (2009)
3. Beethoven's Big Break (2008)
4. Psycho IV (1990)
5. Problem Child 2 (1991)
6. Matinee (1992)
7. The Waterboy (1998)
8. Hoover (1998)
9. House on Haunted Hill (1999)
10. Held for Ransom (2000)

Behind the scenes

Universal Studios Florida® is more than just a tourist attraction. Since opening in 1990, it has also been the production site for thousands of television shows, commercials, music videos, and movies. While TV and film production has been scaled back in favor of theme park rides and live entertainment (such as Blue Man Group at the Sharp Aquos Theatre), there are still five working sound stages, two broadcast studios, casting and makeup services, post-production editing facilities, and various backlot film sets, including re-creations of New York streets, Hollywood Boulevard, a fishing village, and many others. Though these areas are not normally open to the public, if park guests want to be part of some camera action, they can join the studio audience when TV shows shoot episodes at Universal. Tickets for these productions are typically distributed free of charge on the day of taping. Visitors can check in advance with Guest Services to find out if special-event TV shows will be taped during their visit. There are also regular presentations that give a behind-the-scenes look at the movie-making process.

Star Spotting

Universal Studios doesn't just allow you to "ride the movies." Here, you get to meet the stars, too. Actors playing a whole host of silver-screen and TV legends – including Marilyn Monroe, Scooby-Doo, SpongeBob SquarePants, and the Simpsons – can be seen around the park (especially in the Front Lot) and are always willing to pose for photos.

Hollywood Boulevard, Universal Studios Florida®

TOP 10 SeaWorld® Orlando

Opened in 1973, SeaWorld® Orlando is the city's third major attraction. But its unique marine wildlife focus and educational goals puts it in a league all of its own. Guests can get up close and personal with killer whales, sea lions, manatees, rays, and a host of other watery creatures. During 2012 and 2013, SeaWorld® is undergoing a major redevelopment, so some attractions may not be open.

Journey to Atlantis® ride

⭐ **For lunch, head to Sharks Underwater Grill.** This upscale restaurant offers fish and seafood and allows diners to eat under water, surrounded by creatures of the deep.

🎫 **Get a Quick Queue ticket for special access (see p132).**

Beat the heat with mid-day visits to air-conditioned indoor attractions.

Didn't bring a stroller? Rent one at the Children's Store. Two-way radios can also be rented at the maps & education building.

🌐 7007 SeaWorld Dr
• Map T5
• 407-351-3600
• www.seaworldorlando. com/seaworld/fla
• Opens 9am, closes between 5pm and 10pm (depending on the season)
• Adm: adults $97.98, children (3–9) $89.46 (inclusive of tax). Children under 3 go free.

Top 10 Attractions

1. Dolphin Cove
2. Wild Arctic®
3. Kraken®
4. Journey to Atlantis®
5. One Ocean™
6. Shark Encounter
7. Antarctica
8. Pacific Point Preserve
9. Manta
10. A'Lure

2 Wild Arctic®

An impressive and chilly re-creation of the Arctic, with ice walls nearly a half-inch thick. See polar bears *(below)*, beluga whales, harbor seals, and walruses. Guests can opt to "arrive" by a simulated helicopter ride, but the line will be longer.

3 Kraken®

Billed as the "tallest, fastest, longest, and only floorless roller coaster in Orlando," Kraken® is a fearsome thrill. It takes riders up 15 stories, spins them upside down seven times, and goes under water, all at speeds up to 65 mph (104.6 kmph).

1 Dolphin Cove

The joyful spirit of "Flipper" lives on with these playful bottlenose dolphins *(below)*, which romp at the edge of the lagoon where they can be petted.

4 Journey to Atlantis®

The big draw of this flume ride is a 60-ft (18-m) drop, but the surprise bonus is the twisting roller coaster section near the end. Everyone should expect to get wet, especially those in the front of the car.

5 One Ocean™

This show features SeaWorld®'s majestic killer whales playing, leaping, and interacting with each other and their trainers, all set to an original musical score.

For more watery fun in Orlando See pp48–9

SeaWorld® Orlando Park Plan

Shark Encounter

Here, thanks to the world's largest underwater acrylic tunnel, you can stand six inches (15 cm) from a toothy shark and glide on a people-mover through a world of slithery eels, pufferfish, and sleek barracuda.

Antarctica: Empire of the Penguin

Explore the world of penguins in vehicles over the 4-acre (2-ha) "South Pole". You can see the birds up close.

Pacific Point Preserve

On the surf-drenched rocks of this re-created California coast, hundreds of sea lions and seals cavort and squall in a deafening, endless request for lunch.

Park Guide

Upon arrival, grab a map/event schedule at the Information Counter, and plan your visit according to the live shows you wish to see. The thrill rides – Wild Arctic®, Kraken®, and Journey To Atlantis® – have the longest lines, so visit those when major live shows are taking place. Finally, consider visiting in the late afternoon and evening. Lines vanish, temperatures cool, and the park takes on a different character under the evening sky.

Manta

This thrilling ride combines education and fun, with floor-to-ceiling aquariums and a unique roller coaster (left) that allows you to spin, glide, and soar like a manta ray.

A'Lure

Taking place at the Nautilus Theater, this exciting show features flying performers, aerial tumblers, and silk yo-yo artists. It narrates the tale of the mythical sea sirens, who were said to use their hypnotic song to lure sailors to a watery grave by causing them to shipwreck.

Left **Dolphin Nursery** Right **Shamu's Happy Harbor**

☺10 Shows & Other Attractions

1 Pets Ahoy!
A multi-species cast of 18 cats, a dozen dogs, a flock of birds, a den of rats, three little pigs, and one horse prove their stage savvy in this humorous display of skills and tricks.

2 Shamu Rocks
The underwater viewing area for SeaWorld®'s killer whales offers an ongoing show of its own. This spot gives the best glimpse of adult whales tending their young.

3 Turtle Trek
Find out all about a turtle's lifecycle and the hardships it has to overcome from the turtle's point of view in this 3D, 360-degree undersea ride and attraction.

4 Blue Horizons
This show is a breakthrough theatrical spectacular that show-cases graceful dolphins and false killer whales, a rainbow of exotic birds, and a cast of world-class divers and aerialists in elaborate costumes.

5 Stingray Lagoon
Lean over this waist-high lagoon and pet the velvety hides of stingrays. The ever-hungry rays flock to those offering fish – feeding times are displayed next to the booth selling fish.

6 Dolphin Nursery
When park dolphins give birth, they're brought to this shaded outdoor pool to be with their young calves. Just ask, and the staffer on duty will provide lots of fascinating information.

7 Sky Tower
For a marvelous view of the park and its backstage areas, take a guided trip to the top of the 450-ft (137-m) revolving Sky Tower. The once-extra admission fee is now included.

8 Manta Aquarium
Floor-to-ceiling aquariums present thousands of tropical fish, octopus, rare leafy sea dragons, and more than 300 rays. Kids can get a 360-degree underwater view through the pop-up observation dome.

9 Shamu's Happy Harbor
Kids can only focus for so long. After that, bring them to this huge playground, complete with slides, roller-coaster rides, a mini-waterpark, a four-story maze of nets, steel drums, and a separate sandbox for smaller guests.

Stingray Lagoon

10 Turtle Point
Here you can see endangered and threatened species of sea turtles in a natural lagoon complete with beach, dunes, and indigenous plant life.

For information on Discovery Cove®, SeaWorld®'s sister park **See p97**

Top 10 Rescued Animals at SeaWorld® Orlando

1. Sea turtles *(Cheloniidae)*
2. Manatees *(Trichechus)*
3. Pygmy sperm whales *(Kogia breviceps)*
4. Dwarf sperm whales *(Kogia simus)*
5. Pilot whales *(Globicephala)*
6. Bottlenose dolphins *(Tursiops truncatus)*
7. Killer whales *(Orcinus orca)*
8. Sandhill cranes *(Grus canadensis)*
9. Herons *(Ardeidae)*
10. Grackles *(Quiscalus)*

SeaWorld®'s Rescue & Rehabilitation Program

Park staff do more than teach killer whales to splash the audience on command. As part of their commitment to conservation, animal experts at all SeaWorld® parks in Orlando, Texas, and California are on call 24 hours a day to rescue sick or injured sea mammals, birds, and turtles. These animals are sheltered at the parks, nursed back to health, and – whenever possible – released into the wild. Endangered Florida manatees are regular beneficiaries of the rescue program. As a result of motor-boat propellers, tangled fishing lines, and dangerous toxins, numerous manatees are injured or killed each year. When the call goes out, SeaWorld® responds with a specially equipped animal rescue unit, which can begin emergency treatment on the spot. Manatees on the mend, along with those that wouldn't survive in the wild, are housed in the park's Manatee exhibit (see p29). Since SeaWorld® Orlando started its rescue program in 1976, it has been responsible for saving more than 270 manatees, with more than 100 released back into the wild. By the end of 2000, SeaWorld® Orlando's entire program had rescued and cared for 3,251 animals, including those from animal shelters, and released 735 back into the wild.

Breeding program

SeaWorld® also has a hugely successful breeding program: baby penguins, seals, and no less than 10 killer whale calves have been born at SeaWorld® Orlando.

SeaWorld® staff conducting a triple manatee release

Following pages **Kraken® Ride, SeaWorld® Orlando**

TOP 10 Wet 'n Wild®

Opened in 1977 by George Millay, the founder of SeaWorld®, Wet 'n Wild® boasts an awesome collection of rides, family activities, and a beach party atmosphere that visitors of all ages enjoy. There is a refreshing lack of merchandise tie-ins here, even though the park is now owned by Universal Studios®. The focus is on original thrill rides that leave guests breathless and grinning. Despite strong challenges by Disney World in the form of Blizzard Beach and Typhoon Lagoon, Wet 'n Wild® remains the region's best water park, and one of the area's top attractions.

The central Surf Lagoon

🍴 **Bubba's Bar-B-Q & Chicken** is a good bet for lunch. The park's food outlets accept cash, as well as all major credit cards.

👣 Steps to rides and asphalt walkways can get very hot in high temperatures. Be sure to wear non-slip footwear as protection.

Hi-speed rides can leave you uncovered! Ladies, avoid bikinis or consider adding a T-shirt.

Rides have a 36-inch (91-cm) minimum height requirement for kids riding solo.

• 6200 International Dr
• Map T2
• 407-351-1800
• www.wetnwildorlando.com
• Open 10am–5pm daily, call to check seasonal hours • Adm: adults $58.58, children (3–9) $53.25 (including tax), children under 3 go free. Afternoon discounts are available year-round.

Top 10 Features

1. Der Stuka/The Bomb Bay
2. The Storm
3. Black Hole
4. Disco H2O
5. Mach 5
6. The Flyer
7. Lazy River
8. Bubba Tub
9. The Blast
10. Brain Wash

1 Der Stuka/The Bomb Bay

The park's scariest ride has two options. Der Stuka is a six-story free fall down a 78-degree incline; the steeper Bomb Bay *(below)* is just as high but even more terrifying.

2 The Storm

Hurtle down a shoot filled with mist, thunder, and (at night) lightning, then swirl into an open bowl before dropping into a lower pool. Thrilling.

3 Black Hole

Two people in a raft hang on for dear life as they travel 500 ft (153 m) of twisting tubes in pitch-black darkness *(right)*.

4 Disco H2O

Board a four-passenger tube and head toward a watery nightclub, complete with groovy disco hits from the 1970s.

For more Orlando water parks See pp48–9

Mach 5
A solo flume navigated by riders on a foam mat. On tight turns, ride the flowing water as far up the wall as possible.

Entrance

Wet 'n Wild® Park Plan

The Flyer
On this watery toboggan run, four riders mount one raft and plow through 450 ft (137 m) of banked curves and racing straight runs.

Lazy River
A mile-long (1.6-km) circular waterway *(left)*, which gently winds past swaying palms, tropical flowers, and waterfalls. Perfect for slowly floating along in an inner tube or for a refreshing swim that takes you back to where you started.

Bubba Tub
This six-story-high slide *(left)* offers three big drops during its descent. The large circular rafts hold up to four, making it perfect for getting the whole family screaming.

Park Guide

Wet 'n Wild®'s aquatic center is the giant Surf Lagoon, which is encircled by various rides. On entering the park, bear right and head to the Tube, Towel & Locker Rental counter to get a locker for your belongings. You can return to it whenever you need to during the day. Guest Services is located on the left as you go into the park. If you plan to do some tanning or lying around, try to reserve a beach chair with your towel before hitting the rides, and make sure you've got sunscreen. After that, just see which ride has the shortest line.

Brain Wash
Hold on to your inflatable two- or four-person ride *(above)* as it hurtles down an extreme six-story tube, eventually dropping 53 ft (16 m) into a giant domed funnel. Riders must be at least 48 inches (122 cm) tall.

The Blast
A two-person tube ride through a "broken" pipeline. Riders zip through sharp turns, raging rapids, and churning waves, passing colorful machinery and exploding pipes, while the swirling colors and sound effects twist and turn into a waterfall plunge at the end.

Discover more at www.dk.com

TOP 10 Merritt Island

Thanks to the U.S. government's race into space, Merritt Island National Wildlife Refuge at the Kennedy Space Center has become the second-largest reserve in Florida. Founded in 1963 to serve as a security buffer zone for NASA, its 140,000 acres now serve as an important habitat for endangered species and a vital stop-over along the migration path of hundreds of birds. The manatees are the refuge's most popular attraction.

Wildlife drive starting point

🍴 Grab a bite to eat at Paul's Smoke House located directly across the Indian River Lagoon before setting out to the island.

⏰ The best times to spot wildlife on the Black Point Wildlife Drive are one to two hours after sunrise and one to two hours before sunset. At these times, the animals make their way to the impoundments for feeding.

🗺 Located just east of Titusville on SR 402. From I-95, take exit 220 and head east for four miles on SR 402 (Garden Street).
• 321-861-0667
• http://fws.gov/merritt island or www.nbbd.com/ godo/minwr
• Open year-round.
• Closed federal holidays and 4 days prior to spacecraft launches.
• No admission charge ($5 daily pass for boat ramps).

Top 10 Attractions

1. Manatee Observation Point
2. Black Point Wildlife Drive
3. Fishing
4. Boating
5. Bird Tours
6. Hiking
7. Waterfowl Hunting
8. Visitor Center
9. Migrations
10. Beaches

1 Manatee Observation Point
Though more common in spring and fall, manatees (sea cows) frequent the refuge year-round. Visitors can see these herbivorous animals up close in Banana River or from the viewing platform at Haulover Canal.

2 Black Point Wildlife Drive
The best places to spot wildlife here are linked by an easy access drive. Follow the seven-mile, one-way loop to see a variety of waterfowl, wading birds, and raptors.

3 Fishing
With both Florida State and Refuge fishing permits, you can cast your line on the Indian River, Banana River, and Mosquito Lagoon. Red drum, spotted sea trout, and snook are the most common catches.

4 Boating
Boating or canoeing is still the best way to get close to the wildlife. In season, the waterways are filled with wading birds in migratory pit stops and manatees in the depths.

Bird Tours

For those with no bird-watching experience, the reserve offers birding tours for beginners. A well-trained park volunteer teaches visitors to identify many of the different types of birds in the refuge, such as this snowy egret.

Merritt Island Plan

Hiking

There are six hiking trails on offer. Most are quite wet, but none are too strenuous. They range from a quarter of a mile (0.4 km) to five miles (8 km).

Waterfowl Hunting

So large are the numbers of birds involved in the seasonal migration that hunting for ducks and coot is allowed from November to January. Permits and safety cards are required, and all expeditions must return by early afternoon.

Visitor Center

In addition to a 20-minute video of the refuge, the center has wildlife exhibits and educational displays providing a good introduction to the Island. The ponds behind the center are favorite spots for alligators.

Audio Guide

The Visitor Center sells CDs and tape guides for the Black Point Wildlife Drive. You can also pick up a self-guiding brochure near the entrance to the drive. This provides information on the best places to spot wildlife along the route. Unless you want to keep the brochure, you are encouraged to leave it in the box at the end of the drive for other visitors to use.

Migrations

Throughout the year, the refuge plays host to migrating animals. The birds return in May, and during June and July turtles lay their eggs on the beaches. In September waterfowl are plentiful in the rivers.

Beaches

Visitors to the refuge spend more time on land than in water, but Playalinda Beach provides access, parking, and other facilities for swimmers. However, beware of alligators on the road to the beach.

x

Kennedy Space Center

More than any other Florida attraction, the Kennedy Space Center highlights and celebrates the fruits of human inquiry and imagination. Built in 1967, the center's Visitor Complex has become one of Florida's most popular tourist destinations. Each year, it offers a fascinating window on life beyond Earth to more than 1.5 million visitors, and is the site of many dramatic spacecraft launches.

Vehicle Assembly Building

🍴 Grab a hot dog and sit next to a chunk of real moon rock at the Moon Rock Café.

🎟 Kennedy Space Center Tours provides tickets and transportation to the Visitor Complex, with several pick-ups in Orlando and Kissimmee. Call 888-838-8915 or visit www.kennedyspacecentertours.net

🛰 Rte 405, Titusville
• Off map • 321-449-4444 • www.kennedyspacecenter.com •
Open 9am–5pm daily.
• Adm: $50; children (3–11) $40. Children (0–2) free. • Rocket launch tickets must be purchased in advance. Call 321-449-4400 for information on launch viewing tickets. Visit www.kennedyspacecenter.com for more information.
• Call for details of inclusive tour.

Top 10 Attractions
1 Spacecraft Launches
2 Cape Canaveral: Then & Now Tour
3 Shuttle Launch Experience
4 Astronaut Encounter
5 Atlantis
6 IMAX Theaters
7 International Space Station Center
8 Apollo/Saturn V Center
9 Rocket Garden
10 Early Space Exploration

1 Spacecraft Launches
Watching this, the ultimate Florida thrill ride *(below)*, is a once-in-a-lifetime experience. Check the website for up-to-date rocket launch schedules.

2 Cape Canaveral: Then & Now Tour
This three-hour tour visits historic launch pads and the US Air Force Space & Missile Museum.

3 Shuttle Launch Experience
This exciting simulation ride *(above)* allows visitors to experience the unique sights, sounds, and feel of a space shuttle launch.

4 Astronaut Encounter
The Kennedy Space Center is the only place on earth where guests can meet a real astronaut every day *(right)*. Children and adults alike find these 30-minute question-and-answer sessions inspiring.

5 Atlantis
This is the new permanent home of the space shuttle, Atlantis. The $100-million exhibit tells the story of the space shuttle's achievements over its span of 30 years.

Entrance
Kennedy Space Center Plan

IMAX Theaters
The Center's twin, back-to-back, 5.5-story theaters show two films: *Space Station – 3D* and *Hubble 3D*, offering an inspiring look into the far reaches of the universe, and the legacy of the Hubble Space Telescope, the world's first orbiting observatory.

International Space Station Center
Here, visitors can explore detailed, full-scale models of the International Space Station's compartments and see actual components being prepared for use.

Apollo/Saturn V Center
Visitors relive the historic launch of Apollo 8 in the Firing Room Theater and get to walk underneath one of only three Saturn V rockets *(above)* left in existence *(see p40)*.

Rocket Garden
Unlike any other garden you have seen, this area *(right)* houses eight actual rockets, including a Mercury Atlas similar to the one that was used to launch astronaut John Glenn. Red, white, and blue lighting adds drama and patriotic flair to these historic spacecraft.

Early Space Exploration
This exhibit offers visitors the opportunity to look at the actual Mercury Mission Control consoles used for the first American manned flights. It also highlights the Mercury and Gemini space programs and features artifacts from the first manned flights.

Center Guide

About a 45-minute drive from Orlando, the Center forms part of the Merritt Island National Wildlife Refuge *(see p52)*. Admission includes a bus tour to exhibits located away from the Visitor Complex; it's worth renting the tour's audio guide. Boarding areas for the bus tours are just inside the complex, once you pass through the information center. Except for launch days, the center is rarely overcrowded.

Left **Saturn V** Center **X-15** Right **Gemini VII capsule lauched by Titan II**

Rockets: Past, Present, & Future

1 Jupiter C
This early variation of the Mercury Redstone rocket *(see below)* was developed by a team headed by the German scientist Wernher von Braun. The Jupiter C carried the USA's first satellite, Explorer I, which launched on January 31, 1958.

2 X-15
The X-15 rocket plane flew 199 missions from 1959 to 1968, carrying a who's who of astronauts, including moon-walker Neil Armstrong. It reached altitudes of 354,200 ft (107,960 m) and speeds of 4,520mph (7,274 kmph).

3 Mercury Redstone
This rocket carried the first American into space. Alan B. Shepard Jr.'s 15-minute, 22-second ride aboard the Freedom 7 capsule in 1961 was one of six flights in the Mercury program.

4 Mercury Atlas
When the six-flight Mercury program graduated from sub-orbital to orbital flights, the Atlas replaced the Mercury Redstone. This rocket took John Glenn, Scott Carpenter, Wally Schirra, and Gordon Cooper into space in 1962–3.

5 Titan II
When a larger capsule was needed for two-person crews, this rocket earned its place in NASA history. It was used for 10 manned flights (Gemini Titan expeditions) in 1965 and 1966.

6 Saturn 1B
The Saturn 1B launched Apollo lunar spacecraft into Earth orbit in the mid-1960s to train for manned flights to the moon. Later, it launched three missions to man the Skylab space station (1973) as well as the American crew for the Apollo/Soyuz Test Project (1975).

7 Saturn V
At 363 ft (110 m), this was the largest launch vehicle ever produced. The highlight of its career was Apollo 11, the 1969 mission that landed Buzz Aldrin and Neil Armstrong on the moon.

8 Titan Centaur
The Titan Centaur rocket launched Voyager I and II in 1977 on a mission to explore Jupiter and Saturn, Uranus, and, 12 years after its launch, Neptune.

Mercury Redstone

9 Pegasus
Today's version of this winged wonder is capable of flying small communications satellites into a low Earth orbit from the bellies of mother ships such as the L-1011.

10 X-43A Launch Vehicle
These diminutive rockets may one day boost small, unmanned jets at high speeds and altitudes, improving the safety of manned flights.

Discover more at www.dk.com

Top 10 US Crewed Space Program Events

1. **May 5, 1961** Alan B. Shepard, Jr. becomes the first American in space.
2. **Feb 20, 1962** John H. Glenn, Jr. becomes the first American to orbit the Earth.
3. **Jun 3, 1965** Edward H. White, Jr. becomes the first American to walk in space.
4. **Jul 20, 1969** Neil A. Armstrong becomes the first person to walk on the moon.
5. **Apr 11–13, 1970** An explosion nearly causes disaster for Apollo 13.
6. **Apr 12, 1981** The first shuttle is launched.
7. **Jan 28, 1986** Seven astronauts die in the Challenger space shuttle explosion.
8. **May 27–Jun 6, 1999** The space shuttle docks for the first time on the International Space Station.
9. **Feb 1, 2003** Columbia explodes on re-entering Earth's atmosphere, killing seven astronauts.
10. **Jul 21, 2011** The shuttle program ends with the landing of Endeavour at Kennedy Space Center.

The Space Shuttle

The space shuttles were the first fully reusable spacecraft and the best recognized of NASA's vehicles. Five of them ventured into space: Columbia, Challenger, Discovery, Atlantis, and Endeavour. Once in orbit, the shuttles were capable of cruising at 17,500 mph (28,163 kmph), and their cargo bays could hold a fully loaded tour bus, yet the engineless orbiters could glide to a runway more gracefully than a pelican landing on water. Despite the loss of two of the spacecraft and their crews – Challenger in 1986 and Columbia in 2003 – the shuttles were a remarkable success. They were pivotal in building the International Space Station and extending the life of the Hubble Space Telescope, and their crews carried out valuable cutting-edge research while in orbit.

The 100th space shuttle launch

Investigations in Space
The shuttles allowed astronauts to conduct a wide range of experiments. Here, mission specialist Kathryn P. Hire undergoes a sleep study experiment in the Neurolab on board the Earth-orbiting space shuttle Columbia (April 20, 1998).

Left **Dragon Challenge™** Right **Incredible Hulk Roller Coaster®**, both Islands of Adventure®

🔟 Thrill Rides

1 Splash Mountain®
Prepare to get wet on this deep-drop ride. In summer, it's a cooling trip; at any time of year it's one to enjoy as a spectator from the bridge between Frontierland® and Adventureland®. Even in that relative safety you may get drenched. *See p8 (Magic Kingdom®).*

2 Twilight Zone Tower of Terror™
Take the plunge on the phantom elevator that crosses into the Twilight Zone at the Hollywood Tower Hotel. According to legend, in 1939, five passengers on the elevator disappeared during a violent thunderstorm, never to be seen again. Not suitable for young children. *See p16 (Disney Hollywood Studios®).*

3 Rock 'n' Roller Coaster®
This ride accelerates like a military jet. If that isn't enough to make heads spin, each 24-passenger "stretch limo" has 120 speakers that blare Aerosmith hits at a teeth-rattling decibel level. *See p16 (Disney Hollywood Studios®).*

4 Incredible Hulk Coaster®
Possibly the ultimate inversion ride – it's a zero-G-force, multi-looping ride of a lifetime. The net catches personal items riders should have stashed in a locker. *See p20 (Islands of Adventure®).*

5 Dragon Challenge™
The ride climbs 12.5 stories above the ground before you realize it's too late and you're locked in for the duration. To increase the adrenaline rush, try to get one of the two outside seats in the first eight rows of either dragon. Centrifugal force will steal some of your courage. *See p20 (Islands of Adventure®).*

Dr. Doom's Fearfall®

6 The Amazing Adventures of Spider-Man®
More high-tech than Universal Studios' Back to the Future, but tamer than the Dragon and Hulk coasters. Still, it's not for those with heart problems or motion sickness tendencies. Use the single line if alone or split from your group – it's quicker. *See p20 (Islands of Adventure®).*

7 Doctor Doom's Fearfall®
This is a bit like free-falling in a metal harness. As your legs dangle free and you bob to a

Kraken®, SeaWorld®

Many thrill rides are not suitable for young children.

stop, you'll probably be screaming at the top of your lungs.
See p20 (Islands of Adventure®).

Hollywood Rip Ride Rockit®

The tallest (167 feet/51 m) and one of the fastest (65 mph/105 km/h) coasters in Orlando lets you pick a soundtrack and buy a recording of your ride to edit into your own music video later. *See p25 (Universal Studios®).*

Kraken®

Think pure speed as Poseidon's mythological underwater beast breaks free and without warning pulls your 32-passenger train 151 ft (46 m) closer to heaven, then dives 144 ft (44 m) back toward hell at speeds of 65 mph (105 km/h)! If you survive, expect seven loops on a 4,177-ft (1,273-m) course. This may just be the longest 3 minutes, 39 seconds of your existence. *See p28 (SeaWorld®).*

Summit Plummet

No water park ride will tangle up your bathing suit faster than this 120-ft (36-m), partial-darkness ride. It starts slow, but ends in a near vertical drop that has you plummeting at 60 mph (96 km/h). It's not for the weak of heart or those under 48 inches (122 cm). *See p89 (Blizzard Beach).*

Top 10 Thrill Rides for Children

Peter Pan's Flight
Fly over London and on to Never Land with Peter and the Lost Boys. See p8.

Prince Charming Regal Carousel
A 100-year-old beauty with an engaging fairy-tale theme. See p9.

The Many Adventures of Winnie the Pooh
Pooh created controversy when he replaced Mr. Toad's Wild Ride in 1999, but he's since won converts. See p9.

The Magic Carpets of Aladdin
A gentle ride for all ages aboard a flying carpet. See p9.

Flight of the Hippogriff™
Like the Barnstormer and Woody's Nuthouse, this one's corkscrew action is a blast. See p21.

Pteranodon Flyers®
A neat aerial adventure, but it can make some riders queasy. See p20.

The Cat in the Hat™
This ride's dizzying, 24-ft (7-m) tunnel can leave your head and tummy in a spin. See p21.

Caro-Seuss-El™
Seussian characters make this carousel ride truly unique. See p22.

E.T. Adventure®
You may have to wait in line a while before pedaling your bicycle past fantastic scenery and characters. See p26.

Woody Woodpecker's Nuthouse Coaster®
The banked turns of this mini coaster are absolutely exhilarating. See p26.

For more on minimum height requirements **See p139**

43

Left **Titanic – The Experience** Right **Ripley's Believe It Or Not!® Odditorium**

🔟 Smaller Attractions

1 Gatorland®

This park is chock-full of around 800 lurking alligators, honking for mates, and sometimes performing tricks. The gators don't sit up and beg, but they do jump for food – raw chicken, to be exact, dangled over their ponds by a brave employee. Two hundred or so crocodiles are here to add diversity, as are snakes and other reptiles. There is also a fun water park, Gator Gully Splash. *See p107*.

2 The Holy Land Experience

Ancient Jerusalem comes to life at this attraction, which has reconstructions of Jesus' tomb, the temple, and the caves where the Dead Sea scrolls were found. Make no mistake: this is a "Christ-centered ministry," but guests of any religion can get a kick out of cast members acting out biblical scenes and telling stories from both testaments. A café serves up "Goliath burgers" among other fare. *See p98*.

3 Ripley's Believe It or Not!® Odditorium

Cunningly designed, this building looks like it's about to slip into the ground. Inside, kids might squeal – and adults might cringe – over the replicas of human and animal oddities on display. Two-headed cat, anyone? A movie shows people swallowing coat hangers, light bulbs, and more. There are also plenty of quirky displays, such as a rendition of the *Mona Lisa* made out of toast. *See p98*.

4 Titanic – The Experience

The spirit of Leonardo DiCaprio lingers around this impressive recreation of the doomed Titanic. Guided tours by actors playing crew members and passengers bring the displays to life. Among the 200 or so exhibits are life jackets salvaged from the ship, which add a solemn touch. *See p99*.

5 Fun Spot America

Looking for life in the fast lane? The Fun Spot's thrilling go-kart tracks and the huge ferris wheel are especially designed for adrenalin enthusiasts. The addition of two giant roller coasters and the world's biggest SkyCoaster have only made it more attractive to visitors. *See p97*.

Gatorland®

6 iFLY Orlando

If you've always wanted to try sky-diving but don't like the thought of stepping out of a plane, this vertical wind tunnel is for you. More than 100,000 visitors each year immerse themselves in the high adventure of skydiving without ever having to pack a parachute. There are certain weight restrictions and you have to be more than three years old, but other than that no experience is necessary. The price includes a class, gear and equipment, and two 1-minute jumps, which is usually more than enough to exhaust a novice skydiver. ✆ *6805 Visitors Circle* • *800-759-3861* • *Map T2* • *Open 10am–9:30pm daily* • *Adm* • *www.iflyorlando.com*

iFLY Orlando

7 Zip Orlando

Fly over untouched Florida's wilderness choosing from a range of day or night excursions. Take a moonlit or a zipline tour, or opt for the guided ATV tour through the backcountry in search of native animals. *See p107*

8 WonderWorks

Gimmicks abound inside this building, which, like Ripley's, is sinking into the ground, only this time it's roof first. Inside, there's an interactive arcade of some mild scientific educational value. Among the more than 85 hands-on activities, the curious can experience an earthquake or virtual hang gliding, and test their reflexes. For simple fun, the huge laser-tag field is a blast. *See p99*

9 Reptile World Serpentarium

This unique and educational attraction gives visitors the opportunity to watch a snake handler in action as he extracts poisonous venom from deadly snakes. It also contains the largest reptile exhibit in Florida. *See p108*.

10 Winter Park Scenic Boat Tour

Glide through three of Winter Park's lakes on a pontoon boat for this hour-long tour. Nature-lovers can spot birds such as ospreys and herons. The more materialistic can swoon over huge lakeside mansions, sometimes getting close enough to peek in a window. The architecture of Rollins College, and the secluded feel of the canals, make this tour a popular option for the kitschweary. *See p119*.

Left **Swan Boats, Lake Eola** Right **CityWalk®**

📖 Ways to Have Fun on the Cheap

The Peabody Ducks
It all began in the 1930s when a couple of inebriated sportsmen returning from a week-end hunting trip thought it would be funny to put live ducks in the Peabody Hotel's lobby fountain. The joke stuck and now the orig-inal ducks' descendants are local celebrities. They march down from their penthouse at 11am, via the elevator, and return at 5pm. ◈ *9801 International Dr • Map T4 • 407-352-4000 • Free • www.peabodyorlando.com*

HOB Blues Bar
The main room at House of Blues is one of the best spots in town to catch big-name acts *(see p74)*. But the HOB Blues Bar, next door, is an intimate stage for small-scale blues bands that are generally unknown but excellent. Guests ordering dinner get priority for table seating. ◈ *Downtown Disney Westside • Map G2 • 407-934-2583 • Open 11am–11:30pm Sun–Wed (to 1:30am Thu–Sat) • Free*

The Peabody Ducks

Silver Spurs Rodeo
Located inside of Osceola Heritage Park, the Silver Spurs Arena seats 8,300 people. The Silver Spurs Rodeo was founded in 1944 by the Silver Spurs Riding Club to promote good horse-riding skills. The rodeo has bareback bronc riding, barrel racing, bull riding, saddle bronc, steer wrestling, team roping, and tie-down roping. It is the oldest rodeo in the Kissimmee-St. Cloud area. *See p109.*

Downtown Disney®
Undergoing renovation until 2016, the Downtown Disney® area is being rebranded as Disney Springs. It will reopen with a new multilevel shopping arcade, fresh restaurants, and the Splitsville bowling centre along with many other existing attractions. Kids, in particular, like the LEGO® Imagina-tion Center's *(see p92)* outdoor work stations where they can make almost anything.

Disney's BoardWalk®
A recreation of a 1940's seaside resort, Disney's BoardWalk® offers many attrac-tions to visitors, with street performers, good restaurants and bars, and even a leisurely water taxi ride to the back gate of Epcot®. It is a great place to watch Disney's nightly fireworks for free. The ESPN Club is a perfect venue to catch a major league game of any kind on giant TV screens. *See p93.*

6 Center for Birds of Prey

Founded by the Florida Audubon Society, and off the beaten tourist track, this center's primary function is to rescue and rehabilitate wounded and orphaned raptors. Birds of prey that can't be released back into the wild, however, are kept and used to educate the public about wildlife conservation. With knowledgeable staff and the opportunity to stand close to birds such as eagles and vultures, the center is a captivating treat for a handful of dollars. *See p120.*

Silver Spurs Rodeo

7 Universal's CityWalk® & Portofino Bay Boat Ride

By day, visitors stroll through this area of restaurants and shops on their way to Universal Studios® and Islands of Adventure® *(see pp20– 27)*. In the evening, City-Walk® becomes its own sparkling destination, a swinging Downtown with outdoor entertainment and pulsating crowds to rival Disney's BoardWalk®. For 15 minutes of quiet romance, take the free boat ride (which runs until 2am) between CityWalk® and the Portofino Bay Hotel *(see p142)*. In the moonlight, the Portofino's *faux* Italian paint job looks even more convincing. ◈ *Map T1*

8 Swan Boats In Lake Eola

Tucked under the blossoming skyline of downtown Orlando, Lake Eola Park is a charming city oasis *(see p52)*. Those seeking some (inexpensive) time alone can rent a two-person Swan Boat (propelled by pedal power) and cruise about on the lake. *See p114.*

9 Fort Wilderness Petting Farm

For kids who want to ride a pony (for a small charge) or get to pet miniature donkeys, goats, and other farmyard creatures, this splendid little park can't be beaten. ◈ *Walt Disney World • Map F2 • 407-824-2900 • Open 8am–5:30pm daily • Free*

10 Orlando Speedworld Speedway

This racetrack, 17 miles (30 km) east of Orlando, sees eight divisions of highly modified stock cars race each week. However, the most entertaining evenings are those with destructive, madcap races like Schoolbus Demolition Derbys, and Boat and Trailer Races. The price depends on what's on, but it's always a cheap night out. ◈ *Highway 50 (at the 520 Cocoa cutoff), Bithlo • Map F1 • 407-568-1367 • Open 8pm Fri Apr–Nov • Adm • www.orlandospeedworld.org*

Left **Wet 'n Wild®** Right **Discovery Cove®**

🔟 Places to Cool Off

1 Wet 'n Wild®
Orlando's best water park is full of rides and slides to keep the most hardened thrill-seeker's adrenalin pumping. But it's not all action – there are kids' rides and chill-out areas, too. *See pp34–5.*

2 Discovery Cove®
Need to unwind on a tropical beach, swim with dolphins, or snorkel over coral reefs? Well, if you check into Discovery Cove®, you can. This exclusive (daily entry is limited to 1,000 people) and inspired Orlando attraction offers the features and personalized services of an upscale island resort. Admission is not cheap, but includes everything from lunch to wet suits and sun block. Reservations two months in advance are suggested. *See p97.*

Lakefront Park

3 Blizzard Beach
In the battle for water park supremacy, Wet 'n Wild®'s main competitor is this sizeable Disney park. It's what a ski resort would be like if it started to melt, with water slides replacing ski runs. Geared to teens and young adults, the park offers seven water slides and excellent rides, a wave pool, and kids' areas. If park capacity is reached early (as it often is), it closes to new admissions until later in the day. *See p89.*

4 Lakefront Park
The Lakefront Park is very family orientated. The park includes a marina with 143 boat slips, a children's playground, picnic areas with pavilions and grills, a performing arts pavilion for concerts and special events, walking and biking trails, a white sand beach, beach volley ball courts and a water fountain playground, which has a great view of picturesque East Lake Tohopekaliga. *See p108.*

5 Typhoon Lagoon
This Disney water park is an enthralling mix of slides, tubes, and the largest wave pool in the US. It's well-suited to families with pre-teen children who'll appreciate the gentle nature of the attractions here. One stand-out is Shark Reef, a short snorkel course over a coral reef teeming with tropical fish and live sharks. Wannabe surfers *(see p57)* can pay an extra fee to use the wave pool outside of regular opening hours. *See p89.*

6 Orlando Dive & Snorkel Tours
Dive at Florida's most spectacular crystal clear inland springs and rivers, which boast 200 ft (61 m) visibility and a wide variety of marine life. Swim with manatees,

turtles and catfish or enter the 'grand ballroom' 100 ft (30 m) below the surface in a cavern dive. Gear rental, transportation, and lessons are available. ✈ *13800 S.R. 535* • *Map G3* • *407-466-1668* • *Open daily* • *www.diveorlando.com*

7 Sammy Duvall's Watersports Centers

These Disney World-based centers were founded by four-time world champion water-skier Sammy Duvall. The Contemporary Resort branch offers parasailing, water-skiing, wake-boarding, knee-boarding, and tubing. Guests can either rent a boat and driver or take lessons. The slalom course is geared to more hardcore water-skiers. Guests can bring their own gear or rent it. ✈ *Map F1 & G2* • *407-939-0754* • *Open winter: 10am–5pm daily; summer: 8am–6pm daily* • *Adm* • *www.sammyduvall.com*

8 Buena Vista Watersports

This friendly facility, offers water-ski lessons, water-ski and wake-board charters, and rentals of personal watercraft (such as Waverunners and Seaddoos). The center, on the shores of Lake Bryan, is geared to beginners, and kids as young as three can join in. Non-skiers can enjoy the use the lakeside beach, volleyball net, and picnic area.
✈ *13245 Lake Bryan Rd* • *Map G3* • *407-239-6939* • *Open 9.30am–6pm daily (weather permitting)* • *Adm* • *www.BVwatersports.com*

9 Aquatica®

SeaWorld®'s unique waterpark allows you to swim with, under and through sealife, with high-speed tube slides and half-pipes,

Jet skiers, Buena Vista Watersports

competitive mat races, giant wave pools, and the Dolphin Plunge, which zooms along through enclosed slides into a dolphin pool ✈ *5800 Water Play Way* • *Map U5* • *888-800-5447* • *Opening hours vary seasonally* • *Adm* • *www. aquaticabyseaworld.com*

10 Makinson Aquatic Center

On the eastern edge of Kissimmee, this center offers three pools – one for laps, one for kids, and another for the water slide. It's perfect for families with toddlers or youngsters for whom a major water park could be a bit overwhelming (and admission is far cheaper). ✈ *2204 Denn John Lane* • *Map H4* • *407-870-7665* • *Open Tue–Sun Mar–Sep (times vary)* • *Adm* • *www.kissimmee.org*

Following Pages **Discovery Cove**

Left **Canaveral National Seashore** Right **Turkey Lake Park**

🔟 Parks & Preserves

1 Canaveral National Seashore & Merritt Island National Wildlife Refuge
These two federal preserves bordering the Kennedy Space Center are home to scores of species, including endangered ones such as sea turtles, manatees, dolphins, alligators, bald eagles, and ospreys. Explore Canaveral's beaches (including a naturist one, Playalinda) and Merritt Island's trails, driving route, and observation deck *(see pp36–7)*. ◎ Titusville • Off map • Seashore open at least 6am–6pm daily; refuge open at least 9am–5pm daily • Adm (seashore), free (refuge) • www.nps.gov/cana

Lake Eola Park

2 Lake Eola Park
Burn a few calories on the 0.9-mile (1.4-km) trail that circles the lake here. Less energetic pursuits include feeding the birds and cruising Lake Eola in the swan-shaped rental boats *(see p47)*. This 43-acre (17-ha) park is also home to several annual and seasonal events, including the 4th of July fireworks show. Orlando's farmers' market is held here on Sundays. See p114.

3 Wekiwa Springs State Park
These springs provide a fertile habitat for such species as white-tail deer, gray foxes, bobcats, raccoons, and black bears. They also provide some of the best places for paddling in a boat in central Florida. Canoe rentals, and picnic, grilling, camping, and volleyball areas are also available. ◎ 1800 Wekiwa Circle, Apopka • Map A3 • 407-884-2008 • Open 8am–sunset • Adm • www.floridastateparks.org/wekiwasprings

4 Lake Louisa State Park
You can fish, swim, or paddle a canoe, but you'll have to bring your own equipment. The beach has a bathhouse with showers, and there's a picnic area. White-tail deer, wild turkeys, marsh rabbits, opossums, and raccoons are common, and don't be surprised if a polecat (also known as a skunk!) cuts across your path. ◎ State Park Dr, Clermont • Off map • 352-394-3969 • Open 8am–sunset • Adm • www.floridastateparks.org/lakelouisa

5 Lake Kissimmee State Park
This park is one of the best bird-watching areas in the state. You might see bald eagles and snail kites, as well as whooping and sandhill cranes. Other residents include otters, wild turkeys, deer, and fox squirrels. On weekends, the park has a re-created 1876 cattle camp. ◎ Camp Mack Rd, Lake Wales • Off map • 863-696-1112 • Open 7am–sunset • Adm • www.floridastateparks.org/lakekissimmee

6 Bill Frederick Park at Turkey Lake

Unlike many state parks with spartan amenities, this 300-acre (120-ha) city retreat has a swimming pool, picnic pavilions, a lake full of fish, nature and jogging trails, three playgrounds, and a farm-animal petting zoo. It also has camping areas if the call of the wild is too strong to leave. ⚐ 3401 S. Hiawassee Rd • Map D3 • 407-246-4486 • Open 8am–5pm daily (to 7pm Apr–Oct) • Adm

7 Big Tree Park

Though the Senator, a 3,500-year-old cypress tree, burned down in 2012, its companion the 2,000-year-old Lady Liberty, still stands along with Phoenix, a Senator clone, which was planted in 2013. The park has picnic tables and a boardwalk through the cypress swamp. ⚐ General Hutchison Pkwy, Longwood • Off map • 407-665-2001 • Open 8am–sunset • Free

Wekiwa Springs State Park

8 Tosohatchee State Reserve

Swamps dotted with hardwood hammocks (tree islands) and a 19-mile (30-km) stretch of the St. John's River combine to make this one of Central Florida's prettiest and most primitive parks. Photographers will appreciate the scenic locales, some with wild orchids and other flora. Hawks, eagles, fox squirrels, and songbirds can sometimes be seen from the park's trails. ⚐ Christmas, 18 miles (29 km) NE of Orlando • Off map • 407-568-5893 • Open 8am–sunset • Adm

9 Wheatley Park

This city park is more urban oasis than rustic countryside retreat. It features lots of facilities such as basketball, tennis, and sand volleyball courts, and picnic areas with grills for a barbecue. Kids will appreciate the well-equipped playground. ⚐ 18th & Central Ave, Apopka • Off map • 407-886-1441 • Open sunrise–sunset • Free

10 Ralph V. Chisholm Park

This shady park, on the shore of East Lake Tohopekaliga, has various amenities including a beach, swimming area, horse trails, children's playground, softball and baseball fields, sand volleyball courts, and picnic areas. Bring your own equipment, food, and drinks. ⚐ 4700 Chisholm Park Trail, St. Cloud • Off map • 407-343-7173 • Open sunrise–sunset • Free

→ For more on day trips out of the city See pp82–5

Left **Clubhouse, Champions Gate** Right **Falcon's Fire**

Golf Courses

Disney's Osprey Ridge

Arguably the most challenging of Disney's five 18-hole courses, the Tom Fazio-designed Osprey Ridge features native woodlands, elevated tees, fairly large greens, nine water holes, and more than 70 bunkers. *Golf Digest's* "Places to Play" ranks it among Florida's best public and resort courses. (Max yds: 7,101 [6,493 m]. USGA rating: 74.4.) ® *Golf View Dr • Map F2 • 407-938-4653 • www.disneyworld.com*

Grand Cypress Golf Club

Jack Nicklaus designed these highly rated 45 holes; the New Course was actually inspired by the Old Course at St. Andrews in Scotland. The club is semi-private with some public tee times. (Max yds: 6,906 [6,315 m]. USGA rating: 74.4.) ® *1 N. Jacaranda • Map F2 • 407-239-4700 • www.grandcypress.com*

Waldorf Astoria Golf Club

Rees Jones designed this challenging 18-hole course to follow the contours of a wetland preserve. Impressive stands of

pine and cypress trees line the fairways, and a 5-tee system accommodates players of all skill levels. (Max yds: 7,108 [6,500 m]. USGA rating: 74.6.) ® *14200 Bonnet Creek Resort Ln • Map G2 • 407-597-5500 • www.waldorfastoriaorlando.com*

Disney's Magnolia

Here's a course with forgivingly wide fairways that let you hammer the ball. But don't get reckless: 11 of the 18 holes contain water and the course has 97 bunkers, with many waiting to gobble your miss hits. Part of the PGA's Funai Golf Classic *(see p57)* is played here. (Max yds: 7,190 [6,574 m]. USGA rating: 73.9.) ® *Palm Dr • Map F1 • 407-938-4653 • Lessons available • www.disneyworld.com*

Celebration Golf Club

The father-and-son team of Robert Trent Jones, Sr. and Jr. came up with a course that has water on 17 of 18 holes thanks to natural wetlands, so bring an extra ration of balls. There's also a three-hole junior course for 5- to 9-year-olds. (Max yds: 6,786 [6,205 m]. USGA rating: 73.) ® *701 Golf Park Dr • Map G2 • 407-566-4653 • Lessons available • www.celebrationgolf.com*

Champions Gate

Greg Norman created two 18-hole courses (the National and the International)

Villas of Grand Cypress

Make reservations at more than 40 Orlando-area golf courses with Tee Times USA 800-465-3356 or Florida Golfing 866-833-2663.

located in this resort community southwest of Disney, featuring woods, wetlands, and open land. Between them they have 13 water holes, and share double greens at the 4th and 16th holes. (Max yds: 7,048 [6,445 m] and 7,407 [6,773 m], respectively. USGA rating: 75.1 & 76.3.) ✎ *1400 Masters Blvd • Map H1 • 407-787-4653 • Lessons available • www.championsgategolf.com*

Orlando Area Golf Course

7 Orange County National – Panther Lake

The elevation changes as much as 60 ft (18 m) in places on this 18-hole course, one of *Golf Digest's* top "Places to Play". It also gets high marks for course condition and pace of play. The course is surrounded by woodlands, while adjoining wetlands and lakes yield 13 water holes. (Max yds: 7,295 [6,670 m]. USGA rating: 75.7.) ✎ *16301 Phil Ritson Way • Map E1 • 407-656-2626 • Lessons available • www.ocngolf.com*

8 Disney's Palm

This jewel of a course is surrounded by woodlands. Half of its holes have water,

and its 94 bunkers create headaches for those whose shots stray. The 18th hole is one of the toughest on the PGA Tour. (Max yds: 6,957 [6,391 m]. USGA rating: 73.) ✎ *Palm Dr • Map F1 • 407-939-4653 • Lessons available • www.disneyworld.com*

9 Disney's Lake Buena Vista

This tight course with its heavily bunkered fairways and greens also uses dense pine forest to challenge golfers. Its most unusual feature is an island green on the seventh hole. Perennially rated as one of Florida's Top 20 in *Golfweek*. (Max yds: 6,819 [6,325 m]. USGA rating: 72.7.) ✎ *Buena Vista Dr • Map F2 • 407-938-4653 • www.disneyworld.com*

10 Falcon's Fire

With just three water holes, the first nine may convince you to let your guard down, but seven of the last nine holes give you a chance to submerge a ball in two large lakes. This Rees Jones course opened in 1993 and hosts the Senior PGA Tour's qualifying school. (Max yds: 6,901 [6,310 m]. USGA rating: 72.5.) *See p110.*

Most golf courses in Orlando are usually open sunrise to sunset year-round.

55

Left **Playing tennis, Grand Cypress Raquet Club** Right **Cycling along scenic country trails**

🔟 Sports & Outdoor Activities

1 Horseback Riding

Tri-Circle-D Ranch at Disney's Fort Wilderness Resort offers 45-minute guided trail rides on horseback or carriage through the woodlands. Smaller children can tour the stables and take a pony ride. ⊗ *Walt Disney World • Map F2 • 407-824-2900 • Open 8:30am–4pm daily • Adm • www.disneyworld.com*

Tri-Circle-D Ranch, Fort Wilderness

2 Tennis

Disney's Contemporary Resort has six hydrogrid courts and its Grand Floridian Resort & Spa has two clay ones. The nearby Grand Cypress Raquet Club has 12 courts, four of them all-weather. ⊗ *Disney • Map F1 • 407-939-7529 • Open 9am–10pm daily • Adm ⊗ Grand Cypress • 1 N. Jacaranda • Map F2 • 407-621-1991 • Open 8am–5pm daily • Adm*

3 Cycling

Get away on Disney's scenic bike trails. You can rent single, multi-speed, and kids' bikes at the Fort Wilderness Resort's Bike Barn. Tandems and cycles with baby seats and training wheels are also available. ⊗ *Walt Disney World • Map F2 • 407-824-2900 • Open at least 9am–5pm daily • Adm*

4 ESPN Wide World of Sports

Kids and the young-at-heart can play video sports on 40-inch televisions, watch semi-pro baseball, soccer, basketball, and volleyball. Take part in the runDisney marathon and collect merchandise from selected locations. ⊗ *Walt Disney World • Map G2 • 407-828-3267 • Open 9:30am–5pm daily • Adm*

5 Swimming

Most of Orlando's hotels have their own pools, but for a change of scene and a place to swim serious lengths, try an aquatic center. *See p49.*

6 Boating

The man-made lakes around Walt Disney World are perfect for idling away an afternoon. Several of the resorts have small motorboats and pontoon boats for hire. There are also paddle-boats for people who like a more rigorous work-out. ⊗ *Map F1–G2 • Open at least 9am–5pm daily • Adm*

7 Watersports

Test your water-skiing legs at one of Sammy Duvall's Water Sports Centers (which also offers parasailing and wake-boarding). Buena Vista Watersports (which also charters and rents boats) is another option. *See p49.*

Surfing

In land-locked Orlando? You bet. According to the state's surf addicts, who sometimes rent the park after hours, Disney's Typhoon Lagoon *(see p48)* has wave-making down to a fine art. But you don't have to be a pro to give it a try. Carroll's Cocoa Beach Surfing School puts on a twice-weekly class for beginners. ◐ *Walt Disney World • Map G2 • 407-939-7873 • Open 6:45–9:30am Tue & Fri • Adm*

Fishing

Land your dinner (and a good fish story) with Pro Bass Guide Service, a Winter Garden outfit that specializes in guided bass-fishing. Local and regional trips to some of Central Florida's most picturesque rivers and lakes are on offer (pick-up can be arranged), as are offshore expeditions for saltwater species, such as redfish and sea trout. ◐ *407-977-9676 • Open daily • Adm*

Freshwater fishing, Central Florida

Hayrides

For something a little more unusual in the way of outdoor fun, try a 45-minute hay wagon ride around Disney's Fort Wilderness Resort. Expect some singing and dancing, and a good-time atmosphere that makes for a relaxing end to the day. One of Disney's most popular campground experiences. ◐ *Walt Disney World • Map G2 • 407-824-2900 • evenings daily • Adm*

Sporting Events

Florida Citrus Bowl

The annual college football showdown between the No. 2-ranked teams from the Southeastern and Big Ten conferences; preceded by a huge parade. ◐ *407-849-2020 • Jan 1*

Walt Disney World Marathon

A 26.2-mile (42.6-km) race with entrants from around the world. ◐ *407-824-4321 • Early Jan • www.disneyworld.com*

Speedweeks

Two weeks of motor action at Daytona Beach, ending with the Daytona 500. ◐ *866-761-7223 • Early Feb*

Silver Spurs Rodeo

Twice a year rodeo events for cowboys and girls in Kissimmee. ◐ *407-677-6336 • Oct • www.silverspursrodeo.com*

Arnold Palmer Invitational

Golf legend host Arnold Palmer, plus players like Tiger Woods, are the draw. ◐ *407-876-2888 • Mar*

Atlanta Braves Spring Training

Catch baseball's Braves in pre-season training. ◐ *407-939-7712 • Mar • www.braves.com*

Orlando Predators

Grab a chance to support the local arena football team. ◐ *407-648-4444 • Apr–Aug*

Orlando City Soccer

Watch professional sports teams in action here. ◐ *407-478-4007 • Feb–Aug*

Orlando Magic

Don't miss the NBA team if it's the season. ◐ *407-440-7000 • Oct–Apr*

Children's Miracle Network Classic

Disney hosts tour pros in a week of golfing events. ◐ *407-939-4653 • Mid-Oct*

For more Orlando area events **See pp64–5**

Left **nèu lotus spa at Renaissance Orlando Resort** Right **Massageworks Salon & Day Spa**

🔟 Spas

1 Spa at the Buena Vista Palace

Just around the corner from Disney's parks, the Buena Vista Palace offers an upscale experience that's from another world. This full-service, European-style spa has various styles of massage; body treatments (mud masks, wraps, and polishes); facials; and hydrotherapy treatments. It has steam rooms, saunas, and a health-and-fitness center. ◈ 1900 Buena Vista Dr • Map G2 • 407-827-2727 • Usually open 9am–6pm daily

2 Mandara Spa at the Portofino Bay Hotel

A state-of-the-art fitness center with a full-service spa (massages, saunas, facials, a couple's treatment room, and more) are on offer at this Universal resort. If you are a guest, you can choose to have your massage in your room. ◈ 5601 Universal Blvd • Map T1 • 407-503-1000 • Open 9am–6pm daily

3 Grand Floridian Senses Spa & Health Club

The spa at Disney's Victorian-style resort has a whole range of services including water and massage therapies, aromatherapy, body wraps, and masks. There's a couple's treatment room and a well-equipped health club. The

Grand Floridian also offers nutrition and fitness counseling. ◈ 4401 Floridian Way • Map F1 • 407-824-2332 • Open 8am–8pm daily

4 Relâche Spa at Gaylord Palms

This full-service spa offers hair styling along with a range of relaxing treatments including aromatherapy massage with essential oils, organic facial treatments tailored to your skin's needs, moisturizing manicures, and exfoliating pedicures. ◈ 6000 W. Osceola Pkwy, Kissimmee • Map G3 • 407-586-4772 • Open 9am–8pm daily

Relâche Spa

5 nèu lotus spa at Renaissance Orlando at SeaWorld®

There's a full line of traditional spa services here, including massages (Swedish, deep tissue, and reflexology); body treatments (polishes and wraps); and a full line of facials, one of which is designed to introduce teenagers to the basics of skin care. In-room massages are available for an extra charge. ◈ 6677 Sea Harbor Dr • Map T5 • 407-248-7428 • Open 8am–8pm

6 Disney's Saratoga Springs Resort

The spa at this resort has a range of massage therapies (including hydromassage), body treatments, facials, pedicures and manicures. Treatments can be selected individually or as part of a full-day package, and the staff are happy to design personal treatment programs. Reservations must be made by phone in advance. ✆ *1920 Magnolia Dr • Map G2 • 407-827-4455 • Open 8am–8pm • www.relaxedyet.com*

7 Omni Orlando Resort at Champions Gate
This beautiful resort has a first-class spa with state-of-the-art treatments and a deluxe fitness facility. From aromatherapy facials to sports massages, clients can take a break from the crowds at this luxurious secret resort and have a day of pampering. ✆ *1500 Masters Blvd, Championsgate • 407-390-6603 • www.omnihotels.com*

8 Poseidon Spa at Grand Bohemian
The AAA Four Diamond Grand Bohemian is a landmark luxury hotel, and the Poseidon Spa only adds to the acclaim. This relaxing spa offers several therapeutic treatments including facials, manicures, pedicures, and massage. ✆ *325 S. Orange Ave • Map P3 • 407-313-9000 • Open 9am–6pm daily • www.grandbohemianhotel.com*

9 Massageworks Salon & Day Spa
Located in a 100-year-old Kissimmee schoolhouse, this spa has an air of yesteryear. Treatments include massages (Swedish, neuromuscular, reflexology, and sports); therapies (salt scrubs, aroma steam, and mud-aloe); wraps (oil, marine algae, and sea clay); and colonic irrigation. There are sauna, teeth-whitening, and power nap facilities available. It's possible to combine treatments in three- to six-hour packages.

Spa at the Buena Vista Palace

✆ *216 Broadway • Map H4 • 407-932-0300 • Open 8am–7pm Mon–Sat • www.massageworksdayspa.com*

10 Ritz-Carlton Spa
A day spent in this spa is time well spent. Start your day with a facial in one of the Spa's 40 treatment rooms. Go for a swim in the private 4,000-sq ft (375-sq m) heated outdoor lap pool or enjoy a relaxing massage followed by a visit to the boutique. End your outing with dinner at Norman's. ✆ *4012 Central Florida Pkwy • Map F4 • 407-393-4200 • Open 9am–7pm daily • www.ritzcarlton.com/en/Properties/Orlando/Spa*

Left **Exhibit, Mennello Museum of American Folk Art** Right **Orlando Science Center**

ᴛᴏᴘ10 Museums

Orlando Museum of Art
Following a multi-million dollar makeover in 1997, the Orlando Museum of Art (OMA) has earned a reputation as one of the southeast's top arts museums. The fine permanent collection is dominated by pre-Columbian art and American artists such as Georgia O'Keefe, George Inness, and Robert Rauschenberg. These works are supplemented by touring exhibitions from major metropolitan museums, and numerous smaller shows of regional or local significance, although curators tend to avoid overtly controversial works.
See p113.

Orlando Science Center
This huge, attention-grabbing, exploratorium-style museum boasts hundreds of interactive, child-friendly exhibits that are designed to introduce kids of all ages to the wonders of science. The center's four floors are divided into 10 themed zones. These deal with subjects ranging from mechanics to math, health and fitness to lasers, making this an educational and fun break from the usual Orlando theme park distractions. Don't miss the CineDome, which houses the planetarium and the world's largest Iwerks® theatre.
See p113.

Detail, Charles Hosmer Morse Museum of American Art

Orange County Regional History Center
Given the region's relatively short history, this museum has wisely ignored geographic limitations. Exhibits not only feature local photographs and memorabilia, but a re-created Victorian parlor, a 1926 fire station, and fascinating temporary shows that cover themes relating to other parts of Florida, such as pirates and space travel.
See p113.

Charles Hosmer Morse Museum of American Art
Here rests the world's most comprehensive collection of work by American artist Louis Comfort Tiffany, best known for his Art Nouveau stained-glass pieces. The museum's highlights are a spectacular chapel Tiffany made for the 1893 World's Columbian Exposition and a re-creation of Tiffany's grand New York home. *See p119.*

Cornell Fine Arts Museum
Located on the campus of Rollins College, the small but stylish Cornell is Florida's oldest art collection. It showcases European and American paintings, sculpture, and decorative arts ranging from the Renaissance and Baroque periods to the 20th century. Among the highlights

Some museums have different opening hours in school vacations.

Albin Polasek Museum and Sculpture Gardens

are *Madonna and Child Enthroned* (c.1480) by Cosimo Rosselli, and *Reclining Figure* by Henry Moore (1982). *See p119.*

6 Mennello Museum of American Folk Art

This small, lakeside museum houses an unusual and charming collection of paintings by obscure curio-shop owner and Floridian folk artist, Earl Cunningham (1893–1977). In addition to his own work are traveling exhibitions featuring the works of other "outsider" artists. *See p113.*

7 Holocaust Memorial Resource & Education Center

It was founded in 1980 by survivors and witnesses of the Holocaust. It aims to inculcate the value of compassion and generosity in future generations. The museum conducts lectures, hosts a film series, and has a permanent exhibition of remembrances. ⊛ *851 N. Maitland Ave • Map J3 • 407-628-0555 • Open 9am–4pm Mon–Thu, 9am–1pm Fri, 1–4pm Sun • www.holocaustedu.org*

8 Albin Polasek Museum and Sculpture Gardens

Czech-American Polasek (1879–1965) was a sculptor who specialized in European figurative technique. In semi-retirement, he moved to this self-designed house and studio, where he continued working until his death. The beautiful gardens are filled with his sculptures, as are four galleries within the house, which also hold a few pieces from other artists. *See p119.*

9 Zora Neale Hurston National Museum of Fine Arts

Eatonville – the first incorporated African-American municipality in the USA – was the childhood home of Zora Neale Hurston (1903–1960), writer, anthropologist, and folklorist. This modest museum offers exhibitions centered on Hurston and the Eatonville of days gone by. *See p120.*

10 Maitland Historical & Telephone Museums

Artifacts, textiles, and photos from Maitland's pioneer days through to the heydays of the citrus and lumber industries are the focus here. In the same building, the Telephone Museum has vintage phones and memorabilia. ⊛ *221 W. Packwood Ave • Map J4 • 407-644-2451 • Open 12–4pm Thu–Sun • Free (donation) • www.maitlandhistory.org*

Left **Orlando Philharmonic** Right **The Orlando Shakespeare Theater**

Cultural Venues & Organizations

1 Orlando Shakespeare Theater

This nationally recognized theater company performs the Bard's works as well as modern classics and Broadway hits. Their productions can be seen in an 8-month-long season at their state-of-the-art theater at Loch Haven Park. ✆ *812 E. Rollins St • Map M3 • 407-447-1700 • Adm • www.orlandoshakes.org*

2 Orlando Repertory Theatre

Founded as the Orlando Little Theatre in 1926, the Repertory has grown into Orlando's version of a Broadway theater. It has three stages and puts on classic and contemporary plays alike. The year-round schedule is packed with high quality shows. The Theatre for Young People perform educational plays for school children. ✆ *1001 E. Princeton St • Map M3 • 407-896-7365 • Adm*

3 Theatre Downtown

Named as Orlando's Best Local Repertory Company, this volunteer organization has been producing first-rate shows since 1984. In 1989, it moved to a former appliance store, and in this casual setting has presented an array of classics, contemporary works (such as David Mamet's *American Buffalo*), and new plays by local writers. ✆ *2113 N. Orange Ave • Map M3 • 407-841-0083 • Adm • www.theatre-downtown.net*

4 Enzian Theater

Central Florida's only full-time art-house cinema is a unique venue – its single-screen, 250-seat house is arranged like a dinner theater, with waiters serving food and drinks (including beer and wine). Featuring foreign and American independents, and with regular special-interest festivals, plus the Florida Film Festival *(see p65)*, this is a place for true cinephiles. *See p121.*

5 SAK Comedy Lab

A downtown favorite, SAK is Orlando's home of improvisation comedy. Shows are always funny and inventive, and there are two per night. The 8pm shows are usually family-friendly, while the later ones get a bit edgier, although obscene material is strictly avoided. Of particular interest are the series shows, such as *Foolish Hearts*, an on-going, improvised soap opera. ✆ *29 S. Orange Ave • Map P3 • 407-648-0001 • Adm • www.sak.com*

Orlando Ballet

6 Orlando Philharmonic

Orlando's resident orchestra boasts more than 80 conservatory-trained musicians. Venues vary, and include the Phil's home at Symphony Square, Leu Gardens (for outdoor concerts), and even SeaWorld®. Its best-known showcase is the "Phil at Carr", an eight-concert series (Sep–May) at the Bob Carr Performing Arts Center, with guest artists in both classical and pop concerts. ◉ *Symphony Square, 812 E. Rollins St • Map M3 • 407-896-6700 • Adm • www.orlandophil.org*

7 Orlando International Fringe Festival

The 14-day Orlando Fringe follows in the footsteps of the grand-daddy of fringe: the Edinburgh (Scotland) Fringe Festival. Like Edinburgh, the Orlando Fringe presents uncensored, unjuried music, dance, and other perfomances, and pays 100 percent of box office sales to the artists. The Orlando Fringe is held at the Lowndes Shakespeare Center, the Orlando Rep, and other nearby sites. *See p64.*

8 Orlando Ballet

This small, but growing, company presents four major productions annually, including a version of *The Nutcracker*, choreographed by company artistic director Fernando Bujones. Smaller shows are held on community stages, but the major productions are at the Bob Carr Performing Arts Centre. ◉ *1111 N. Orange Ave • Map P3 • 407-426-1739 • Adm • www.orlandoballet.org*

9 Osceola Center for the Arts

Kissimmee's home of high culture offers a theater, art gallery, and special events. The Osceola Center for the Arts (OCFTA) has an engagingly diverse schedule, eagerly offering a little bit of everything, from Broadway to Barbershop, storytelling to sculptures. ◉ *2411 E. Irlo Bronson Memorial Hwy • Map P3 • 407-846-6257 • Adm • www.OCFTA.com*

10 Mad Cow Theatre

A favorite among local actors, this mainstay theatrical group has developed a reputation for small, high-quality shows. With a passion for both classic and contemporary productions, the theater represents the best from American and World literature. Past plays have ranged from Chekhov to Neil Simon. ◉ *54 W Church St • Map P3 • 407-297-8788 • Adm*

Mad Cow Theatre

For dinner shows **See pp80–81**

Left **Orlando International Fringe Festival** Right **Blue Skies Balloon Festival**

Festivals & Events

1 Renninger's Antique Extravaganzas

From Victorian furnishings to vintage political campaign buttons, you can find all things old and valuable sold at the 1,400 antique stalls spread across a meadow here. The prime goods go fast, so get here early (it opens around 9am). *Renningers Antique Center, Hwy 441 • Off map • 352-383-8393 • 3rd weekend of Jan, Feb, & Nov*

2 Blue Skies Balloon Festival

Over 20 exotic hot air balloons, some in the shape of animals or even a space shuttle, can be seen taking to the skies at this festival. Capture this view on camera from below. You can also take a ride on one of the hot air balloons which will take you over the theme parks and untouched Florida territory. *Formosa Gardens, 7836 W. Irlo Bronson Memorial Hwy • Map G1 • 800-831-1844 • Jun*

Poster, Florida Film Festival

3 Central Florida Fair

This massive 11-day shindig takes place close to Downtown Orlando, but its cowpoke attitude is a world away. The country-style attractions include carnival rides, livestock shows, country music, farming exhibits, and more fried food than you'll ever care to eat. *4603 W. Colonial Dr • Map C3 • 407-295-3247 • Early Mar • www.centralfloridafair.com*

4 Winter Park Sidewalk Arts Festival

For three days, this prestigious outdoor festival sees hundreds of artists exhibit on sidewalk stalls. Traffic comes to a standstill as the crowds mill around. *Cranes Roost Park, Altamonte Springs • Map A5 • 407-592-0002 • Mid-Feb • www.uptownartexpo.com*

5 Uptown Art Expo

This fine art and craft expo enjoys a pretty setting on the shore of Cranes Roost Lake, and showcases the juried work of 125 artists. There are also children's activities, and a chalk street art competition for adults and teens *Cranes Roost Park, Altamonte Springs • Map A5 • 407-592-0002 • Mid-Feb • www.uptown artexpo.com*

6 Orlando International Fringe Festival

With over 500 performances in 14 days, the Fringe offers improvised comedy, drag shows, stand-up, and more. Inspired by the Edinburgh festival, this premier event draws enthusiastic local crowds. *Various venues • 407-648-0077 • May • www.orlandofringe.org*

7 Zellwood Sweetcorn Festival

Eat as much sweetcorn as you can while listening to excellent country bands. A huge machine, Big Bertha, cooks up to 1,650 ears of corn every 9 minutes. There are also some fairground rides and a crafts fair. ⚑ *4253 Ponkan Rd • Off map • 407-886-0014 • Mid-May • www.zellwoodcornfestival.com*

Florida Film Festival

This 10-day festival is packed with more than 100 features, documentaries, and shorts. Film-makers introduce their works, and a few Hollywood names make guest appearances. ⚑ *Enzian Theater, 1300 S. Orlando Ave, and other venues • Map D4 • 407-629-1088 • Apr • www. floridafilmfestival.com*

Gay Days

Gay Days is a week-long blowout of parties and theme park visits for more than 130,000 gay and lesbian guests. By day, gay and straight mix in the parks; at night, parks and clubs are rented for evening raves. ⚑ *Various venues • 888-942-9329 or 407-896-8431 • www.gaydays.com • Early Jun*

Anime Festival Orlando

This gathering of "Japanimation" fanatics has screenings, Japanese video games, dance and costume contests, and dozens of dealers offering hard-to-find collectibles. ⚑ *Renaissance Orlando at Seaworld • Map F3 • 3 days in Jun, Jul or Aug • www.animefestivalorlando.com*

Gay Days

Attraction Events

1 Mardi Gras at Universal
The ultimate "Big Easy" party, with parades, music, and lots of beaded necklaces. ⚑ *Universal Studios® • Feb–Mar*

2 Disney Hollywood Studios Star Wars Weekends
Four consecutive weekends of *Star Wars*-inspired frolics. ⚑ *Disney Hollywood Studios® • May*

3 Night of Joy
A two-night showcase of contemporary Christian music. ⚑ *Disney World® • Early Sep*

4 Bands Brew & BBQ
Combines beer, grilled food, and top musical acts. ⚑ *SeaWorld® • Feb–Mar*

5 Halloween Horror Nights
Universal is transformed into a ghoulish home for the undead. ⚑ *Universal Studios® • Oct–Nov*

6 Epcot® International Food & Wine Festival
Disney chefs and sommeliers strut their stuff. ⚑ *Epcot® • Oct–Nov*

7 Epcot® International Flower & Garden Festival
Meet master gardeners and HGTV stars. ⚑ *Epcot® • Mar–May*

8 Disney World Festival of the Masters
Daytime art exhibits and nighttime big-name jazz shows. ⚑ *Downtown Disney® • Nov*

9 Mickey's Very Merry Christmas Party
Evening seasonal fun complete with snow and enchanting parades. ⚑ *Magic Kingdom® • Dec*

10 Grinchmas
Enjoy a live performance of *How the Grinch Stole Christmas* at Seuss Landing. ⚑ *Islands of Adventure® • Dec*

Left **Downtown Disney Store** Right **Nike Factory Store, Orlando Premium Outlets International**

🔟 Places to Shop

1 Orlando Premium Outlets

This terrific 150-store complex is located just across I-4 from the east entrance of Disney World. It boasts high-end designer outlets by Versace, DKNY, and Barney's New York, as well as a mix of popular brands including Nike, Timberland, and Banana Republic. ⑨ *8200 Vineland Ave • Map F3 • 407-238-7787 • www. premiumoutlets.com*

2 Orlando Premium Outlets International

This 180-store mall offers upscale shopping from stores such as Eddie Bauer, Betsey Johnson, Perry Ellis, Lacoste, Juicy Couture, Hugo Boss, Coach, Kate Spade, Ugg, Movado, and Le Creuset. ⑨ *4951 International Drive • Map U2 • 407-352-9600*

3 Mall at Millenia

Upscale and slightly uptown, the Mall at Millenia offers luxury retailers including Tiffany & Co., Louis Vuitton, Neiman Marcus, and Jimmy Choo, as well as mid-price stores like Macy's, Pottery Barn, and Gap. Valet parking and currency exchange are available, and there's also a US Post Office in the mall, which is handy for mailing purchases home or sending gifts. Special events at the mall include fashion expos and interactive children's activities. Central Florida's only IKEA store is across the road from Millenia. ⑨ *4200 Conroy Road • Map E4 • 407-363-3555*

4 Florida Mall

Sure, it's a big enclosed suburban mall, but it's also one of the best in Central Florida and hugely popular with visitors and locals. Stores include Dillard's, JC Penney, Macy's, Saks Fifth Avenue, Sears, Nordstrom, Lord & Taylor, and more than 200 others. ⑨ *8001 S. Orange Blossom Trail • Map E4 • 407-851-6255 • www.simon.com*

Park Avenue

5 Park Avenue

This eight-block stretch of downtown Winter Park retains a times-gone-by quality. A canopy of live oak trees shades the brick-paved street, which is surrounded by low buildings and flanked by relaxing Central Park. Many of the stores on this upscale avenue are independents, but there are some national chains too, such as Williams & Sonoma and Lilly Pulitzer. There's no food court, but the sidewalks are lined with places for lunch or dinner. ⑨ *Park Ave bet Fairbanks Ave & Swoope Ave • Map L4*

Factory outlets – which sell last season's stock and imperfect goods at discounts of at least 30 percent – generally open 9am–9pm daily.

Pointe Orlando

Pointe Orlando is a complex of shopping, dining, and entertainment venues. It offers something for everyone – a 21-screen cinema, a Wonderworks entertainment center, several upscale restaurants, plus more than 20 retail stores, including Victoria's Secret, Armani Exchange, and lots of specialty stores. The landscaped outdoor layout makes this a pleasant place for a shopping spree. ✪ 9101 International Dr • Map T4 • 407-248-2838 • www.pointeorlando.com

Ivanhoe Row

Downtown Disney®

There are two shopping options in Downtown Disney®. On the glittery West Side is the massive RideMakerz car shop and the House of Blues store. The more serene Marketplace is highlighted by World of Disney (the planet's largest Disney store) and the LEGO® Imagination Center, an enormous superstore. ✪ Downtown Disney • Map F2 • 407-824-4321 • www.disneyworld.com

Flea World

Claiming to be America's largest flea market, Sanford's Flea World is a Byzantine maze of more than 1,700 sales booths, which are bursting with bargains every weekend. The mostly new goods are already cheap, but you can haggle to lower prices still. In addition to an A to Z list of goods for sale, Flea World also has live bands, bingo, and an a old-style amusement park, Fun World, for the kids. ✪ 4311 S. Hwy 17/92, Sanford • Off map • 407-330-1792 • Open 9am–6pm Fri–Sun

Renninger's Antique & Flea Markets

Spread across a bucolic country meadow, Renninger's offers a large, folksy flea market, and a diverse indoor and outdoor antique market. The flea market offers everything from clothing to vinyl. The antique market has permanent dealers who specialize in excellent furnishings and jewelry. Renninger's also hosts the massive Antique Extravaganzas (see p64). ✪ 20651 Hwy 441, 1 m (1.6 km) E. of Mount Dora • Off map • 1-352-383-8393

Ivanhoe Row

This stretch of antique shops has thinned out due to rising rents, but there are still more than a dozen stores offering vintage linens, clothing, jewelry, and various collectables. Imported furniture from Bali and vintage LPs can also be found here. ✪ N. Orange Ave • Map N3

Factory outlet stores often have sales at the same times of the year as regular shops (Mar–Apr and Aug–Oct).

Left **The Boheme** Right **Park Plaza Gardens**

High-End Restaurants

Victoria & Albert's
The high price can limit this to very special occasions, but trust the first-class food, fine wine, and faultless staff to make a memorable visit. It's decorated like Queen Victoria's dining room, and each table gets its very own Victoria and Albert as servers. Changing menus offer seven courses of international dishes, including apple-smoked Colorado bison and black bass with couscous. Take advantage of the wine-pairings (a glass with each of the five courses); it's cheaper and more varied than buying a bottle. See p94.

Primo
Housed in the sprawling J.W. Marriott Hotel, Primo has an elegant and warm dining area. Chef Melissa Kelly creates delicious dishes with Mediterranean accents using fresh local ingredients, including herbs and vegetables from the garden behind the hotel.

Emeril's of Orlando

Sit on the outdoor patio and sample the chargrilled Moulard duck for a special treat. ◈ 4040 Central Florida Pkwy • Map T6 • 407-393-4444 • Dinner only • No kids' menu • Pre-arrange vegetarian entrées • $$$$

California Grill
The 15th-floor vista here gets top marks from both critics and diners. The redesigned kitchen and menu has only helped further that general opinion. Popular choices are seared grouper in a noodle bowl with ginger-crab salad and some of the most inventive sushi in town. They also offer an interesting menu for people who prefer vegetarian. It's hard to get a table on weekends. See p94.

Emeril's of Orlando
Famous US TV chef Emeril Lagasse owns this place, but only appears once a month, leaving the day-to-day cooking of the creole-inspired menu to his chefs. They create treats such as quail stuffed with Louisiana oyster dressing, andouille-crusted redfish, and a kosher salt and cracked black pepper rib-eye steak. This lofty place has a 12,000-bottle wine cellar. Book well in advance for dinner; there's a similar lunch menu at two-thirds of the price. ◈ CityWalk • Map T1 • 407-224-2424 • $$$$$

Norman's
A high-end restaurant located in the Ritz-Carlton, Norman's specializes in a fusion of Latin,

Todd English's bluezoo

European, and Floridian cuisine. World-renowned chef Norman Van Aken holds court when in town, but the kitchen turns out his New World cuisine regardless. The highlights here are the Brazilian conch chowder and barbequed veal chops.
⊛ *4012 Central Florida Pkwy • Map F4 • 407-343-4333 • Pre-arrange vegetarian entrées • $$$$$*

Fiorella's Cucina Toscana
Inside the Westin Hotel, this is hand-crafted Tuscan and northern Italian cuisine with a modern flair, served in a relaxed atmosphere. The striking dining room features colorful contemporary art glass, and has views of the open kitchen. Specialties include seafood dishes based on seasonal local produce, and the signature "Globo" brownie in a chocolate dome. *See p105.*

The Boheme
The signature restaurant of the Westin Grand Bohemian Hotel is a key business venue and a prime romantic destination. Serving classic dishes with a modern twist, menu highlights range from Southern crab cakes to filet mignon and rack of lamb. Sip a Martini before dinner in the hip Bösendorfer Lounge. *See p117.*

Todd English's bluezoo
Celebrate the "blue zoo" of the ocean in a glass-accented dining room that feels like an underwater scene. Asian, Tuscan, and American touches appear in innovative dishes created with superb fish selections. Meat dishes are also available.
⊛ *Dolphin Hotel, 1500 Epcot Resorts Blvd, Lake Buena Vista • Map G2 • 407-934-1111 • Dinner only • No kids' menu • Pre-arrange vegetarian entrées • $$$$*

Park Plaza Gardens
For a touch of class, book a table at the exquisite Park Plaza Gardens. The glorious cuisine (such as blackened deep sea grouper with red lentils and curry vinaigrette) is enjoyed in a divine garden, much like a French courtyard. Take your pick from one of the best wine lists in Orlando, and finish off with towering desserts such as the triple chocolate cake. *See p123.*

Napa
This California-themed upscale restaurant in the Peabody Orlando Hotel *(see p143)* includes superb seafood, local and seasonal organic ingredients, and a wide-ranging international wine list. The restaurant overlooks the inviting, palm-ringed Grotto Pool.
⊛ *9801 International Dr • Map T3 • 407-345-4570 • $$$$$*

Unless stated, all restaurants advise reservations, are non-smoking, take credit cards, and have DA, kids' menus, A/C, and vegetarian dishes.

Left **Outback Steakhouse** Right **Café Tu Tu Tango**

🔟 Family Restaurants

1 Rainforest Café
This jungle-themed restaurant provides noisy fun and a California-style menu. The mixed grill includes barbecued ribs, soy-ginger steak skewers, chicken breast, and peppered shrimp. Kids get their own special menu, the cartoon-like decor is good fun, and a "volcano" erupts every now and then. *See p95.*

Romano's Macaroni Grill

2 Romano's Macaroni Grill
Despite being part of a chain, Romano's has a neighborhood feel. The modestly priced Italian menu includes thin-crust pizzas cooked in a wood-burning oven, sauteed salmon scaloppini, and chicken marsala. Paper tablecloths and crayons will keep kids happy for hours. ◈ *12148 Apopka-Vineland Rd • Map F2 • 407-239-6676 • $$$*

3 Coral Reef Restaurant
A 600,000-gallon (272,600-liter) floor-to-ceiling aquarium is a calming backdrop to this themed restaurant. Despite the highbrow, mainly fish and seafood menu, it's very child-friendly. Try the sauteed rock shrimp in a lemon cream sauce. *See p95.*

4 Outback Steakhouse
Tasty seared steaks are the headliners here; choose from ribeyes, strips, fillets, and porterhouses. The Outback also serves good smoked ribs, shrimp and chicken over fettucine, rib-and-chicken combos, pork chops, and hamburgers. ◈ *4845 S. Kirkman Rd • Map D3 • 407-292-5111 • $$$*

5 Restaurant Marrakesh
Mosaic tiles and a painted Moorish ceiling set the Moroccan scene. The food is flavorsome, with delights such as roast lamb *au jus* with couscous, and marinated beef shish kabobs. A belly dancer shimmies around and kids love to join her. *See p95.*

6 Café Tu Tu Tango
The menu in this lofty space is Spanish tapas in name but more international in flavor, with such diverse nibbles as baked goat's cheese, tuna sashimi, alligator bites, and snapper fingers. Performers (from sword eaters to artists at work) provide the entertainment. *See p105.*

7 Boma – Flavors of Africa
This all-you-can-eat, African-themed restaurant is in Disney's Animal Kingdom® Lodge. Dishes from more than 50 African countries are served from the open kitchen for breakfast and dinner. There's a good selection of fire-grilled meats, salads, and African pastries for dessert. The dinner

Unless stated, all restaurants advise reservations, are non-smoking, take credit cards, and have DA, kids' menus, A/C, and vegetarian dishes.

buffet is a family-friendly option.
◈ 2901 Osceola Parkway • Map G1
• 407-939-3463 • $$$

Baja Burrito Kitchen
The draw here is the fresh and healthy Californian and Mexican cuisine, such as tacos, quesadillas, fajitas, and burritos, stuffed with lean meat and sour cream and cheese.
◈ 2716 E. Colonial Dr • Map N4
• 407-895-6112 • $$

Panera Bread
There are no preservatives in the dough used in the sandwiches and baked goods here available to eat in or take away; there's everything from whole-grain to focaccia and sourdough. Soup is also available. ◈ 7828 Sand Lake Rd
• Map F3 • 407-226-6992 • $

Chili's Grill & Bar
This international Tex-Mex chain serves scrumptious Cajun chicken sandwiches, margarita-grilled chicken topped with lime shrimp, and Cadillac fajitas with black beans and rice. See p105.

Chili's Grill & Bar

Dining with Disney & Universal Characters

1 Chef Mickey's
Mickey hosts American buffet breakfasts and dinners in the Contemporary Resort.

2 Restaurantosaurus
Donald Duck and pals host the Breakfastosaurus in the Animal Kingdom every morning.

3 Wonderland Tea Party
Every weekday at 2pm, Alice in Wonderland characters join guests in the Grand Floridian resort for tea and cakes.

4 1900 Park Fare
Have breakfast with Mary Poppins or a sit-down dinner with other Disney favorites at the Grand Floridian Resort.

5 Mickey's Backyard BBQ
Disney characters keep you entertained at this hoedown and all-you-can-eat American buffet dinner in Fort Wilderness.

6 Cinderella's Royal Table
A whole host of Disney characters join you for the "Once Upon a Time" breakfast in Magic Kingdom®'s Cinderella castle (park adm required).

7 Circus McGurkus
The Cat in the Hat, the Grinch, Thing One, and Thing Two turn up at Seuss Landing in Islands of Adventure at 2:45pm daily for a late lunch.

8 The Crystal Palace
Meet Pooh and his cohorts for American buffet breakfasts, lunches, and dinners in Magic Kingdom (park adm required).

9 Liberty Tree Tavern
Mickey and Goofy host the sit-down dinner "Liberate your Appetite" in the Magic Kingdom (park adm required).

10 Cape May Café
Join Goofy for a breakfast buffet at the Beach Club Resort.

For character meals, call seven days in advance (Disney: 407-939-3463; Universal: 407-363-8000). Expect to pay $ for kids, $$–$$$ for adults.

Left **Bösendorfer Lounge** Right **Downtown bar scene**

🔟 Places to Have a Drink

1 Lucky Leprechaun
A lively, welcoming Orlando institution. As its name suggests it has Irish connections and a friendly Irish flair. They offer a huge selection of great beers, including all the Irish beers you could hope for, and also food. There is karoke every night, live entertainment, and big-screen televisions showing all the important sporting events. Very popular hangout with the locals. *See p104.*

2 Independent Bar
A relaxed and hip place where you can dance to great tunes without the stuffiness of many other clubs. Fabulous mix of music from classic pop and hip hop to indie and jazz. Plenty of room at the long bar and on the spacious dance floor. *See p116.*

3 Cowboys Orlando
Kick up your heels at this popular country music dance venue, located near downtown Orlando. This huge club has four bar areas and state-of-the-art sound and lighting. It's open Thursday to Saturday to guests over 18 years old, and has nightly drink specials and dance contests. *See p116.*

4 The Bar at California Grill
This bar is a fabulous place to kick back, enjoy a bottle of wine and watch the fireworks over the Magic Kingdom®. The secret is out, though, so come early for a table. Finding a spot at other times isn't too hard as long as you avoid the dinner rush. *See p94.*

5 Fiddler's Green
A big, noisy Irish pub, Fiddler's Green has an excellent beer selection, a homey, shabby ambience, and a bartender who pours faster than anyone in town. Darts and occasional live music form the entertainment, but people come here just to down a few beers and shoot the breeze. Lunch and dinner are served. *See p123.*

Bar-B-Q Bar

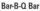 *Most bars tend to open betweem 4–8pm and close around 2am.*

6 Bar-B-Q Bar

It's little more than an average beer joint with sticky floors and loud crowds, but Bar-B-Q is *the* place to see and be seen for the more creative set. A favorite venue with local musicians, the bar gets packed whenever there's a good band on stage. People-watch clubbers cruising the Orange Avenue strip from a sidewalk table. ✪ *64 N Orange Ave • Map P3 • 407-648-5441*

7 Sky 60

Located above The Social *(see p74)*, this rooftop bar is an Orange Avenue hotspot, attracting folks who prefer not to mingle with the masses but rather look down on them. Covered in whitewash, this airy spot is a classier option for folks who usually drink downstairs or at the Bar-B-Q Bar. Entertainment is typically provided via a DJ who leans toward refined, less aggressive grooves. *See p116.*

8 The Bösendorfer Lounge

Luxury is a tough sell Downtown, partly because the club crowd tends to be well under 30 and lacking serious funds. However, this swanky hotel bar is thriving, confirming that an older, upscale, and urbane crowd is more than willing to pay the price for a suave evening of fancy cocktails. *See p74.*

9 Dexter's of Thornton Park

A white-collar after-work crowd frequents this hugely popular bar/ restaurant in a spacious, loft-like room. On fine nights, drinkers often head for the small outdoor space or spill out onto the sidewalk, jostling and juxtaposing with the congregations from the fundamentalist church and a working-class beer joint that are located on the same street.

Fiddler's Green

Dexter's is also known for its great New American menu, and for serving lots of wines by the glass. There's another branch in Winter Park *(see p122)*. ✪ *808 E. Washington St • Map P3 • 407-648-2777*

10 The Courtesy

This trendy, speakeasy bar serves hand-crafted cocktails concocted with local and fresh ingredients. Pick your choice of liquor from a fine collection of cocktails, absinthe, beer, and wine. Its cozy ambience, and the friendly and knowledgeable staff make the visit very pleasurable. The Courtesy also offers catering services and cocktail classes on select Saturdays. Go early to avoid crowds. ✪ *114 N. Orange • Map P3 • 407-704-9288*

The minimum age requirement for drinkers in Florida is 21 years. Be sure to bring photo ID to avoid being turned away at the door.

73

Left **Hard Rock Live** right **Blue Martini**

Live Music Venues

The Social
This intimate downtown club serves up an eclectic mix of live music from established acts to up-and-coming artists. Sounds range from alternative rock to funk, jazz, and dance, with local DJs also gracing the club's legendary stage. For years, the club's policy of booking top national touring acts meant it was the shining light of Orlando's live music scene. Competition from much larger clubs is stiffer now, but this tiny spot, with its stylishly raw decor, remains O-Town's favorite venue to enjoy live music. *See p116.*

House of Blues
Wall-to-wall original folk art gives this giant venue a funky look. But like all things in the Disney empire, the decor hides a modern, smooth-running machine. HOB books amazing acts in every genre, from hip-hop to death-metal. Unlike many clubs, shows start and end on time, and the sound system is crystal clear. The one flaw is an incredible lack of seating with stage views, so be prepared to be on your feet all night. *See p93.*

Hard Rock Live
The yin to HOB's yang, Hard Rock has a more comfortable room, with balcony seating and good stage views. The grand ballroom decor is more appropriate for acts that want to perform in an elegant setting, so it's not surprising that top R&B artists such as Maxwell and Erykah Badu play here. The Hard Rock schedule is more erratic, with fewer top name bookings. *See p104.*

Blue Martini
They sell 29 different types of Martini here, of every color and description. This vibrant spot – they have live music every night – is popular with young professionals unwinding after work as well as at weekends. Tapas and a light meal menu are also on offer. The outdoor patio bar is a good place to mix and mingle. ◈ *4200 Conroy Rd • Map M3 • 407-447-2583*

The Bösendorfer Lounge
The lounge music craze that once swept the nation is now only for serious practitioners. This elegant hotel bar is a swell place to sip cocktails and dig the duo in evening dress who sing near the $250,000 Bösendorfer Grand piano. Maybe it's the heavy drapes, the dark wood, or the well-tuned ennui of some patrons, but you feel wealthy just being here. *See p116.*

Blues Bar at House of Blues
Before it evolved into a chain of mega-clubs, the original HOB concept was closer to

Almost everyone needs to show ID to get into Orlando's clubs, most of which are for over 21's only; others set higher age limits.

this casual roadhouse place, which offers bayou-inspired eats, cold beer, and live blues bands on a low stage. Though they get little promotion, the bands booked here are excellent. And even if dinner prices are inflated (*à la* everything at Disney), the cover charge is zero. *See p46.*

Live music at the House of Blues

7 Adobe Gilas

The downside to Gilas is that they book mostly cover bands. The upside is a young, good-looking crowd getting smashed on tequila and dirty dancing with near strangers. The band usually sets up on the patio, but it's more fun and sweaty when it rains and the band crams itself into an inside corner. Sure, the southwestern theme decor gets old fast, but if you need to relive the days of dorm parties, this is the place to go. *See p104.*

8 Atlantic Dance Hall

Travel back in time to the glamorous dance halls of the 1930s and '40s and dance the night away! A great venue featuring wonderfully kitsch Art Deco interiors and grown-up entertainment, Atlantic Dance Hall is ideally located for those staying at a Disney resort. Dueling DJs spin on Thursday and Friday nights, while dance-along videos play on Tuesdays, Wednesdays and Saturdays. *See p93.*

9 Backstage at the Rosen Plaza

This swinging nightclub is located within the Rosen Plaza Hotel on International Drive.

Dance the night away to live bands and top DJs who play popular hits from the 1970s, the 1980s and the 1990s. Valet parking is also available. ◊ *Rosen Plaza Hotel, 9700 International Dr • Map F3 • 407-996-9700 • www.rosen plaza.com*

10 Bongo's Cuban Café

This lively venue combines Old Havana and Miami. In addition to delicious Cuban food, Bongo's serves up furious salsa rhythms on the sound system. There is multilevel indoor and outdoor seating, dancing every night, and great live music on Fridays and Saturdays. *See p93.*

Left **Firestone Live** Right **Downtown nightlife scene**

Hip Clubs

Hard Rock Live
Located at Universal's CityWalk®, this vibrant and huge venue looks like a Roman Coliseum and offers seating for up to 2,000 people – great for a mildly decadent but definitely fun night out. The first floor has a standing-room only dance floor. Hard Rock Live's stunning sound systems are state of the art, as is its lighting technology. Emerging local musical performers, as well as big national and international touring acts, make regular appearances here. *See p104.*

Hard Rock Live

The Beacham Theater
Housed in a downtown Orlando building that once hosted the famous Vaudeville acts of the 1920s, the Beacham Theater is a 1,250-seat live music venue and a buzzing nightclub, with high-tech sound, and light systems and a large dance floor. National touring acts appear regularly; on other evenings, DJs set the pace. Friday night is Ladies' Night. A dress code is enforced. *See p116.*

Firestone Live
Once named top club in the US by *Rolling Stone* magazine, Firestone Live occupies the interior of one of Orlando's oldest buildings. Its vast size, an awe-inspiring light and sound system, and an international DJ lineup still make this the best night out in Orlando. The club attracts a mixed crowd that is very gay-friendly. The sounds run from trance to hip-hop to Latin, depending on the night of the week. *See p116.*

Revolution Nightclub
With more than 14,000 sq ft (1,300 sq m) of dancing space, multiple bars, and three separate rooms of music, Revolution is tailored for the alternative local crowd. Live bands and world-class DJs play Miami salsa, hip- hop, and techno until the early hours, while the Hydrate Video Bar area features giant video screens. ◈ 375 S. Bumby Ave • Map D5 • 407-228-9900 • Adm

Monkey Bar
A sign outside the Wall Street complex of bars and restaurants may proclaim the existence of Monkey Bar, but it takes a walk through the downstairs Tiki Bar and a ride on the elevator to enter this upstairs hideaway. Trendy and cozy, Monkey Bar offers food as well as quirky drinks and live music. Enjoy half-priced Martinis during happy hour (4–7pm Tue–Fri). ◈ 19 N. Orange Ave • Map D4 • 407-849-0471 • Closed Sun, Mon • Adm

Samba Room

This South Orlando club is upscale and hip. It's a restaurant during the week, but on Friday and Saturday nights it also has live Latin and Reggae music, and dancing until 2am. The menu features Latin fusion cuisine and there's also a cigar lounge. ◈ *7468 W. Sand Lake Rd • Map S3 • 407-226-0550 • Adm • www.sambaroom.net*

Rok Room

A rock-themed "Ultra lounge", Rok Room is hidden in an alley behind larger and swankier night-clubs. Look for the sign on the sidewalk and be ready to climb some stairs. It plays a wide variety of music such as rock, dance, dubstep, top 40, hip-hop, and house. The service is very friendly. Wednesdays, Fridays, Saturdays, and Sundays are special nights. Over 21s only; no cover charge. ◈ *41 W. Church St • Map P2 • 407-992-0398 • www.rokroom.com*

The Groove

The theme changes every night at this Universal CityWalk® dance club, with music from the 1970s and '80s, current dance hits, Latin, techno, and more. The club area features a giant psychedelic dance floor, but the smaller areas – the Candle Room, Blue Room, and Red Room – are great for more intimate partying. The Groove is an attractive alternative for teens, too, with dedicated teen nights on Mondays and Wednesdays. *See p104.*

The Social

This intimate live music venue is located in the heart of Downtown's party district. It regularly features big name acts and there's live music most nights. It also has one of the best Martini bars in town. *See p116.*

Roxy

Roxy

Tucked into an after-dark desert area of town, Roxy is a big multi-floor dance club, with impressive hip-hop, Latin, and house DJs playing nightly. The loyal following tends to be less self-consciously trendy and more hetero than the usual Downtown club mix. For example, Monday Night Fights see amateur boxers from the crowd knock back a few beers then jump in a ring to fight each other. Well, the crowd *is* different from that found in Downtown. ◈ *740 Bennett Rd • Map N5 • 407-898-4004 • www.roxyorlando.com*

For more information on nightlife **See pp72–5**

Left **Firestone Live** Right **Carmello, the Orlando drag queen diva**

Gay & Lesbian Nightlife

Parliament House Resort
Parliament is one of the southeast's premier gay resorts, boasting non-stop entertainment. Beside a 130-room hotel, there's a pulsating dance club, a piano bar, a country and western bar, a video bar, lakeside beach parties, and more. ◈ 410 N. Orange Blossom Trail • Map P2 • 407-425-7571 • Free (Adm to club)

The New Phoenix
Claiming to be Winter Park's oldest gay bar, Phoenix holds drag queen and king shows on weekends. It also hosts karaoke and free pool nights. ◈ 7124 Aloma Ave • Map C6 • 407-678-9070 • Adm

The Brink
This downtown hotspot does not charge cover before 10:30pm which means that you need to arrive early. Located behind Firestone Live, The Brink courts a young crowd with happy hours specials, Friday night drag shows and "pants optional" nights. ◈ 47 W. Amelia St • Map P3 • 407-388-4384

Revolution Nightclub
Revolution is a mega-club that combines the Revolution Nightclub, the Hydrate Video Bar, and the Majestic Theatre and Lounge under one roof. Diverse crowds hit the dance floor at Revolution, enjoy drinks and the hottest videos at Hydrate, or watch live theater, music, and female impersonators at the Majestic. There's also an outdoor patio for unwinding and relaxing, and a game room with pool tables, darts, and video games. ◈ 375 S Bumby Ave • Map P3 • 407-228-9900

The Peacock Room
The Peacock's jazzy ambience is a welcome respite

The Peacock Room

from the thump of techno. This is a small, stylish lounge in the heart of Orlando's gay-friendly ViMi district. The decor is muted Art Deco and a small jazz band often plays. The cool vibe also attracts straights, making for a nice mix. ◈ 1321 N. Mills Ave • Map N4 • 407 228-0048 • Free

Savoy Orlando
A sophisticated North Orange lounge that caters for an upscale crowd of mostly professional gay men. High bar tables, black leather stools, and crystal chandeliers give the club a classy air. ◈ 1913 N. Orange Ave • Map P3 • 407-898-6766 • Free

Parliament House

Firestone Live
Ensconced within a former Firestone garage, this giant venue has long been rated one of the southeast's top dance clubs, particularly with gays, ravers, and all types trendy. Although gay-only nights are gone, Firestone continues to pump out house, hip-hop, and trance music for "the community." The upstairs Glass Chamber is a relaxing chill-out room with comfy couches. See p116.

Pulse
This is an Orlando hot spot for gays, with DJs spinning music from the 1970s and 80s. Tuesday night is Karaoke Night, while Wednesday is College Night. Hip-hop music is featured on Thursday nights, but whatever type of music you enjoy, you will find it here. This welcoming establishment is a firm favorite

for the Orlando gay crowd. ◈ 1912 S. Orange Ave • Map Q3 • 407-649-3888 • Adm

Stonewall
Everything from leather-clad dancers to "under-wear nights" makes this a go-to for the local gay communi-ty. There are daily happy hours, bingo and poker nights, and karaoke on Fri-day nights. ◈ 741 W. Church St • Map P3 • 407-373-0888 • Free

Hanks
Hanks has been open for over 20 years and is one of Orlando's oldest gay bars. Pool tables, darts, video games, and a juke-box make this unpretentious beer and wine bar a casual hangout. The Back Room, the adjoining adult store, is open nightly. ◈ 5026 Edgewater Dr • Map L1 • 407-291-2399 • Free

For more on Orlando's clubs See pp76–7

Left **Medieval Times** Right **Sleuth's Mystery Dinner Theatre**

🔟 Dinner Shows

1 Hoop-Dee-Doo Musical Revue

Book early for Disney's most popular "chow-and-cheer" night. The jokes are silly, the stars dress in costumes from Broadway's *Oklahoma!*, and if you don't join in the sing-along fun, the actors and audience will keep on at you until you do. Dinner is all-you-can-eat fried chicken and barbecue ribs; a vegetarian menu is available with 24 hours' notice. *See p93.*

2 Arabian Nights

Horses steal this show. Several breeds such as chiseled Arabians and muscular Belgians thunder through a performance that includes Wild West trick riding, chariot races, a little slapstick comedy, and bareback daredevilry. Horse fans can pet the four-legged stars after the show. ❧ *6225 W. Irlo Bronson Memorial Hwy • Map G2 • 407-239-9223 • 7:30pm nightly*

3 Medieval Times

Horses take a secondary role at this spectacle. Instead, the action heroes are knights who get into sword fights, joust, and otherwise raise the roof while you feast on the likes of barbecued ribs, and roasted chicken with your fingers (after all, this is the 11th century). If you arrive early, you can tour a re-created medieval village. ❧ *4510 W. Irlo Bronson Memorial Hwy • Map G3 • 407-396-1518 • Show times vary*

4 Spirit of Aloha Dinner Show

High-energy performers from Hawaii, New Zealand, and Tahiti show off their hula, ceremonial, and fire-dancing in an open-air theater. Meanwhile, tuck into the all-you-can-eat meal, which includes roast pork and chicken, fried rice, vegetables, and fruit. Learn how to make *leis* and do the hula in the pre-show. ❧ *Disney's Polynesian Resort • Map F1 • 407-824-2000 • 5:15 & 8pm nightly*

5 Pirates Dinner Adventure

The swashbuckling actors entertain with comedy, drama, and music, on a set that is a full-size pirate ship on a water-filled "lagoon". The dinner buffet features roast chicken, braised beef, herbed rice, and more. After the show, there's a Buccaneer Bash

Arabian Nights

All shows charge admission, which sometimes varies depending on whether the performance is midweek or on the weekend.

Dance Party to help you burn a few of those spare calories. ✆ *6400 Carrier Dr • Map U2 • 407-248-0590 • 7:45pm nightly*

Titanic Dinner Event
Experience first-class dining aboard the recreated ship, Titanic, as participants re-enact the retirement dinner of Captain E.J. Smith on that fateful night when it sank. Complete with a tour of the ship, this trip will be one to remember. A three-course dinner and a theatrical evening are included. ✆ *7324 International Dr • Map E3 • 407-248-1166 • Pre-arrange vegetarian entrées • 7pm Wed, Fri & Sat*

Sleuth's Mystery Dinner Theatre
The theater's cast stages eight different shows over the course of a month, all with a suspicious death and a twist before the mystery is uncovered. Meals include hors d'oeuvres before the show, then your choice of honey-glazed Cornish game hen, prime rib, or lasagna with side dishes, dessert, and unlimited beer, wine, and sodas. ✆ *8267 International Dr • Map T1 • 407-363-1985 • Show times vary*

Capone's Dinner & Show
Settle into the 1930s and visit Al Capone's notorious speakeasy, a place where pseudo-mobsters and their molls entertain guests with a lot of song and dance. The all-you-can-eat buffet offers pasta, sausage with peppers and onions, baked chicken and ham, vegetables, potatoes, and whatever beer, wine, coffee, iced tea and sodas you care to drink.

Pirates Dinner Adventure

✆ *4740 W. Irlo Bronson Memorial Hwy • Map G3 • 407-397-2378 • 8pm nightly*

Outta Control Magic Comedy Dinner Show
The audience becomes a part of the show in Tony Brent's 90-minute interactive mixture of magic and fast-paced improvisational comedy. Impersonations and mind-reading are accompanied by all-you-can-eat hand-tossed pepperoni pizza, popcorn, beer, soda, and desserts. The show is suitable for all ages. ✆ *Wonderworks, 9067 International Dr • Map T4 • 407-351-8800 • 6 & 8pm nightly*

Treasure Tavern
This adults-only alternative to the kid's Pirates show combines circus, burlesque, comedy, magic, live music, and prime rib dinner with a full bar. ✆ *6400 Carrier Dr • Map U2 • 407-206-5102 • 8pm Tue–Sat*

There is no minimum age limit for dinner shows, although some may be unsuitable for younger children.

Left **Clearwater Beach, Gulf Coast** Right **Florida Aquarium**

Day Trips South & West

1 Busch Gardens
With six roller coasters, three water rides, and many other attractions, this park is a close second to Islands of Adventure *(see pp20–23)* on the thrill front. Roller coaster addicts rate the park's SheiKra ride very highly - it's a floorless 70-mph (120-km/h) coaster. Nature lovers will enjoy the animal interactions, of the Jungala attraction and the truck ride through the plains of the Serengeti Safari. Ask about the free shuttle from Orlando for ticketholders. ⓢ *3000 E. Busch Blvd, Tampa • 813-987-5082 • Hours vary seasonally • Adm • www.buschgardens.com*

Busch Gardens

2 Florida Aquarium
Florida's native species are just a fraction of the more than 10,000 animals and plants on display in this modern attraction. Wetlands, bays, coral reefs, and their creatures are featured in several galleries, and you can watch divers feed sharks and other marine creatures. ⓢ *701*

Channelside Dr, Tampa • 813-273-4000 • Open 9:30am–5pm daily • Adm

3 Lowry Park Zoo
Tampa's first zoo has 1,500 creatures, including Malayan tigers, African elephants, and Komodo dragons. It also serves as a rehabilitation center for injured manatees *(see p31)* and as a sanctuary for Florida panthers and red wolves. A free-flight aviary and petting zoo provide a chance to touch some tamer species. ⓢ *1101 W. Sligh Ave, Tampa • 813-935-8552 • Open 9:30am–5pm daily • Adm • www.lowryparkzoo.com*

4 Ybor City/Centro Ybor
The Latin heart of Tampa contains the Ybor State Museum, plus trendy art galleries and lively cafés. Take the opportunity to try a Cuban sandwich, and strong *café cubano*, or to salsa and *merengue* into the small hours in one of the district's dozen or so clubs. ⓢ *Seventh Ave, Tampa • Off Map • www.ybor.org*

5 Henry B. Plant Museum
In the late 1800s, railroad magnate Henry B. Plant built an opulent Moorish palace in the swamps of Tampa, attracting tourists and celebrities alike. Now part of the University of Tampa, this museum honors the life and times of Plant. Take a tour through its authentically restored rooms. ⓢ *410 W. Kennedy Blvd • 813-254-1891 • Open 10am–5pm Tue–Sat, noon–5pm Sun • Adm • www.plantmuseum.com*

The Gulf Beaches
6 Western Pinellas County has more than 30 miles (48 km) of white-sand, low-surf, warm-water beaches that are highly popular throughout the year. St. Pete Beach, Treasure Island, Madeira Beach, and Clearwater Beach are among the many headliners. ✆ *St. Pete Beach to Clearwater Beach • Off Map*

Historic Bok Sanctuary
7 This National Historic Landmark has nearly 250 acres (100 hectares) of gardens and grounds surrounding a 205-ft (62-m) bell tower and Mediterranean Revival mansion. The visitor center has a museum, video, café, and gift shop. ✆ *1151 Tower Blvd, Lake Wales • 863-676-1408 • Adm • Dis. access • www.boksanctuary.org*

Salvador Dali Museum
8 The world's most comprehensive collection of Salvador Dali's work from 1914 to 1970 can be found at this world-class museum. The art on display includes oils, watercolors, and sculptures by the great Surrealist. There's a café and an interesting outdoor space, the Avant-Garden. ✆ *1 Dali Blvd, St. Petersburg • 727-823-3767 • Open 10am–5:30pm Mon–Sat (to 8pm Thu), noon–5:30pm Sun • Dis. access • www.thedali.org*

Caladesi Island State Park
9 This 3-mile (5-km) island, accessible by ferry from Honeymoon Island, is a lovely outdoor retreat traversed by a nature trail. A ban on cars helps keep it much as it was a century ago. In

Annie Pfeiffer Chapel, Florida Southern College

season, beach areas are dotted with the tracks of loggerhead turtles that nest here. ✆ *Ferry to island • 3 Causeway Blvd, Dunedin • 727-469-5918 • Ferry runs 10am–5pm daily • Adm • Off Map*

Florida Southern College
10 In the late 1930s, renowned architect Frank Lloyd Wright designed 12 campus buildings at this college – the world's largest collection. Highlights include the Annie Pfeiffer Chapel, the Roux Library, the Danforth Chapel, and the Esplanades. Pick up a walking-tour map from the visitor center. ✆ *111 Lake Hollingsworth Dr, Lakeland • 863-680-4110 • Visitors center open 11am–4pm Tue–Fri, 10am–2pm Sat, 2–4pm Sun • Free*

For Day Trips North & East See pp84–5

Left **Daytona Beach** Right **Ron Jon Surf Shop, Cocoa Beach**

Day Trips North & East

Kennedy Space Center
This well-conceived monument to America's space program impresses visitors with exhibits both mammoth, such as the Saturn V Rocket, and minuscule, such as antiquated space suits. Bus tours are a good way to take in the installations. *See pp38–41.*

Cocoa Beach
Just 60 miles (96 km) east of I-4 via the Beachline Expressway, Cocoa Beach is the seashore closest to Orlando. The beach is picturesque, although the surrounding town is less so (apart from the lovely Cocoa Village near US Hwy 1). Surfing is taken seriously here, due in part to the presence of the Ron Jon Surf Shop, a vast surfing mecca that sells surf wear, beach gear, boards, and every imaginable beach accessory. ◈ *Off map*

Daytona Beach
During the annual "Spring Break," this legendary beach (just 90 minutes from Orlando along I-4) is the destination for thousands of vacationing college students, who drink and party until they drop. But sun and fun isn't all that's offered. Beach Street is lined with shops, restaurants, and clubs; and of course, there's the Daytona Speedway, home to the Daytona 500 and other NASCAR races (see p57). ◈ *Off map • Tourist info 386-255-0415*

New Smyrna Beach
Just south of Daytona Beach, New Smyrna is a smaller, calmer town that lacks Daytona's party scene. The white sand beach is picture perfect – but as at Daytona, cars share the space with sunworshipers. For food, the place to go is JB's Fish Camp, a raucous and friendly shack beside Mosquito Lagoon, which serves some of the state's tastiest fish, seafood, and key lime pie. ◈ *Off map*

Rivership Romance on St. John's River

Cassadaga Spiritualist Camp
Buried deep in the woods near exit 54 off I-4, tiny Cassadaga was founded more than 100 years ago as a community of clairvoyants, mediums, and healers. Resident spiritualists promote the science, philosophy, and the religion of Spiritualism; offer contacts with the deceased in the Spirit World; and provide a variety of healing services for the body, mind, and spirit. Staff at the Cassadaga Camp Bookstore can put visitors in touch with on-call mediums in the area and even provide a phone to make appointments.

*Off map • Cassadaga Camp Bookstore, 1112 Stevens St • Open 10am–6pm Mon–Sat, 11:30am–5pm Sun • 386-228-2880 • www.cassadaga.org

Crystal River Manatee Swim and Snorkel Tour

Three covered boats tour year-round down the pristine Crystal River, allowing guests to view – and swim with – endangered manatees *(see p33)*. Sightings of these gentle creatures are most frequent from late October to late March. *Pete's Pier, 1 SW 1st Place, Crystal River • Off map • Tours daily, call for times • 352-628-3450 • Adm • www.crystalrivertours.com*

Merritt Island National Wildlife Refuge

This 140,000-acre (56,000-ha) wildlife sanctuary (the second-largest in Florida) has more federally-endangered species than any other refuge in the United States. A six-mile (10-km) driving tour with shaded board-walks weaves through lush pine and oak hammocks. See p52.

St Johns Ridership Company

Operating out of historic Sanford, this 1946-built triple-decked boat offers daily cruises along the scenic St. John's River. It's a truly civilized way to catch a glimpse of the Florida that tourists rarely see. *433 N. Palmette Ave • 321-441-3030 • Adm • No DA • www.stjohnsridershipco.com*

Central Florida Zoo and Botanical Gardens

Beneath this zoo's dense canopy of foliage, visitors can observe the residents (from howler monkeys

Local architecture, Mount Dora

to bald eagles, llamas, and zebu) at close quarters. Some areas fall short – the pacing big cats obviously need bigger cages – but on the whole, this makes for a rewarding trip. *3755 N.W. Hwy 17–92, Sanford • Off map • Open 9am–5pm daily • 407-323-4450 • Adm • www.centralfloridazoo.org*

Mount Dora

Just 25 miles (40 km) from Orlando, charming Mount Dora seems plucked from the 1950s. The cozy downtown is unmarred by strip malls or chain stores. Instead, the local industry is antiques, with dozens of small shops on and around Donnelly Street as well as Reninger's Antique & Flea Markets *(see p67)* on the edge of town. Train buffs can enjoy a ride on the Mt. Dora trolley for a guided tour, and Lake Dora offers plenty of boating opportunities. *Tourist info 1-352-383-2165 • Off map*

AROUND TOWN

Walt Disney World® Resort & Lake Buena Vista 88–95

International Drive Area 96–105

Kissimmee 106–111

Downtown Orlando 112–117

Winter Park, Maitland, & Eatonville 118–123

ORLANDO'S TOP 10

Left **Lake Buena Vista** Right **Lake Buena Vista environs**

Walt Disney World® Resort & Lake Buena Vista

THERE WAS ONLY ONE *drawback to California's Disneyland, Walt Disney's first theme park, which opened in 1955: the area was prime real estate and there was no free space around the park in which to expand. So, following an aerial tour of Central Florida in 1965, Disney began covertly to buy large tracts of land. At the time, this patch of the Sunshine State was little more than cow pastures, citrus groves, and swamps, and was of little interest to anyone. Today, the 47-sq-mile (121-sq-km) Walt Disney World® Resort is a self-contained and virtually self-governing entity (call 911 here and you get a Disney employee) containing four major theme parks, two water parks, several smaller attractions, and many hotels and resorts, which also spill over into the adjoining Lake Buena Vista area. For some of the 43 million guests who visit annually, it's a once-in-a-lifetime vacation, but many can't get enough of this enchanted fantasyland and return time and again to relive the experience.*

🔟 Sights

1. **Magic Kingdom®**
2. **Epcot®**
3. **Disney Hollywood Studios®**
4. **Disney's Animal Kingdom® Park**
5. **Water Parks**
6. **Cirque du Soleil**
7. **DisneyQuest**
8. **Richard Petty Driving Experience**
9. **Fantasia Gardens & Winter Summerland Miniature Golf**
10. **ESPN Wide World of Sports®**

Magic Kingdom®

Who's the leader of the theme-park pack? Disney's first Florida park is the most popular in the US. *See pp8–11.*

Epcot®
Walt Disney's guys knew something had to appeal to curious adults and techno kids. Epcot® is that something. *See pp12–15.*

Disney Hollywood Studios®
A park that combines front-of-house fun with behind-the-scenes explanation. *See pp16–17.*

Disney's Animal Kingdom® Park
Disney's fourth Orlando park is a place where elusive animals roam. *See pp18–19.*

Water Parks
Disney World has two water parks. The hugely popular Typhoon Lagoon, designed to resemble a beach resort devastated by a tropical storm, can hold more than 7,000 people at once, and has plenty of rides and attractions. Blizzard Beach's theme is a ski resort that melted and is a favorite among water slide fans. But whatever extreme weather they represent, these parks have similar features: long drops to build up speed and darkened tubes to confuse you before spilling you, laughing or screaming, into a wading pool below. The parks have seasonal opening hours, so call to check. *See p48.* ◈ *Typhoon Lagoon • Map G2 • 407-560-4141 • Adm* ◈ *Blizzard Beach • Map G1• 407-560-3400 • Adm*

Cirque du Soleil
Nowadays, circuses without animals are all the rage, and the Canadian company Cirque du Soleil is one of the best of its kind. So popular are its shows that, in addition to world tours, there are now permanent venues, too. Orlando's high energy, 90-minute show, La Nouba, climaxes with a finale in which more than 70 performers execute an extraordinary trampoline routine. The ticket is quite pricey, but you're unlikely to be disappointed. ◈ *Downtown Disney West Side • Map G2 • 407-939-7600 • Shows at 6 & 9pm Thu–Mon • Adm*

Cirque du Soleil

Walt Disney

Walter Elias Disney was just 26 years old when his most famous cartoon character, Mickey Mouse, was introduced in the film *Steamboat Willie* (1928). Despite escalating success in the film world as he embraced first sound then technicolor, Disney had his sights set on more than just animation. He was the man who created the theme park, which he envisaged as a kind of 3-D movie where each individual could spin his or her own story in a totally safe, controlled, and upbeat enviroment. His first, California's Disneyland Park, was the perfect vehicle for bringing Disney's clean-living family values and nostalgia for tradition to the masses. It was also the only one of his parks that came to fruition before his death in 1966 from lung cancer, 11 years after it opened.

7 DisneyQuest

This interactive, indoor theme park is divided into five floors and entertains adults as much as it does kids. Highlights of the Explore Zone include Pirates of the Caribbean®: Battle for Buccaneer Gold, and Aladdin's Magic Carpet Ride. The former puts you on the deck of a two-master schooner to play cat-and-mouse with foul-playing pirates and foul-smelling sea monsters. Aladdin's Magic Carpet involves wearing a virtual reality helmet and taking a ride through the 3-D Cave of Wonders in search of the genie. In the Score Zone, it's all about testing your game-playing skills. Don't miss Buzz Lightyear's Astroblasters, where you get to fly a space ship and blast gigantic robots, or the Mighty Ducks Pinball Slam, a life-size, sure-fire hit for pinball fans. The Create Zone unleashes the designer within:

build your own roller coaster (and then ride it in a simulator), or take a short course in cartooning at the Animation Academy. The Replay Zone is filled with games where for an extra charge, you can win tickets that can be redeemed for prizes you can live without. Crowds are worse after lunch. ◎ *Downtown Disney West Side • Map G2 • 407-828-4600 • Open 11:30am–10pm Sun–Thu, till 11pm Fri, Sat • Adm*

8 Richard Petty Driving Experience

Ever wanted to drive one of those souped-up, 600-horsepower NASCAR race cars, or even just be a co-pilot? Well, here's your chance to try for your dream – and a new land-speed record. The two-page waiver form that riders need to sign may shake your nerve, but there's nothing virtual about this attraction. There are two options: ride or drive. For the first, take the passenger seat while a professional drives off around the track at 145 mph (233 kmph); minimum age for this option is 16. Alternatively, spend a few hours or (if you have lots of cash to spare) days learning how to drive, and then race others for up to 30 laps (minimum age is 18 years). ◎ *Walt Disney World Speedway • Map F1 • 800-237-3889 • www.drive petty.com • Opening times vary • Adm*

9 Fantasia Gardens & Winter Summerland Miniature Golf

Orlando in general and Walt Disney World® Resort in particular have some great golf courses *(see pp54–5)*, but not everyone likes to take the game so seriously, or has the makings of a pro. These two miniature golf courses offer a total of 72 holes of putting fun. Inspired by the classic Disney cartoon, *Fantasia*, Fantasia Gardens'

Fantasia Gardens & Winter Summerland Miniature Golf

18 holes have an animal theme. Located near Disney Hollywood Studios®, it's the more forgiving of the two courses, and so the best choice for young kids or beginners. Winter Summerland is a scale model of a large course, complete with bunkers, water hazards, frustrating putting greens, and holes that are up to 75 ft (23 m) long. Choose between the winter and summer themed courses. ◎ *Fantasia Gardens • Map G2 • 407-560-4582 • Open 10am–11pm daily • Adm* ◎ *Winter Summerland • Map G1 • 407-560-3000 • Open 10am–11pm daily • Adm*

10 ESPN Wide World of Sports®

Disney's sports complex is the spring training home of Major League baseball's Atlanta Braves (Feb–Mar) and minor league baseball's Orlando Rays, a farm team for the Tampa Bay Devil Rays (Apr–Sep). It's also a winter home for basketball's Harlem Globetrotters. Other facilities in the 220-acre (90-ha) complex, which is used for all kinds of amateur sports and athletics,

include: a fitness center; basketball, volleyball, and tennis courts; softball, soccer, and lacrosse fields; a martial-arts venue; and a golf-driving range. ESPN Wide World of Sports® is also the home of the NFL Experience *(see p50)*. There is an extreme sports area catering for skateboarders, in-line skaters, and cyclists, which is now open for special events. ◎ *Map G2 • 407-939-1500 • Opening times vary • Adm*

Hidden Mickeys

Hidden Mickeys started many years ago as a joke among park designers. Today they're a Disney tradition. They're images of the world's most famous mouse: silhouettes of Mickey's ears, his head and ears or his whole body, semi-hidden throughout the parks and resorts. They can be any-where: in the landscaping, in the murals you pass while waiting in ride lines, and even overhead, for example on the Earffel Tower in Disney Hollywood Studios®. See how many you can spot (www.hiddenmickeys.org).

Mitsukoshi Department Store

🔟 Best Shops

1 House of Good Fortune
Here's an excellent source for all things Asian, from jade figurines to silk robes, and inlaid mother-of-pearl furnishings to wind chimes. ✪ *China Pavilion, World Showcase, Epcot® • Map G2 • Adm*

2 Berber Oasis
Hand-tied Berber rugs, camel-bone boxes, and more are on offer in this square, which has the bustle but not the hustle of the real thing. ✪ *Morocco Pavilion, World Showcase, Epcot® • Map G2 • Adm*

3 LEGO® Imagination Center
Kids love the play area, which has enough LEGO® pieces to build almost anything. Inside, the cash registers sing as parents buy the latest Lego gadgets. ✪ *Downtown Disney Marketplace • Map G2*

4 Mitsukoshi Department Store
An amazing selection of kimonos, samurai swords, bonsais, Japanese Disneyana, and kites is sold here. ✪ *Japan Pavilion, World Showcase, Epcot® • Map G2 • Adm*

5 Harley-Davidson
Motorcycle lovers can buy everything from baby clothes to personalized leather vests with the iconic Harley logo, or hop on a real "hog" for a photo op. ✪ *Downtown Disney West Side • Map G2*

6 French Marketplace
Pick up fine soaps, wine, designer fragrances, kitchen gadgets, and even a dashing black beret. ✪ *France Pavilion, World Showcase, Epcot®. • Map G2 • Adm*

7 Art of Disney
This large gallery is one of a kind in Florida. You'll find Disney sculptures, animation cels, and other collectibles. ✪ *Downtown Disney Marketplace • Map G2*

8 Hoypoloi Gallery
This small but sensory gallery sells sculptures, ceramics, and other imaginative oddities made of metal, stone, clay, and wood. ✪ *Downtown Disney West Side • Map G2*

9 Mickey's Mart
Everything in this shop located between Disney Tails and Disney at Home is $10 or less. Every week there is a featured sale item. ✪ *Downtown Disney Marketplace • Map G2*

10 TrenD
The stylish side of Mickey Mouse, with edgy, trendy, one-of-a-kind clothes and accessories, including organic loungewear, embroidered hand-bags, jeweled sun-glasses, and exclusive creations by cutting-edge designers. ✪ *Downtown Disney Marketplace • Map G2*

➡ *Forget to buy something? Call 407-363-6200, give the item's description and where you saw it. You can probably order it by phone.*

Downtown Disney®

1 House of Blues®

One of Orlando's best venues for live music with a wide variety of musical acts. *See p74.* ◈ *Downtown Disney West Side • Map G2 • Map G2 • 407-934-2583 • Adm*

2 Disney's BoardWalk®

By night, this "seaside" boardwalk is thronged with guests enjoying the buzzing vibe and some great restaurants and clubs. *See p46.* ◈ *Map G2 • Free*

3 Downtown Disney®

Probably Disney's best spot for night owls, with lots of bars and clubs to choose from. *See p46.* ◈ *Map G2 • Free to walk around*

4 Cirque du Soleil

In a tent-like theater in Disney's West Side, this avant-garde circus troupe spotlights superhuman acrobats. *See p89.*

5 DisneyQuest

Heaven for video gamers, here kids can design their own roller coaster and ride it, or steer a ship in Pirates of the Caribbean. *See p90.*

6 Bongo's Cuban Café

This venue evokes images of Havana of the 1940s and '50s, and has live music at weekends. *See p75.* ◈ *Downtown Disney®, 1498 E. Buena Vista Dr • Map G2 • 407-828-0999 • Adm on Sat*

7 ESPN Club

Watch big games on a giant screen, play arcade games, and join the audience for live shows at this sports bar, which serves burgers and steaks. ◈ *2101 Epcot Resorts Blvd • Map G2 • 407-939-1177*

8 Hoop-Dee-Doo Musical Revue

This family show combines an all-you-can-eat dinner with country & western dancing, singing, and comedy. Unlimited draft beer, wine, and soft drinks are included. *See p80.* ◈ *Disney's Fort Wilderness Resort • Map F1 • 407-WDW-DINE • 5, 7:15 & 9:30pm nightly*

9 Atlantic Dance Hall

This glorious kitschy 1930s-style dance hall has been repositioned as a place to dance along to music videos and dueling DJs. *See p75.* ◈ *Disney's BoardWalk® • Map G2 • Closed Sun & Mon • Adm*

10 Chip 'n' Dale's Campfire Sing-A-Long

Enjoy songs and marshmallows around a campfire, followed by a different Disney movie every night. It is open to all – just park at the River Country entrance and take the bus to the party. ◈ *Meadow Trading Post, Fort Wilderness Campground • Map G2 • 407-824-2900 • Free • 8pm (summer), 7pm (rest of the year)*

Around Town – Walt Disney World® Resort & Lake Buena Vista

 Guests must be 21 or over to get into clubs and bars in Orlando, and need to have picture ID (driving license or passport) to prove it.

93

Sanaa

ᵀᴼᴾ10 Resort Area Restaurants

1 Victoria & Albert's
This romantic gem has an international menu that is served by staff dressed as Queen Victoria and Prince Albert. *See p68.*
Ⓢ *Disney's Grand Floridian Resort & Spa • Map F1 • 407-824-1089 • Pre-arrange vegetarian entrées • No kids' menu • $$$$$*

2 California Grill
This vegetarian-friendly restaurant offers delicious California cuisine in a romantic 15th-floor space. *See p68.*
Ⓢ *Disney's Contemporary Resort • Map F1 • 407-824-1576 • $$$$*

3 Be Our Guest
Modeled along the film, *Beauty and the Beast*, this high-end restaurant serves casual lunches and sit down dinners. Reserve ahead to enjoy French cuisine and wine. Ⓢ *Magic Kingdom Dr • Map F1 • 407-934-5277 • $$$$$*

4 Jiko – The Cooking Place
Jiko features a show kitchen and an inventive menu: banana-leaf steamed sea bass is a typical dish. Ⓢ *Disney's Animal Kingdom Lodge • Map G1 • 407-938-3000 • $$$$*

5 Artist Point
Bison rib-eye steak and nut-and-herb crusted lamb chops are a few of the delicious options here. There's patio dining as well.
Ⓢ *Disney's Wilderness Lodge • Map F1 • 407-824-3200 • $$$$*

6 Emeril's Tchoup Chop
The Polynesian fare here has a New Orleans twist. Menu highlights include dumplings and pot stickers followed by fish cooked in clay pots, and Kona-glazed duck. Ⓢ *Royal Pacific Resort, 6300 Hollywood Way • Map T2 • 407-503-2467 • No kids' menu • $$$$*

7 Sanaa
The Indian-spiced African menu here is loaded with slow-cooked delights, grilled over a wood fire or roasted in a tandoor oven. Ⓢ *Disney's Animal Kingdom Lodge • Map G1 • 407-WDW-DINE • $$$$*

8 Columbia Restaurant Celebration
Come here for a taste of old Havana. Indulge in crab-stuffed pompano or dive into the exquisite calamari. Ⓢ *649 Front St • Map G2 • 407-566-1505 • $$$*

9 Wolfgang Puck's Café
Grilled pizza, spicy tuna rolls, and pumpkin risotto are some of the eclectic options made here by the acclaimed California chef.
Ⓢ *Downtown Disney West Side • Map G2 • 407-938-9653 • $$$$*

10 Portobello Yacht Club Restaurant
This classy eatery is sure to please with thin crust pizzas, pastas, and Italian food such as slow-roasted pork loin.
Ⓢ *Downtown Disney • Map G2 • 407-934-8888 • $$$$$*

Unless stated, all restaurants advise reservations, are non-smoking, take credit cards, and have DA, kids' menus, A/C, and vegetarian dishes.

Price Categories

For a three-course meal for one, a glass of house wine, and all unavoidable extra charges including tax.	**$** under $20
	$$ $20–$30
	$$$ $30–$45
	$$$$ $45–$60
	$$$$$ over $60

Coral Reef

🔟 Theme Park Restaurants

1 Via Napoli
Authentic pizzas are made with ingredients from Italy in giant wood-burning ovens at this wonderful family-style restaurant. ◐ *Italy Pavilion, Epcot®* • *Map G2* • *407-939-3463* • *$$$$*

2 Rainforest Café®
American cuisine inspired by Mexican, Carribean, and Asian flavors is served in an indoor rainforest setting. If you don't like volume and kids, this isn't for you. ◐ *Disney's Animal Kingdom* • *Map G1* • *407-939-3463* • *Park adm not required* • *$$$$*

3 Coral Reef
Classical music and aquarium visuals are the setting here. Try the roasted snapper with veggies. ◐ *Living Seas Pavilion, Epcot* • *Map G2* • *407-939-3463* • *$$$$*

4 Cinderella's Royal Table
This restaurant in a castle has a great menu, with tasty prime-rib pastry-pie leading the way. ◐ *Fantasyland, Magic Kingdom* • *Map F1* • *407-939-3463* • *Pre-arrange vegetarian entrées* • *No alcohol* • *$$$$*

5 Akershus
Hunker down for traditional Norweigian dishes (herring, potato salad, gravlax in mustard sauce, venison stew, and more) in a medieval castle setting. ◐ *Norway Pavilion, Epcot* • *Map G2* • *407-939-3463* • *$$$*

6 Hollywood Brown Derby
Polish off SoCal dishes such as skillet-seared tuna and grapefruit cake with cream-cheese icing. ◐ *Disney Hollywood Studios* • *Map G2* • *407-939-3463* • *Reserve ahead; pre-arrange vegetarian entrées* • *$$$$*

7 San Angel Inn
Try *mole poblano* (chicken with spices and chocolate) or beef with black beans and fried plantain at this massive south-of-the-border eatery. ◐ *Mexico Pavilion, Epcot* • *Map G2* • *407-939-3463* • *$$$*

8 Rose & Crown Pub & Dining Room
A pub-grub joint offering British staples such as bangers and mash, rib with Yorkshire pudding, and Cornish pasties. ◐ *UK Pavilion, Epcot* • *Map G2* • *407-939-3463* • *Pre-arrange vegetarian entrées* • *$$$*

9 Chefs de France
Meet Remy from *Ratatouille* at this brasserie-style restaurant full of Gallic flare and flavor. ◐ *France Pavilion, Epcot* • *Map G2* • *407-939-3463* • *Pre-arrange vegetarian entrées* • *$$$$*

10 Liberty Tree Tavern
Buffet-style American fare, such as roasted turkey, flank steak, and ham, is served in a colonial setting. ◐ *Liberty Sq, Magic Kingdom* • *Map F1* • *407-939-3463* • *Pre-arrange vegetarian entrées* • *No alcohol* • *$$$*

For information on Priority Seating in Walt Disney World Resort See p134

Left **Wet 'n Wild®** Right **Universal Studios®**

International Drive Area

CONSIDERED THE TOURIST CENTER OF *Orlando, International Drive is a brash 10-mile (16-km) strip boasting five theme parks, countless attractions open day and night, including Universal's CityWalk® entertainment complex, and the USA's second-largest convention center. Added to the mix are hundreds of hotels and resorts catering to all budgets, shopping malls and outlet stores, and themed and fast-food restaurants. As a package, the result is a frenetic zone, which, despite its wall-to-wall neon signs and visual overload, has become a serious competitor of Disney World, appealing to visitors who prefer to stay away from the clutches of Mickey but want to be in the thick of the action.*

CityWalk®, Universal Orlando®

🔟 Sights & Attractions

1. Islands of Adventure®
2. Universal Studios Florida®
3. Wet 'n Wild®
4. SeaWorld® Orlando
5. Discovery Cove®
6. Fun Spot Action Park
7. Ripley's Believe It or Not®! Odditorium
8. The Holy Land Experience
9. WonderWorks
10. Titanic – The Experience

Discover more at www.dk.com

Islands of Adventure®

Islands of Adventure®
The addition of the Wizarding World of Harry Potter™ to the rides here makes this a popular destination. *See pp20–23.*

Universal Studios Florida®
Part studio and part attraction, the movie-themed rides and shows here really let visitors step inside the movies. *See pp24–7.*

Wet 'n Wild®
It's hard to out-do Disney and SeaWorld®, but Wet 'n Wild® is among Orlando's best sun-and-swim water park attractions, with plenty of slides and rides to amuse. *See pp34–5.*

SeaWorld® Orlando
Orcas, dolphins, and other animal attractions offer a refreshing change of pace from fast rides and cartoon characters. *See pp28–31.*

Discovery Cove®
You might be in land-locked Orlando, but you can still fulfill those tropical island fantasies of swimming with dolphins and snorkeling over coral reefs if you check in to Discovery Cove®. The dolphin swim is the biggest draw (each session lasts about one hour), but the white-sand beaches, snorkeling opportunities in fresh and

salt-water lagoons, and soothing beach-resort vibe elicits just as much praise. Admission is not cheap (largely because there are never more than 1,000 visitors daily), but you get almost everything you need for the day thrown in, including sun block, lunch, and snorkel gear, as well as a seven-day pass to SeaWorld®. Kids might miss the lack of thrill rides, but they will not be short of things to do. Redevelopment work on the park during 2012 and 2013 may affect some attractions. *See p48.* ◈ *6000 Discovery Cove Way • Map T6 • 407-370-1280 • Open 9am–5:30pm daily • Adm*

Discovery Cove®

Fun Spot America
This arcade/amusement-park has something for everyone who has a little bit of the child in them. The park has four go-kart tracks, two giant roller coasters, as well as the world's biggest SkyCoaster. In addition, there are bumper boats and cars, a 100-ft (30-m) Ferris wheel, 100 arcade games, and a kid zone that has swings, a train, spinning tea cups, and flying bears. *See p44.* ◈ *5551 Del Verde Way, Orlando • Map U2 • 407-363-3867 • noon–11pm Mon–Fri, 10am–11pm Sat–Sun • Free (but ride and game prices vary) • Min age for solo go-karting is 10 yrs*

Fun Spot America

Ripley's Believe It or Not!® Odditorium

7 Ripley's Believe It or Not!® Odditorium

If you're a fan of the bizarre, you'll love Ripley's. This worldwide chain of attractions displays the unbelievable finds of Robert Ripley's 40 years of adventures, the reports of which were published in more than 300 newspapers and read by more than 80 million people. The Orlando branch has a full-scale model of a 1907 Silver Ghost Rolls Royce (with moving engine parts) built out of 1,016,711 match sticks and 63 pints (36 l) of glue; a flute made of human bones; a mosaic of the Mona Lisa made of toast; shrunken heads; a five-legged cow; and a portrait of Van Gogh made from 3,000 postcards. You'll also see a holographic 1,069-lb-(485-kg) man, plus films of strange feats such as people swallowing coat-hangers. *See p44.* ✆ *8201 International Dr • Map T3 • 407-363-4418 • Open 9am–midnight daily • Adm*

The Peabody Ducks

Their existence came about because of a practical joke, but now these five mallards, which reside in the Peabody Hotel *(see p143)*, are among the best known and most unusual celebreties in I-Drive. As befits VIPs (Very Important Poultry), they spend much of each day in their $100,000 glass-enclosed home, called the 'Duck Palace'. But what draws the crowds is their twice daily procession (at 11am and 5pm), when they waddle through the hotel lobby, led by their own red-coated duck master, on the way to and from the lobby fountain.

8 The Holy Land Experience

Marvin J. Rosenthal, a Christian convert and Baptist minister, created quite a stir when he opened this religious theme park. Set in a half-scale reconstruction of the Temple of the Great King, which stood in Jerusalem in the 1st century AD, the park aims to take visitors 7,000 miles (11,200 km) away and 3,000 years back to the ancient Jerusalem of biblical times (BC 1450 to AD 66 to be exact). The attraction has models of the limestone caves where the Dead Sea Scrolls were discovered and of Jesus's tomb. It also has displays of rare antique Bibles and biblical manuscripts, an outdoor stage where actors portraying biblical personalities tell stories from the Old and New Testaments, and a café that serves Middle Eastern food. *See p44.* ✆ *4655 Vineland Rd • Map D4 • 407-872-2272 • Open 10am–6pm, sometimes later, closed Sun & Mon • Adm*

The Holy Land Experience

9 WonderWorks

You can't miss this attraction from the outside: it looks as though a classical building has landed upside down on top of a warehouse. Inside, there are 85 hands-on exhibits. Highlights include an earthquake simulator; a Bridge of Fire, where you can

WonderWorks

literally experience the hair-raising effects of 250,000 watts of static electricity; and Virtual Hoops, which uses some of the latest cinema technology to put you on TV to play basketball against one of the NBA's top players. You can also try Virtual Hang Gliding, which sends you soaring like a bird through the Grand Canyon, and WonderCoaster,

Titanic – The Experience

which challenges your roller coaster-designing skills and then your nerve to ride your creation in a simulator. WonderWorks also runs a laser-tag venue and a twice-nightly magic show, both of which cost extra. *See p45.*
❂ *Pointe Orlando, 9067 International Dr*
• *Map T4* • *407-351-8800* • *Open 9am–midnight daily* • *Adm*

10 Titanic – The Experience

This exhibit's 200 artifacts include a real life jacket and an old deck chair, which were both recovered from the wreckage of the fateful liner, as well as the Titanic's second-class passenger list. The attraction also has full-scale re-creations of some of the ship's rooms, including its grand

staircase, as well as memorabilia from three major Titanic movies – including one of the costumes worn by Leonardo DiCaprio. Actors in period garb play out events that occured on the fateful journey, telling the story of the White Star Line's supposedly unsinkable ship. Most of the artifacts came out of private collections from both the United Kingdom and the USA. *See p44.*
❂ *8267 International Dr*
• *Map T3* • *407-248-1166* • *Timings vary* • *Adm*

I-Ride Trolley

One of the best things about I-Drive itself is the tourist-oriented I-Ride Trolley, which offers an easy way to ogle some of the area's oddities and its high-density visual overload. It is also an excellent and extremely cheap way to get around this part of town while avoiding the need to get involved in fighting I-Drive's frustratingly heavy traffic, or walking any distance in the heat. There are 78 stops on the circuit, serving all the local major attractions, shopping malls, hotels, and restaurants. *See p127.*

Left **Ice Bar** Center **Ripleys Believe It or Not®! Odditorium** Right **WonderWorks**

🔟 Eye-Openers on I-Drive

1 Four Points by Sheraton Orlando Studio City

This distinctive 21-story circular hotel has a huge globe sitting on top of it. ✆ *5905 International Dr • Map T2*

2 Titanic – The Experience

Relive the tragedy, share in the inspirational personal stories of those aboard, and marvel at the splendor of this luxurious liner that has been impressively re-created. *See p99.*

3 Pirate's Cove Adventure Golf

The view of pirate ships and waterfalls at this mega-mini-golf spot, not to mention the sound of cannon fire, is unexpected on I-Drive. ✆ *8501 International Dr • Map T3 • 407-352-7378*

4 Bargain World

The doorway to this shop is straddled by a large flying saucer. Alighting from a nearby rocketship is a giant green Martian wearing casual clothes and holding a stick. ✆ *8520 International Dr • Map T2 • 407-352-7100*

5 King's Bowl

There are 22 bowling lanes over several levels on offer here, along with two full bars, a full service restaurant, and 60 giant TVs. ✆ *8255 S. International Dr • Map E3 • 407-363-0200 •11–2am daily*

6 Ice Bar

There's always something cool happening at this frozen cocktail bar, from karaoke and swing dance lessons to DJs. Be sure to grab your coat before you visit! ✆ *8967 International Dr • Map T2*

7 Ripley's Believe It or Not®! Odditorium

This place is built to look as if one of Florida's sinkholes opened up and nearly swallowed the building. *See p98.*

8 iFLY

Take a close look at this blue and purple building and you might see people floating in front of you – look closer and you will see they are actually flying. *See p45.*

9 WonderWorks

As the marketing story goes, a tornado picked up this four-story building and sent it crashing upside down on top of a 1930s-era brick warehouse. Silly perhaps, but it stops traffic. *See p99.*

10 Air Florida Helicopters

With flights starting at just $20 (plus $4 for fuel) per person, there's no reason not to enjoy a panoramic birds-eye view over the city. ✆ *8990 International Dr • Map T4 • 407-354-1400 • 9:30am–8pm daily*

For tips on shopping in Orlando **See p132**

Left **Edwin Watts Golf National Clearance Center** Right **Stores on I-Drive**

TOP 10 I-Drive Stores & Outlet Centers

1 Nike Factory Store
A gigantic collection of things adorned with the famous "swoosh," at discount prices. ◈ *Orlando Premium Outlets International, 5201 W. Oak Ridge Rd • Map U1 • 407-351-9400*

2 Kenneth Cole
Choose from recent lines of Cole shoes; bags and clothes also vie for attention with about 25 percent discount. ◈ *Orlando Premium Outlets International, 5247 International Dr • Map U1 • 407-903-1191*

3 Orlando Premium Outlets International
With more than 170 stores bursting with bargains, there's something for everyone. ◈ *5401 W. Oakridge Rd • Map U1 • 407-352-9611*

4 Bass Pro Shops Outdoor World
Overflowing with fishing, golf, camping, and hunting supplies and apparel, this is a vast shrine to the great outdoors. ◈ *5156 International Dr • Map U1 • 407-563-5200*

5 Coach Factory Store
Leather rules at this spacious store, and deals abound on current and last season's handbags, jackets, and luggage. ◈ *Orlando Premium Outlets International, 5269 International Drive • Map U1 • 407-352-6772*

6 Edwin Watts Golf National Clearance Center
Like cars, golf clubs also have model years. This store offers last season's hot drivers and putters at deep savings. ◈ *7024 International Dr • Map T3 • 407-352-2535*

7 Brooks Brothers Outlet
Slim pickings for suits, but there's a great range of casual sportswear for men and women, discounted by at least 40 percent. ◈ *Orlando Premium Outlets International, 5247 International Dr • Map G3 • 407-363-5918*

8 Off 5th
Like Saks Fifth Avenue's regular stores, this outlet is heavy on high fashion brand names and has a rapid turnover. ◈ *Orlando Premium Outlets International, 5253 International Dr • Map U1 • 407-354-5757*

9 Oshkosh B'Gosh
This American company has sturdy kids' clothes, including its trademark overalls. ◈ *Orlando Premium Outlets International, 5401 International Dr • Map U1 • 407-352-6414*

10 Divers Direct Outlet
This deep discount outlet carries everything needed for underwater adventures. ◈ *5368 International Dr • Map U1 • 407-363-2883*

Most stores on I-Drive are open 10am–10pm Mon–Sat and noon–6pm Sun.

Left **Bob Marley – A Tribute To Freedom** Center **Red Coconut Club** Right **Hard Rock Live**

🔟 Bars, Clubs, & Entertainment

1 Hard Rock Live
One of the best spots in to see live music (national/local rock and R&B acts), with a top-notch sound system. *See p74.* ◎ *City-Walk • Map T1 • 407-351-5483 • Adm*

2 The Groove
This powerhouse dance club has slamming DJs, as well as several quiet chill-out lounges. *See p77.* ◎ *CityWalk • Map T1 • 407-224-3663 • Over 21 yrs • Adm*

3 Jimmy Buffet's Margaritaville
A mecca for Parrot Heads or anyone who wants to have a good time in the ultimate tropical setting. Great drinks, food, and live entertainment most evenings. ◎ *Universal CityWalk • Map T1 • 407-224-2155*

4 Howl at the Moon
Rock 'n' roll dueling pianos and signature drinks make this high-energy nightclub a fun adult getaway. ◎ *8815 International Dr • 407-354-5999 • Map T4 • Adm varies*

5 Lucky Leprechaun
Karaoke every night at this lively and popular Irish-themed bar – great selection of Irish beers. ◎ *7032 International Dr • Map T4 • 407-352-7031*

6 Latin Quarter
Expect anything Latin – from food to dance lessons – at this energetic venue. A 13-piece Latin band is on most nights. ◎ *CityWalk • Map T1 • 407-224-2800 • Adm after 10pm Thu–Sat*

7 Adobe Gilas
Crowds of 20-somethings swarm this restaurant/bar (with 65 varieties of tequila) and dance the night away. *See p75.* ◎ *Pointe Orlando, 9101 International Dr • Map T4 • 407-903-1477 • Free • DA*

8 Bob Marley – A Tribute To Freedom
Live outdoor reggae music is the big draw here, and the bands are often excellent. ◎ *CityWalk • Map T1 • 407-224-2690 • Over 21 yrs only after 10pm • Occasional evening adm*

9 Cricketers Arms Pub
A little piece of England, with European soccer on the TVs, darts, and nearly 20 ales, lagers, bitters, and stouts on tap. ◎ *Mercado, 8445 International Dr • Map T3 • 407-354-0686 • Free*

10 Red Coconut Club
A hip 50s retro lounge with three bars on two levels, plus live music and DJs. ◎ *CityWalk • Map T1 • 407-224-3363 • Occasional adm*

Age restrictions (18 or 21 years) for shows and clubs vary. Bring your photo ID to make sure you are not turned away at the door.

Price Categories

For a three-course meal for one, a glass of house wine and all unavoidable extra charges including tax.

$	under $20
$$	$20–$30
$$$	$30–$45
$$$$	$45–$60
$$$$$	over $60

Cuba Libre

🔟 Places to Eat

1 Café Tu Tu Tango
Local artists' work adorns the walls of this vaguely Latin-style eatery. Dishes include black bean soup, shrimp fritters, and quesadillas. ✎ *8625 International Dr • Map T3 • 407-248-2222 • $$*

2 Fiorella's Cucina Toscana
Choose from high-end, hand-crafted Italian specialties in this hotel restaurant inside The Westin Imagine Orlando. *See p69.* ✎ *9501 Universal Blvd • Map T4 • 407-233-2950 • $$$*

3 Roy's
On the menu here are Hawaiian fusion dishes such as sesame-oil-seared mahi-mahi with red Thai curry sauce. ✎ *7760 W. Sand Lake Rd • S3 • 407-352-4844 • $$$$*

4 Everglades
A casual, intimate hotel restaurant with an imaginative chef and superb steaks and seafood. ✎ *9840 International Dr • Map T3 • 407-996-2385 • $$$*

5 Seasons 52
The seasonally inspired menu includes grilled vegetables, crab-stuffed mushrooms, and rosemary and parmesan cheese flatbreads. All dishes have a low calorie content. ✎ *7700 W. Sandlake Road • 407-354-5212 • No kids' menu • $$$*

6 Cuba Libre
Located in a Cuban hacienda courtyard, Cuba Libre serves Cuban cuisine and has choreographed floor shows on Saturday nights. ✎ *Pointe Orlando, 9101 International Dr • Map T4 • 407-226-1600 • $$$$*

7 NBA City
This is the place where you can cheer for your favorite team on TV while you eat. Enjoy the NBA memorabilia on the walls during the ad breaks. ✎ *Universal CityWalk • Map T1 • 407-363-5919 • $$*

8 Bahama Breeze
Trust the Caribbean menu and spirits to create some fun, but expect to wait up to two hours for a table. ✎ *8849 International Dr • Map T4 • 407-248-2499 • No reservations • $$$*

9 Chili's Grill & Bar
One of the better chains offering Tex-Mex food including fajitas, sandwiches, and grills, with low-fat options. ✎ *7021 International Dr • T2 • 407-352-7618 • $$$*

10 The Palm
Think high-end steaks, often belly-busters (up to a 36-oz [1.2-kg] strip for two) but don't overlook the lobster option. ✎ *Hard Rock Hotel, 5800 Universal Blvd • Map T1 • 407-503-7256 • $$$$$*

Unless stated, all restaurants advise reservations, are non-smoking, take credit cards, and have DA, kids' menus. A/C, and vegetarian dishes.

Left **Osceola County Historical Museum & Pioneer Center** Right **Gatorland**

Kissimmee

WHAT USED TO BE A COW TOWN *has in the past few decades evolved into an inexpensive hotel enclave for Disney World tourists. But there's more to Kissimmee than cheap places to sleep. Though U.S. 192 (also called the Irlo Bronson Memorial Highway) is dense with strip malls and hotels – and looks like a grim vision of tourist hell – downtown Kissimmee (centered on Broadway and Emmet streets) was built in the early 1890s and boasts attractive low-slung buildings, which house several antique and gift shops. The land surrounding U.S. 192 is relatively undeveloped, providing Kissimmee visitors with easy access to Florida's rich, natural beauty. A terrific variety of outdoor pursuits is available to the visitor who is willing to spend time away from the theme parks.*

Downtown Kissimmee

Sights & Attractions

1. Gatorland
2. Celebration
3. Zip Orlando
4. Osceola County Pioneer Village & Museum
5. Green Meadows Petting Farm
6. Lakefront Park
7. Old Town
8. Reptile World Serpentarium
9. Forever Florida – Florida Eco-Safaris
10. Silver Spurs Rodeo

Discover more at www.dk.com

Celebration

Gatorland

Gatorland, Orlando's original theme park, opened more than 50 years ago as a swampy roadside stand, and is now home to well over 1,000 alligators, crocodiles, and snakes. Its appeal? A chance to gaze, just steps away from these mysterious creatures, who remain curiously similar to their prehistoric relatives. Visitors can stroll along a boardwalk over lakes full of cranky gators and buy hot dogs to throw into their mouths. A bizarre and unique attraction. *See p44.* ☒ *14501 S. Orange Blossom Trail • Map G4 • 800-393-5297 • Open 9am–sunset daily • Adm*

Celebration

When Walt Disney conceived of Epcot® *(see pp12–15)*, he imagined it as a residential community happily engaged in road-testing futuristic technologies. After his death, that dream went out the window only to resurface years later here. However, instead of looking to the future, Celebration salutes the past in a cliché of small town USA (think *The Truman Show*). The houses are pretty, the downtown has some good restaurants and a cinema, and everything is upscale. This is not an attraction, but it is quite a sight. ☒ *Located E. of I-4 at Exit 25. Turn right at Celebration Ave and follow the signs • Map G2*

Zip Orlando

Zip on a 950-ft (290-m) long line over deer, raccoons, and alligators. Choose from a wide range of night or day activities including night-time tours and guided ATV tours. Moonlit zip-line excursions are available for a headlamp-lit experience. *See p45.* ☒ *4509 S. Orange Blossom Trail • Map H3 • 407-808-4947 • Open 9am–6pm Mon–Sat, 12:30–6pm Sun • Adm*

Osceola County Pioneer Village & Museum

This homespun outdoor museum gives a glimpse of Kissimmee life before Disney. The focal point is a pair of late 1800s "Cracker-style" cypress wood buildings, complete with "possum trot" breezeway – an early form of air-conditioning. One showcases a simple home, while the other is reconfigured as a general store, selling local history books, crafts, and guides for the nature preserve located across the street. ☒ *750 N. Bass Rd • Map H3 • 407-396-8644 • Open Thu–Sun 10am–4pm • Adm*

Green Meadows Petting Farm

This educational spot is perfect for anyone who might enjoy milking a cow, riding a pony, or learning about over 300 friendly farm animals. A two-hour guided tour is included and picnic facilities are available. ☒ *1368 S. Poinciana Blvd • Map H3 • 407-846-0770 • Open 9:30am–4pm daily • Adm*

Green Meadows Petting Farm

6 Lakefront Park

This park offers a range of amenities, such as pavilions, picnic areas, and playgrounds, and hosts many community events and concerts. There are several miles of pathways for walkers, joggers, skaters, and bicycles, including a sidewalk by Lake Tohopekaliga that is popular with birdwatchers.

Lakefront Park

It also has a superb white sand beach, a fishing pier, and impressive marina. The park has easy access to Kissimmee's historic district, and is close to Chisholm Park and Peghorn Nature Park. *See p48.*

⊗ 1104 Lakefront Blvd, St. Cloud • Map H6

7 Old Town

Essentially, this is a tourist-oriented shopping mall filled with around 75 stores covering the usual array of gifts, novelty items, and souvenirs – kitsch or otherwise. What sets Old Town apart from other gift-shop strips are the numerous entertainment options: a cheerful 18-ride amusement park, Laser Tag, a Haunted House, carousel, live music performances, and a vintage car show every Friday and Saturday night. It's very much about family fun, and there's no charge for admission, although the carnival rides are priced separately. On a warm Florida night, the feeling is one of strolling the bustling midway of a state fair. ⊗ 5770 W. Irlo Bronson Hwy • Map G2 • Open 10am–11pm daily • Free

8 Reptile World Serpentarium

This is a unique and educational attraction providing all the right ingredients to make your skin crawl. Visitors can watch a snake handler extracting poisonous venom from cobras, rattlesnakes, and other deadly serpents. The indoor exhibits house more than 60 species of reptiles, and it's the largest of its kind in central Florida. *See p45.* ⊗ 5705 E. Irlo Bronson Memorial Hwy (3.5 miles east of St. Cloud) • Map H6 • 407-892-6905 • Open 9am–5:30pm Tue–Sun • Adm

9 Forever Florida – Florida Eco-Safaris

Go back in time to Old Florida on this working cattle ranch and nature preserve. The Forever Florida experience is based on the heritage of the Florida Cracker Cowboy. Take a tour on horseback or ride aboard an elevated cracker coach, then in the evening enjoy a

Forever Florida – Florida Eco-Safaris

Vintage cars, Old Town

meal at the Cypress Restaurant.
⊛ 4755 N. Kenansville Road, St. Cloud
• 407-957-9794 • Eco-Safaris on Safari
Coaches at 10am and 1pm daily
• www.foreverflorida.com

Silver Spurs Rodeo

The largest rodeo held east of the Mississippi, attracts all the top professional cowboys and is held several times a year. The Silver Spurs Rodeo dates back to 1944 and was from 1950 held in a specially constructed open-air arena, until that was replaced by the state-of-the-art, climate-controlled Silver Spurs Arena in 2002. The arena is also used for many other events, such as concerts and sports, but will always be chiefly associated with the excitement of bronc riding, steer wrestling, and bull riding.
⊛ Osceola Heritage Park, 1875 Silver Spur Lane • Map H5 • 407-67-RODEO
• www.silverspursrodeo.com

Silver Spurs Rodeo

A Day in Kissimmee

Morning

There are countless breakfast buffets in the area, all offering mounds of food, from fresh fruit to omelets. Find the one closest to you and start the day there. As mornings tend to be cooler and a bit less insect-ridden than afternoons, follow your meal with a self-guided tour of swamp life at **Airboat Rentals You Drive** (see p110). Head as far away as possible from the road, cut the engine, and enjoy the silence. Most of Florida used to be like this. For lunch, head to Kissimmee's historic Downtown and pop in to Azteca's (809 N. Main St), a tiny and original Tex-Mex restaurant. Be careful ordering anything "very hot"; the cook takes this as a personal challenge and will likely spice the dish so your head explodes.

Afternoon

From Downtown, it's a short drive north to **Gatorland**. The massive gators prowling the front lakes are the big attraction. But smart guests will take the Swamp Walk, check out the crocodile pens, and survey the alligator breeding marsh from the observation tower. There are four live animal shows but if time is tight, Gator Jump-A-Roo and Gator Wrestling are the essentials.

Evening

For dinner, the slightly camp **Pacino's Italian Ristorante** (see p111) is popular for its home-style Italian favorites and delicious pizza. Afterwards, take another short drive to **Old Town** where kids can play on the rides while adults watch from a bench enjoying an ice cream.

Around Town – Kissimmee

Left **Airboat ride, Boggy Creek** Center **Fishing, Kissimmee** Right **Warbird Adventures**

TOP 10 Leisure Pursuits & Activities

1 East Lake Fish Camp
This lakeside facility provides everything from fishing poles to boats, bait, and bunks. Large mouth bass and sometimes game fish hit the lines. ◈ *3705 Big Bass Rd • Off map • 407-348-2040 • Adm • No DA*

2 Extreme Jet Ski
Rent a Jetski or three, and race the family on Lake Cecile. ◈ *4914 W. Irlo Bronson Memorial Hwy • Map G3 • 407-390-9200 • Adm • No DA*

3 Warbird Adventures
Have a flight in a vintage North American T-6 Texan or a Bell 47 helicopter. You'll even get the chance to take the controls and have the whole experience recorded on dvd. ◈ *233 N. Hoagland Blvd • Map H3 • 407-870-7366*

4 Thompson Aire
Hover high over Disney, and the wilds of Kissimmee in a hot-air balloon. Daily flights at sunrise. ◈ *13825 Avalon Rd • Map G1 • 407-421-9322 • Adm • No DA*

5 Osceola Center For The Arts
Here, culture mavens will find anything from theater to music events, and exhibitions. ◈ *2411 E. Irlo Bronson Memorial Hwy • Map H5 • 407-846-6257 • Adm*

6 Boggy Creek Airboat Rides
These 18-passenger flat-bottomed skiffs powered by giant fans make regular daylight wildlife tours and special one-hour night tours. ◈ *3702 Big Bass Rd • Off map • 407-344-9550 • Adm*

7 The Ice Factory
Get out of the Florida sun and do a few laps on this ice rink, which also has a kids' play area. ◈ *2221 Partin Settlement Rd • Map H5 • 407-933-4259 • Adm • No DA*

8 Falcon's Fire Golf Club
This immaculately groomed public golf course is said to be one of the best in Florida. ◈ *3200 Seralago Blvd • Map G3 • 407-239-5445 • Adm • No DA • www.falconsfire.com*

9 Central Florida Guide Service
This professional guide service takes clients fishing in some of the best big bass waters in Florida. ◈ *1326 Sweetwood Blvd • Map H4 • 407-908-4600 • Adm • www.floridabassfishing.com*

10 Horse World Riding Stables
Enjoy horse riding on 750 acres (300 ha) of peaceful sandy trails. There are pony and hay rides, as well as friendly farm animals. ◈ *3705 S. Poinciana Blvd • Off map • 407-847-4343 • Adm*

Price Categories

For a three-course meal for one with a glass of house wine, and all unavoidable extra charges including tax.

$	under $20
$$	$20–$30
$$$	$30–$45
$$$$	$45–$60
$$$$$	over $60

Tarantino's Italian Restaurant

TOP 10 Places to Eat

1 Charley's Steak House
Charley's uses an Indian cooking method, yielding steaks that are charred outside, juicy inside. ✍ *2901 Parkway Blvd • Map G2 • 407-239-1270 • Closed lunch • $$$$*

2 Azteca's Mexican
Authentic Mexican and Tex-Mex is served in an extravagantly decorated room. ✍ *809 N. Main St • Map H4 • 407-933-8155 • $$ • No DA*

3 Tarantino's Italian Restaurant
This delightful Italian venue wins praise for charming ambience and well-prepared Italian classics. ✍ *4150 W. Vine St • Map H3 • 407-870-2622 • Closed lunch • $$$*

4 Chef John's Place
John Walker's casual retreat serves fresh local fish which highlights the menu of grouper, catfish, smoked ribs and pork, and grilled steak. ✍ *3753 Pleasant Hill Rd • off map • 407-343-4227 • Open daily • $$$$*

5 Pacino's Italian Ristorante
Sicilian specialties here include hand-cut steaks, veal chops, and great pizza and pasta. ✍ *5795 W. Irlo Bronson Memorial Hwy • Map G2 • 407-396-8022 • $$$$*

6 Puerto Rico Café
It's a bit of a dive, but don't let that put you off trying the delicious *mojo*-enhanced steaks and seafood. ✍ *507 W. Vine St • Map H4 • 407-847-6399 • Open daily • $$$ • No DA*

7 Celebration Town Tavern
A quiet local neighborhood gathering spot, which serves great seafood and burgers. Family-friendly yet grown-up happy hours are on offer, and football games are shown on the big-screen TV. ✍ *721 Front St • Map G2 • 407-566-2526 • $$*

8 Black Angus Restaurant
Melt-in-your-mouth steaks are the focus of this award-winning, family eatery, but ribs and fried chicken are also popular. There's a great breakfast buffet, too. ✍ *7516 W. Irlo Bronson Memorial Hwy • Map G1 • 407-390-4548 • $$$$*

9 Logan's Roadhouse
With its neon signs and country jukebox, the vibe here is 1940s, honky-tonk, roadside grill. Try the mesquite-grilled steaks or honey sweet rolls. ✍ *5925 W. Irlo Bronson Memorial Hwy • Map G2 • 407-390-0500 • $$$*

10 Taste of Punjab
A perfect place for an authentic and reasonably priced Indian buffet, offering both meat and vegetarian dishes for lunch and dinner. ✍ *4980 W. Irlo Bronson Memorial Hwy • Map G3 • 407-507-3900 • $$*

Left **Downtown Skyline** Right **Orange County Regional History Center**

Downtown Orlando

*O*RLANDO IS NOT JUST about Walt Disney and amusement parks. Long a hub of the banking and citrus-growing industries, Downtown Orlando is also a historic district, and a cultural and natural retreat. It contains several of the city's leading museums, as well as its best-known park, a lovely green

oasis that surrounds Lake Eola, which boasts dramatic skyline vistas and hosts festivals and seasonal celebrations. By day Downtown is a relaxed southern enclave, but by night it transforms into a throbbing club scene – despite the decline of the famous entertainment, dining, and shopping zone, Church Street Station. Orange Avenue is the main street and most evenings, herds of party people, both gay and straight, migrate from club to club in search of cheap drinks and hot DJs – and there are plenty of both.

Orlando Science Center

🔟 Sights

1. Orlando Science Center
2. Orlando Museum of Art
3. Orange County Regional History Center
4. Harry P. Leu Gardens
5. Mennello Museum of American Folk Art
6. The Vietnamese District
7. Lake Eola Park
8. American Ghost Adventures
9. Church Street
10. Colonial Lanes

Orlando Science Center

The workings of the natural world, from the infinitesimal to the overwhelming, are on display here. Big interactive fun awaits at the Body Zone, where a huge mouth introduces an exhibit about the digestive system. The vast Cinedome shows movies about topics such as Egyptian treasures and ocean life, and on weekend evenings, stargazers can pick out the planets through a telescope. ✆ 777 E. Princeton St • Map M3 • 407-514-2000 • Open 10am–5pm Sun–Tue & Thu–Sat • Adm • www.osc.org

Orlando Museum of Art (OMA)

The focus of exhibitions in this big, bright museum is American art from the 19th century onward, art from the ancient Americas and Africa, and blockbuster traveling shows. On the first Thursday evening of every month, you can enjoy music, food, and the work of local artists for an inventively themed get-together. ✆ 2416 N. Mills Ave • Map M3 • 407-896-4231 • 10am–4pm Tue–Fri, noon–4pm Sat–Sun • Adm • www.omart.org

Orange County Regional History Center

From the informative to the kitsch, the History Center highlights the formative periods and industries of Central Florida. Dioramas show scenes of early Native Americans, and a re-created Florida Cracker house can be inspected. There's also a display called The Day We Changed, which chronicles the impact of the arrival of the Disney theme parks. Some exhibits fall a little flat, but many elements, such as the stuffed alligators and pink flamingos, betray a sense of fun. ✆ 65 E. Central Blvd • Map P3 • 407-836-8500 • 10am–5pm Mon–Sat, noon–5pm Sun • Adm • www.thehistorycenter.org

Harry P. Leu Gardens

Well-tended pathways weave through this elegant 50-acre (20-ha) park. Earthy scents waft from an herb garden, while another contains plants that attract butterflies. Depending on the season, visitors might catch roses in bloom (in Florida's largest rose garden) or the grace of camellias. Guides conduct tours of the early 20th-century Leu House. ✆ 1920 N. Forest Ave • Map M4 • 407-246-2620 • Open 9am–5pm daily • Adm • www.leugardens.org

Fountain, Lake Eola Park

Mennello Museum of American Folk Art

Half of the Mennello is devoted to the work of Florida folk artist Earl Cunningham (1893–1977), who created vibrant, whimsical pastoral paintings glowing with orange skies and yellow rivers. The other half houses traveling exhibits of folk art. The lakeside grounds contain wonderfully quirky sculptures scattered here and there. ✆ 900 E. Princeton St • Map M3 • 407-246-4278 • 10:30am–4:30pm Tue–Sat, noon–4:30pm Sun • Adm • www.mennellomuseum.com

Mennello Museum of American Folk Art

6 The Vietnamese District

This area, also known as the ViMi district (for the crossroads at Virginia and Mills avenues), is a less obvious ethnic enclave than, say, New York's Chinatown. Nevertheless, it is still clustered with Vietnamese restaurants and shops, as well as delights from other Asian countries. The thickest concentration is south of Virginia, at Colonial Drive. ◎ *Mills Ave bet Virginia Ave & Colonial Dr • Map N3*

7 Lake Eola Park

A pedestrian-only path encircles Lake Eola, offering a pleasing view of Downtown's skyline. Those willing to exert their leg muscles can rent swan-shaped paddle boats *(see p47)*. Real swans drift along in the lake's shallow water and will venture onto dry land if offered a handful of the food that can be bought for small change. Concerts are performed at the Walt Disney Amphitheater, a bandshell with surprisingly decent acoustics. The landmark illuminated fountain in the middle of the lake is computerized and produces on a light show of changing colors. ◎ *Map P3*

Signs, Vietnamese Disctrict

8 American Ghost Adventures

A guide leads walking tours through Downtown Orlando, telling tales of the city's scandals, unsolved mysteries, and hauntings dating back to 1886. The two-hour walk circles back around to its starting point, the Orange County Regional History Center, where participants can carry out their own amateur ghost hunt with the help of handheld "ghost detectors". ◎ *Depart from Orange County Regional History Center • Map P3 • 407-256-6225 • 8pm nightly • Adm*

9 Church Street

The Amway Center Arena has brought life and activity back to Church Street. The influx of new restaurants, the renowned drama company Mad Cow Theatre, and the upcoming SunRail station have made it even more popular. The Amway Center attracts big-name touring acts, and the stretch of Church Street that lies between Orange Avenue and I-4 once again has enough retail stores, restaurants, and bars to keep visitors interested. The area's original anchor is Church Street Station, a three-level complex constructed around the attractive historic building that was the city's original train station. The complex holds a variety of bars, restaurants, and shops, and it is easy to zigzag between watering holes. ◎ *Church St bet. Orange Ave & I-4 • Map P3*

Lake Eola Fountain, Lake Eola Park

Church Street

Colonial Lanes

10 For more than 50 years, the venerable Colonial Lanes has offered patrons the sociable and quintessential blue-collar pastime of bowling. This 32-lane facility is a friendly and noisy place to knock over a few pins, so rent some shoes, pick out a ball, and let the computer keep score – but bear in mind that league bowling takes over the place between 6pm and 9pm every night, so

Bowling balls, Colonial Lanes

avoid those times, unless you're happy to watch. After the game, the place to go is the Colonial Lanes Bar & Restaurant, parts of which resemble a giant sunken living room (with bartenders standing on a lower floor than customers). Drinks are cheap, and the concept of rounding off prices never caught on here, so don't be surprised if your tab is a quirky $4.38. ◎ *400 N. Primrose Dr • Map P4 • 407-894-0361 • Timings vary • Free, but pay to play*

A Day Downtown

Morning

Begin with a big healthy breakfast at JP's Everyday Gourmet (63 E. Pine St) before visiting the **Orange County Regional History Center**, a homespun place that reveals the pre-Disney history of the region. For lunch, wander over to **Café Annie** *(see p117).* This authentic café has Greek and Lebanese food, including mixed platters. This kind of food usually has lots of vegetarian options.

Afternoon

After lunch, jump in the car or grab a cab to Loch Haven Park, where the **Orlando Museum of Art**, the **Orlando Science Center,** and the **Mennello Museum of American Folk Art** *(for all see p113)* reside within easy walking distance of each other. The Science Center, with its four floors of interactive fun, is the best bet for kids. Art lovers can easily hit the Mennello and the OMA in the same afternoon but if time is short, the OMA deserves priority. Make a dinner stop in the Vietnamese district where Ha Long Restaurant (1231 E. Colonial Dr) serves up a top-notch bowl of comforting *pho*, a traditional, and delicious noodle soup.

Evening

The downtown club scene starts late, so kick off with an early cocktail at **The Bösendorfer Lounge** *(see p116).* Fans of live music should head to **The Social** *(see p116),* where shows start around 10pm. Die-hard clubbers should try **Firestone Live** *(see p76),* where the DJs play well into the early hours.

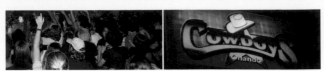

Left **The Social** Right **Cowboys Orlando**

🔟 Nightspots

1 The Social
Orlando's best club for live music, bar none. The stage hosts an incredible variety of performers, from jazz to electronica. *See p74.* ✆ *54 N. Orange Ave • Map P3 • 407-246-1419*

2 The Beacham
This historic building in Downtown Orlando houses a state-of-the-art nightclub and live music venue showcasing a variety of musical styles. ✆ *46 N. Orange Ave • Map P3 • 407-246-1419*

3 Cowboys Orlando
This gigantic country music hot spot has four huge bars and nightly dance contests. ✆ *1108 S. Orange Blossom Trail • Map P2 • 407-422-7115 • Closed Sun–Wed*

4 The Bösendorfer Lounge
With upscale elegance, this lounge is perfect for sipping cocktails in stylish surroundings. Lounge singers and pianists play around the $250,000 Bösendorfer piano (Tue–Sat). *See p74.* ✆ *Westin Grand Bohemian Hotel, 325 S. Orange Ave • Map P3 • 866-663-0024*

5 Howl at the Moon
Dueling pianos, nightly sing-alongs and a full bar make this a pleasant nightspot. ✆ *8815 International Dr • Map E3 • Open till 2am • 407-354-5999 • Adm*

6 Sky 60
South Beach-style hip bar with a DJ every night. Great rooftop terrace with mood lighting. ✆ *64 N. Orange Ave • Map P3 • 407-246-1599*

7 Church Street
A two-block strip of bars, restaurants, and clubs that draws party people wanting to steer clear of the trendiness of other downtown clubs. ✆ *Church St, bet Orange Ave & I-4 • Map P3*

8 Firestone Live
This club offers lively techno, rave, and house dance beats. The best time to go is on the weekends, especially Saturday nights when there is a big crowd and occasional live acts. ✆ *578 N. Orange Ave • Map N3 • 407-872-0066*

9 NV Lounge
A small basement venue with dark decor and atmospheric lighting. A good place to hang out, and sample the terrific boutique beer and wine. ✆ *27 E. Pine St • Map P3 • 407-649-0000*

10 180 Grey Goose Lounge
Located in the Amway Arena, this is a before-, during-, and after-game hotspot for drinks and casual conversations on the balcony. ✆ *400 W. Church St • Map D4 • 407-913-0180 • Open on event nights till 2:30am*

➥ *Unless indicated Downtown's nightspots are open seven nights a week.*

Price Categories

For a three-course meal for one with a glass of house wine, and all unavoidable extra charges including tax.

$	under $20
$$	$20–$30
$$$	$30–$45
$$$$	$45–$60
$$$$$	over $60

The Boheme

🔟 Restaurants & Cafés

1 K Restaurant and Wine Bar
Downtown's best dining experience mixes bistro warmth with an adventurous menu of Asian, French, and Italian influences. ◈ 1710 Edgewater Dr • Map M2 • 407-872-2332 • Closed Sun • $$$$

2 The Boheme
This outstanding restaurant, with its sensual paintings and dark woods, serves game, steaks, and seafood to an upscale clientele. See p69. ◈ 325 S. Orange Ave • Map P3 • 407-581-4700 • $$$$$

3 Napasorn Thai Restaurant
This family-owned restaurant serves traditional Thai dishes and interesting pan-Asian variations. ◈ 5G E. Pine St • Map P2 • 407-245-8088 • $$$

4 Graffiti Junction American Burger Bar
The graffiti-covered exterior belies a great, high-energy burger joint within. Order the huge "Lone Star" for a messy delight. There is karaoke on Sunday afternoons. ◈ 900 E. Washington St • Map P2 • 407-426-9502 • $$

5 Café Annie
Head here for authentic Greek and Lebanese food, especially Zorba's platter, the chicken and beef kebabs, couscous and falafel. ◈ 131 N. Orange Ave • Map P3 • 407-420-4041 • Closed Sun • $$$

6 Dexter's of Thornton Park
A favorite after-work hangout, Dexter's offers exotic sandwiches, hearty salads, and entrées such as seared tuna and steak. ◈ 808 E. Washington St • Map P3 • 407-648-2777 • $$$

7 Ceviche Tapas Bar & Restaurant
Huge, noisy, and loads of fun, this restaurant offers an enormous menu, a tapas bar, and a large lounge with live flamenco music. ◈ 125 W. Church St • Map P2 • 321-281-8140 • Closed lunch • $$$

8 Little Saigon
This venue stands out in the city's thriving Vietnamese area for its huge bowls of pho, fragrant soup brimming with meat, seafood, noodles, and spices. ◈ 1106 E. Colonial Dr • Map N3 • 407-423-8539 • $$

9 White Wolf Café
This café serves great salads and Middle-Eastern-inspired fare in a former antiques store. It also sells most of its vintage furnishings. ◈ 1829 N. Orange Ave • Map N3 • 407-895-5590 • $$$

10 Pine 22
Choose your own combination of organic, grass-fed beef and dozens of locally sourced toppings at this relaxed, upscale burger joint. ◈ 22 E. Pine St • Map P2 • 407-574-2160 • $

Unless stated, all restaurants advise reservations, are non-smoking, take credit cards, have DA, kids' menus, A/C, and vegetarian dishes.

Left **Winter Park street scene** Right **Cornell Fine Arts Museum**

Winter Park, Maitland, & Eatonville

TRUE TO ITS NAME, *Winter Park was chartered in 1887 as a winter resort for wealthy – and cold – Northerners. Now nearly surrounded by metropolitan Orlando, it still retains the charm and character of a wealthy, small town, with excellent shops, bars, and restaurants, and a sprinkling of interesting museums. The towns of Maitland and Eatonville, to the north and east, are more residential, but also have some worthwhile attractions, which make a pleasant change from south Orlando's mass-market theme parks.*

Winter Park Scenic Boat Tour

🔟 Sights & Attractions

1. Park Avenue
2. Charles Hosmer Morse Museum of American Art
3. Cornell Fine Arts Museum
4. Winter Park Scenic Boat Tour
5. Albin Polasek Museum & Sculpture Gardens
6. Waterhouse Residence & Carpentry Museum
7. Birds of Prey Center
8. Zora Neale Hurston National Museum of Fine Arts
9. Winter Park Farmers' Market
10. Enzian Theater

1 Park Avenue

The stretch of Park Avenue between Fairbanks and Webster avenues is a thriving and delectable slice of urban living. This is the kind of manageable, old-style downtown, which is usually erased in the rush to suburbanize the Sunshine State. There's bucolic Central Park; buildings are rarely over three stories and contain fashionable shops or eateries at ground level; and all around, the sidewalks are full of people enjoying the day. ◈ Map L4

Park Avenue

2 Charles Hosmer Morse Museum of American Art

This museum contains the world's largest collection of beautiful glass windows and objects by American artist Louis Comfort Tiffany. Other highlights include American ceramics and representative collections of late-19th- and early-20th-century paintings, graphics, and decorative arts. ◈ 445 N. Park Ave • Map L4 • 407-645-5311 • Open 9:30am–4pm Tue–Sat (to 8pm Fri Nov–Apr), 1–4pm Sun • Adm • www.morsemuseum.org

3 Cornell Fine Arts Museum

The art collection at this museum, located on the scenic Rollins College Campus, is one of the oldest in the state. The range of European and American

Charles Hosmer Morse Museum of American Art

art – from the Renaissance to the 20th century – is impeccably presented and of an unusually high quality for a small college art museum. ◈ 1000 Holt Ave • Map L4 • 407-646-2526 • Open 10am–4pm Tue–Fri, noon–5pm Sat–Sun • Adm • www.rollins.edu/cfam

Albin Polasek Museum & Sculpture Gardens

4 Winter Park Scenic Boat Tour

The wealthiest sections of Winter Park were built around a series of lakes and along small, winding canals. This boat tour has been running since 1938, and is part nature trip and part local history lesson. It cruises lazily past Winter Park landmarks and lakeside mansions encountering wildlife, while the skipper tells stories about the area's legendary society crowd. *See p45.* ◈ Morse Blvd at Lake Osceola • Map L4 • 407-644-4056 • Tours depart on the hour 10am–4pm daily • Adm

5 Albin Polasek Museum & Sculpture Gardens

Sculptor Albin Polasek moved here to retire, but in fact he kept producing his figurative works until his death in 1965. Now listed on the National Register of Historic Places, the museum and its sculpture gardens contain works spanning Polasek's entire career. ◈ 633 Osceola Ave • Map L4 • 407-647-6294 • Open 10am–4pm Tue–Sat, 1–4pm Sun • Adm • www.polasek.org

Waterhouse Residence & Carpentry Museum

6 Historic Waterhouse Residence & Carpentry Shop Museum

William H. Waterhouse was a carpenter who came to Central Florida in the early 1880s and built this lovely home overlooking Lake Lily. Pristinely restored and maintained by the Maitland Historical Society, the home, Waterhouse's carpentry shop, and the property's remarkable collection of handcrafted furniture offer a glimpse into Maitland's past. Woodworking buffs will be wowed by Waterhouse's extensive use of heart of pine, a wood rarely seen today. Tours lasting about 40 minutes are offered. The Waterhouse facilities complement the Maitland Historical Museum, Maitland Art Center, and Telephone Museum *(see p61)*, all just a few blocks away and also run by the Maitland Historical Society. ◊ *820 Lake Lilly Dr • Map K3 • 407-644-2451 • Open noon–4pm Thu–Sun • Adm • artandhistory.org/waterhouse-museum*

7 Audubon National Center for Birds of Prey

Think of this place as a halfway house for some of Florida's most impressive birds. It was created by the Florida Audubon Society to rescue, rehabilitate, and release wounded raptors (birds of prey). Those that wouldn't survive being released into the wild are kept here, living a pampered existence in a lovely lakeside location, while helping to educate visitors about wildlife issues and conservation. Guests aren't allowed to observe the rehabilitation process, but permanent residents on view usually include vultures, bald eagles, screech owls, hawks, ospreys, and more. ◊ *1101 Audubon Way • Map K3 • 407 644-0190 • Open 10am–4pm Tue–Sun • Adm • www.audubonofflorida.org*

8 Zora Neale Hurston National Museum of Fine Arts

Zora Neale Hurston earned fame as one of the brightest stars of Harlem's literary heyday in the 1920 and 1930s. Many of her most famous writings (including the 1937 novel, *Their Eyes Were Watching God*) reflected life in Eatonville, the first incorporated African-American municipality in the USA. The front porches and stores of Eatonville, where Zora's characters lived and spun their tales, have long since disappeared, but she is not forgotten. This museum keeps the writer's memory alive, and plays a big part in the annual cultural Zora! Festival held in January. The museum also exhibits work by contemporary African-American artists. ◊ *227 E. Kennedy Blvd • Map K3 • 407-647-3307 • Open 9am–4pm Mon–Fri, 1 1am–1pm Sat • Free • www.zoranealehurstonmuseum.com*

Birds of Prey Center

9 Winter Park Farmers' Market

Some farmers' markets are serious business, packed with old trucks and farmers selling mountains of vegetables just pulled from the earth. The Winter Park Farmers' Market is altogether a different affair. More of a social gathering on the village green, Winter Park's yuppies come here to mingle, buy potted flowers, preserves, and herbs, and indulge in fresh croissants, muffins, and breads. Yes, the required vegetables are here, too, but this is more of a coffee and brunch gathering. ⊗ 721 W. New England Ave • Map L4 • 407-599-3397 • Open 7am–1pm Sat • Free

Exhibit, Zora Neale Hurston National Museum of Fine Arts

10 Enzian Theater

The art of film tastes different at the Enzian. This not-for-profit 250-seat theater doesn't just show American independent and foreign films, but also offers a full menu with beer, wine, and table service. Relax with dinner or snacks and enjoy films with all the comforts of your own living room (if that living room has a 33-ft (10-m) wide screen). The Enzian also produces the 10-day Florida Film Festival (see p65) and smaller niche festivals throughout the year. ⊗ 1300 S. Orlando Ave • Map K3 • 407-629-1088 • Open evenings daily & weekend afternoons • Adm • www.enzian.org

A Day in Winter Park

Morning

🕐 Begin with a hearty breakfast at the **Briarpatch Restaurant** (see p123). You'll probably have to wait a bit, especially on weekends, so grab a newspaper. Then take time to wander the north end of **Park Avenue** (see p119), where a multitude of charming one-off boutiques cater to upscale shopping tastes. At Canton Avenue pop in to the **Charles Hosmer Morse Museum** (see p119); its outstanding collection of Tiffany glass is a must-see. Follow this with a relaxing trip on the **Winter Park Scenic Boat Tour** (see p119), which departs from a dock on Morse Street, just a 15-minute walk away. On your return, lunch options are plentiful, but if the weather is good, grab one of the sidewalk tables at the **Park Plaza Gardens** (see p122) for some good food and people-watching.

Afternoon

After lunch, continue south on Park Avenue to Rollins College, home of the excellent **Cornell Fine Arts Museum** (see p119) and spend the rest of the afternoon enjoying this small but excellent collection.

Evening

Then, it's a 10-minute car ride north to Maitland's **Enzian Theater** where you can settle in to enjoy the latest in US and foreign independent films with a bottle of wine and a cheese plate. End the day at the bustling **Brio Tuscan Grille** (see p123) just a few minutes south by car, savoring a pink cosmopolitan or a gorgonzola-encrusted steak.

Left **Hillstone** Right **Fiddler's Green**

TOP 10 Bars & Nightspots

1 Brio Tuscan Grille
The trendy grill at Brio is wildly popular, but a lot of people come just to hang out at the bar here. Cocktails flow fast and furious for a crowd of well-heeled locals. *See p123.*

2 Dexter's of Winter Park
Home to a serious collection of wines, this branch of Dexter's is more upscale than Downtown's, except on Thursdays when there's a band playing classic rock. ✆ *558 W. New England Ave • Map L4 • 407-629-1150*

3 Fiddler's Green
This energetic Irish pub has darts, music, and a full selection of draft beers and stouts. It stays open until 2am most nights, making it popular for a last round. The food is good, too. *See p123.*

4 Park Plaza Gardens
With tables spilling out onto Park Avenue, this café bar is the bar of choice for those seeking live bands. Popular with the university crowd. *See p123.*

5 Hannibal's on the Square
Part café, part casual upscale bar, Hannibal's shares space with a tremendous French restaurant, Chez Vincent. ✆ *511 W. New England Ave • Map L4 • 407-629-4865*

6 Copper Rocket Pub
With a small stage that hosts jazz jams to psycho rock, Copper Rocket is the only true music bar in the area. Microbrews and import beers fuel the young audience. ✆ *106 Lake Ave • Map K3 • 407-645-0069*

7 Eola Wine Co.
An extensive menu of 70 wines by the glass is on offer at this wine shop and bar. Drinks are complemented by a wide range of snacks and desserts. ✆ *136 Park Ave • Map L4 • 407-647-9103*

8 Hillstone
At one of Winter Park's top spots in which to be seen, the draw may be the generous glasses of wine, or the fact that the entire restaurant menu is available at the bar. *See p123.*

9 Shipyard Emporium
A microbrewery and café in one, which brews its own Shipyard beers in big copper stills. Wooden beams and white-washed walls give a nod to the brewery's New England roots. ✆ *200 W. Fairbanks Ave • Map L3 • 321-274-4045*

10 Mellow Mushroom Beer Bar
This friendly bar offers an extraordinary selection of beers. It serves very good pizza as well. ✆ *2015 Aloma Ave • Map L5 • 407-657-7755*

Winter Park's nightspots are usually open seven days a week.

Brio Tuscan Grille

Price Categories

For a three-course meal for one with a glass of house wine, and all unavoidable extra charges including tax.

$	under $20
$$	$20–$30
$$$	$30–$45
$$$$	$45–$60
$$$$$	over $60

🔟 Cafés & Restaurants

1 Cask & Larder
Local, organic, and Southern food made by James Beard-nominated chefs is served alongside a wide choice of drinks at this brewery and kitchen. ◈ *565 W. Fairbanks Ave • Map L4 • 321-280-4200 • $$$$$*

2 Panullo's Italian Restaurant
From the crispy calamari to the lobster ravioli, this reasonably priced neighborhood eatery is a great place to bring the whole family ◈ *216 S. Park Ave • Map L4 • 407-629-7270 • $$*

3 Park Plaza Gardens
The menu at this garden restaurant is regional Americana with a focus on seafood, such as blue crab cakes with mustard sauce. *See p69.* ◈ *319 S. Park Ave • Map L4 • 407-645-2475 • $$$$*

4 Fiddler's Green
A wooden bar imported from Ireland, weekly folk bands, and authentic Gaelic dishes contribute to Fiddler's real Irish atmosphere. ◈ *544 W. Fairbanks Ave • Map L3 • 407-645-2050 • $$*

5 4Rivers Smokehouse
Widely acclaimed as the best BBQ in town, this bustling place is always crowded, and worth the wait. ◈ *W. Fairbanks Ave • Map L3 • 407-474-8377 • No vegetarian dishes • $$*

6 Briarpatch Restaurant
Winter Park's homey breakfast landmark is known for big omelets and fresh fruit platters, but the creative, healthy American menu will make you consider returning for lunch. ◈ *252 N. Park Ave • Map L4 • 407-628-8651 • $$*

7 Hillstone
Here, various cuts of meat are chopped thick and cooked on a wood-burning grill. Portions are huge, particularly the salads and desserts. There are also seafood options. ◈ *215 S. Orlando Ave • Map L3 • 407-740-4005 • $$$$*

8 Brio Tuscan Grille
This local favorite has a huge dining room that buzzes with chatter and the sizzle of grilling in the open kitchen. ◈ *480 N. Orlando Ave • Map L3 • 407-622-5611 • $$$*

9 Luma on Park
Superlative cuisine, a head-spinning wine list, and an ultra-hip environment can be found at Luma on Park, which throbs with beautiful people. ◈ *290 S. Park Ave • Map L4 • 407-599-4111 • No kids' menu • Dinner only • $$$$*

10 Café de France
Despite the name, this eatery has an international menu served in an upbeat setting. ◈ *526 S. Park Ave • Map L4 • 407-647-1869 • No kids' menu • No vegetarian dishes • $$$$*

Unless stated, all restaurants advise reservations, are non-smoking, take credit cards, have DA, kids' menus, A/C, and vegetarian dishes.

123

STREETSMART

Things to Know
Before You Go
126

Tips on Getting
Around Orlando
127

Sources of Information
128

Behind-the-Scenes
Tours
129

Useful Addresses
130–31

Tips on Shopping
& Tickets
132

Tips for the Budget
Conscious
133

Tips on Eating &
Drinking
134

Health Tips
135

Communication &
Money Tips
136

Safety Tips
137

Tips for Seniors &
Disabled People
138

Tips for Families
139

Things to Avoid
140

Accommodation Tips
141

Places to Stay
142–149

ORLANDO'S TOP 10

Left **Monorail, Orlando International Airport** Right **Summer theme park crowds**

TOP 10 Things to Know Before You Go

1 Orlando International Airport

Serving more than 100 cities worldwide, and handling 35 million passengers a year, Orlando International is the city's busiest airport. Forty scheduled airlines use it: the major domestic carriers include Delta, American, Spirit, US Airways, JetBlue, Frontier, and Southwest. British Airways, Virgin Atlantic, Air Canada, and Lufthansa are some of its international carriers. Check the website *(see p130)* for information and maps to make sure you don't spend more time there than you need to. The airport is located about a 30-minute drive from Walt Disney World® – if traffic is good.

2 Orlando Sanford International

Orlando's second airport, used primarily by international flights, is around an hour's drive from the Disney resorts. It is far smaller (used by just 1.2 million passengers per year) and promises a less crowded, less hectic start to a vacation.

3 Orlando Executive Airport

Situated just 3 miles (5 km) from the city's business center, Orlando's original airport is today used by private charters for both business and pleasure travelers.

4 US Entry Requirements for Canadian Visitors

Canadians need a passport to travel to the US.

5 US Entry Requirements for Overseas Visitors

International visitors must register with the Electronic System for Travel Authorization (ESTA) well in advance of travel; this can be done online (http://esta.cbp.dhs.gov) or at a travel agents. Citizens from the UK, South Africa, Australia, New Zealand, and many European countries may visit for up to 90 days without a visa if they have a valid passport. Other nationals should apply for a visa from their local US consulate or embassy well before they travel. Visit www.state.gov for the latest information.

6 Arriving by Train & Bus

Two Greyhound bus terminals and four Amtrak rail stations (including Sanford's Auto train terminal) serve the Orlando area. Bus lines such as Red Coach transports visitors within Florida.

7 Consolidators & Packagers

Consolidators buy bulk airline seats (and sometimes rooms) to sell at cheaper prices. Try 800-FLY-CHEAP (800-359-2432; www.1800 flycheap.com). Packagers sell full or partial packages that can include flight, room, rental car, and theme park tickets. Some parks have their own; or try www.vacation packager.com. ✪ *Disney packages • 407-828-8101 • www. disneyworld.com* ✪ *Sea-World packages • 407-351-3600 • www.seaworld parks.com/seaworld-orlando/vacations* ✪ *Universal packages • 407-224-7000 • www.universalorlando.com*

8 Beat the Crowds

Theme park crowds are thinnest from the second week in September to the third week in November, the first two weeks of December, mid-January to mid-March, and late April through the third week of May. Weekends are always busy.

9 Weather Wise

Heat and humidity can be oppressive in summer, when temperatures easily hit 90°F (32°C) and lightning is another summer threat. High pollen counts in spring can make life hell for allergy sufferers and hurricane season is from August to November.

10 Online Planning

USA Tourist (www.usatourist.com) has multilingual information on attractions, hotels, restaurants, and more. Search engines are also useful for planning a trip, while Map Quest (www.mapquest.com) can help you plan a route once you've arrived.

Left **I-Ride Trolly** Center **Lynx Bus Stop** Right **Taxi**

TOP 10 Tips on Getting Around Orlando

1 Renting a Car
Most major car rental companies have offices at or near both major airports, as well as in town. Many also have shuttles serving the Amtrak and Greyhound stations. Most agencies offer special deals via their websites *(see p130)* or packagers. Local maps are provided, and staff can help plan the route to your hotel.

2 Navigating Orlando
The city's major north–south artery is Interstate Highway 4 (Hwy I-4), which connects the main tourist areas. The Beachline Expressway (Hwy 528) is an east–west tollway useful for reaching the Kennedy Space Center *(see pp38–41)*. Most main roads suffer gridlock during rush hour (7–9am and 4–6pm daily).

3 Shuttle Options
Mears shuttle buses travel from Orlando International Airport to hotels (the price varies according to distance), and around the tourist areas, including the Kennedy Space Center. Quick Transportation offers the same service, and can carry up to six people but offers personalized pickup and takes you straight to your destination. ⑧ *Mears*
• *407-423-5566* • *www. mearstransportation.com*
⑧ *Quick Transportation*
• *407-354-2456* • *www. quicktransportation.com*

4 Hotel Shuttles
Some hotels offer an airport shuttle service, and many offer transport to and from theme parks and other attractions several times per day. The service is usually free of charge to the parks nearest them, or available for a small charge to get to the others. Inquire about services when booking or planning your vacation.

5 Taking a Taxi
Taxis can be an economical way to get around for groups of four or five people. The fares from Orlando International and Orlando Sanford International airports to Walt Disney World® are around $60 and $150 (plus tip) respectively. Extra charges apply at nights, weekends, and on public holidays. Cabs are easily found at airports and major hotels – otherwise call *(see p131)*, as they are not that easy to flag down in the street.

6 The Disney Transportation System
Disney's free transportation system (monorail, buses, water taxis, and ferries) means you can save money by not renting a car and paying for gas and parking. It's best for guests who will spend most of their time with Mickey. But the circuits are set in stone and it can sometimes take an hour to reach some destinations in the resort.

7 The I-Ride Trolley
This service is a convenient and cheap way to get from A to B along the Universal, Sea-World®, and International Drive corridor. Trolleys run every 20–30 minutes, 8am–10:30pm daily, and make 42 stops. Exact change is required.
⑧ *407-248-9590*
• *www.iridetrolley.com*

8 Lynx Buses
Other than walking or cycling, Orlando's public bus system is the least popular way for most visitors to get around: buses can be frustratingly slow. Bus stops are marked with a paw print. Exact change is required. ⑧ *Lynx Downtown Bus Terminal*
• *78 W. Central Blvd*
• *407-841-8240*
• *www.golynx.com*

9 Hiring a Limo
The least economical but most luxurious way to get around is by limousine – an option for travelers who want to be pampered and who have deeper pockets.
⑧ *Advantage Limousine Service • 407-438-8888*
• *www.advantagelimo.com*

10 Walking
This is one of the USA's most dangerous cities for pedestrians: apart from wide highways with fast-moving traffic, there's a shortage of sidewalks, crosswalks, and street lights.

Left **Newspaper vending machines** Right **Kissimmee Convention & Visitors Bureau**

🔟 Sources of Information

1 Orlando/Orange Co. Convention & Visitors Bureau

Billed as "the official destination marketing organization for Orlando", this group provides an impressively comprehensive service. Their website is outstanding, offering up-to-date information and on-line booking, while the office can provide maps, directions, and answer questions. ✆ 8723 International Dr • 407-363-5872 • www.visitorlando.com

2 Kissimmee/St. Cloud Convention & Visitors Bureau

Focusing on the south of Orlando, this organization offers an excellent website and an office stocked with brochures from area attractions. ✆ 215 Celebration Pl • 407-742-8200 • www.visitkissimmee.com

3 Orlando Sentinel

The sole major daily newspaper in town is conservative in political matters, but the Friday edition carries an excellent arts and events section called the Calendar. There's an on-line version too (www.orlandosentinel.com).

4 Orlando Weekly

O-Town's primary "alternative" paper is this free weekly, which carries excellent and extremely detailed club and arts listings. The columnists – all good, some hilarious – know the local scene intimately. The paper's website (www.orlandoweekly.com) offers all the articles as well as terrific search capabilities for movie and music listings. The paper is available in restaurants, shops, clubs, convenience stores, and street boxes all over town.

5 Watermark

This free bi-weekly newspaper is the voice of Orlando's extensive gay and lesbian community. Not particularly radical, it offers splendid coverage of arts and events and is the best resource for clubs, shows, and more for the community. Available at gay-friendly businesses and in street boxes. There's also an on-line version: www.watermarkonline.com.

6 Lesbian, Gay, Bisexual & Transgender Community Services of Central Florida

This LGBT community center is the city's clearinghouse for gay community information, ranging from art openings to health alerts. The organization regularly sponsors a variety of cultural events around town. ✆ 407-228-8272 • www.thecenterorlando.com

7 News Channel 13

This is Orlando's own version of CNN – a 24-hour cable news channel devoted to O-Town. It is probably most useful to visitors for the weather update that runs every ten minutes (1:01, 1:11, 1:21, etc). ✆ Only available on TVs subscribed to Time Warner Cable

8 WTKS 104.1-FM

The weekday schedule of this radio station is filled with local talk radio personalities hosting shows including "Monsters in the Morning," "SBK Live," and "The Phillips Phile." All offer an interesting window into Orlando's current state of mind. On weekends, the format switches to classic rock.

9 WMFE 90.7-FM

This station is the area's outlet for all-day programming from National Public Radio, including intelligent hourly news. It's a respite from the fanatical talk shows and light pop music broadcast by many of the other local radio stations.

10 Brochure Racks

Virtually every hotel, restaurant, and attraction offers a huge lobby display packed with brochures and tourist guides covering almost all the hotels, restaurants, and smaller attractions in the area. Besides the maps and general information, discount coupons are common in these publications, so they're worth picking up (see p133).

SeaWorld® Adventure Camp

TOP 10 Behind-the-Scenes Tours

1 Backstage Magic
Disney's most complete but expensive tour is ideal for guests who have to know what makes things tick. The seven-hour visit explores the inner workings of Epcot® technology, the Tower of Terror at Disney Hollywood Studios®, and the Magic Kingdom®'s underground operations hub. ✆ 407-939-8687 • Max 20 people, 16 yrs & over • 9am Mon–Fri

2 Keys to the Kingdom
A useful, 4–5 hour Magic Kingdom® taster tour for guests who'd like to see what's on offer before they really get started. It gives a basic park orientation as well as a glimpse of some of the usually hidden high-tech magic. ✆ 407-939-8687 • Min age 16 yrs • Cost does not include park adm • 8:30am, 9am & 9:30am daily

3 Around the World at Epcot®
This 2-hour Segway tour offers a closer view than most park guests get of Epcot®'s multi-cultural treasures. ✆ 407-939-8687 • Max 10 people, min age 16 yrs • Cost does not include park adm • 7:45am, 8:30am, 9am, 9:30am

4 Family Magic Tour
Kids love this two-hour scavenger hunt in Disney World's most child-friendly park, the Magic Kingdom®. Characters also meet guests at the end of the tour. ✆ 407-939-8687 • Cost does not include park adm • 10am daily.

5 VIP Tours
Both Disney and Universal offer VIP tours – at a price. Disney's lets guests create their own itinerary, which could take in one or more parks, meals, golf, spa treatments, and more. The tour includes reserved show seating and expedited access to rides. Universal's five-hour fixed tour offers line-cutting privileges at up to eight rides and shows. ✆ Disney • 407-560-4033 • Up to 10 people per tour, 5-hour min • Universal • 407-363-8000 • 10am & noon daily

6 Scenic/Eco Lake Tours
See the real Florida and its wildlife during a fascinating one-hour narrated tour in a 24-ft (7-m) pontoon boat. Fishing and private charters, as well as island and gator tours, are also available. ✆ 101 Lakeshore Blvd, Kissimmee • 800-244-9105, 407-908-5688 • www.fishingchartersinc.com

7 Yuletide Fantasy
It's hard to beat Disney's Christmas celebration. This 3-hour tour gives guests a front-row look at how the four theme parks and resorts are transformed into a winter wonderland. Highlights include a candlelight procession and Epcot®'s massed choir. This tour is guaranteed to get visitors into the holiday spirit. ✆ 407-939-8687 • Park adm not required • 9am Mon–Sat Nov 30–Dec 24

8 SeaWorld® Adventure Camp
During the summer, SeaWorld® offers several day programs to suit all budgets. The camps are divided by age from preschool through 8th grade (13 yrs) and are designed to help kids better understand the marine animal world. There are family sleep-over programs, too. ✆ 407-370-1380 • Jun–Aug

9 Up-Close Tours
Get a close-up look at SeaWorld®'s penguin, dolphin, and sea lion habitats, with opportunities to feed or touch the animals, in 45–60-min walking tours. ✆ 407-351-3600 • Cost does not include park adm • Times vary

10 Family Fun Tour
A 4-hour tour behind the scenes at SeaWorld®, including reserved seats at the One Ocean show, front-of-the-line access to some family rides, and a light meal at Happy Harbor. Kids will enjoy visiting Shamu the killer whale. ✆ 407-351-3600 • Cost does not include park adm • Times vary

Tours should be reserved at least one month in advance.

Useful Addresses

Tourist Information

Orlando/Orange County Convention & Visitors' Bureau
6700 Forum Dr, Ste 100 (I-D)
• 407-363-5872 • www.visitorlando.com

Tourist Information Center
8723 International Dr (I-D)
• 407-363-5872

Websites

Orlando's Weekly Calendar
http://calendar.orlandoweekly.com

Citysearch
orlando.citysearch.com

The Daily City
www.the dailycity.com

Inside Central Florida
www.wftv.com/icflorida

Theme Park Insider
www.themeparkinsider.com

Visit Orlando
www.visitorlando.com

Airports

Orlando Executive Airport (ORL)
501 Herndon Ave • 407-894-9831 • www.orlando airports.net/orl

Orlando International Airport (MCO)
1 Airport Blvd • 407-825-2001
• www.orlando airports.net

Orlando Sanford Airport (SFB)
2 Red Cleveland Blvd, Sanford
• 407-322-7771 • www.orlandosanfordairport.com

American Automobile Association (AAA)

783 S. Orlando Ave • 407-647-1033 • www.aaa.com

Amtrak Train Stations

1400 Sligh Blvd (DO)
• 407-843-7611
• www.amtrak.com

150 W. Morse Blvd (WP)
• 407-645-5055
• www.amtrak.com

600 S. Persimmon Ave (Sanford) • 407-330-9770
• www.amtrak.com

111 E. Dakin St (K)
• 407-933-1170
• www.amtrak.com

Greyhound Bus Terminals

103 E. Dakin Ave (K) • 888-332-6363; 407-847-3911
• www.greyhound.com

555 N. John Young Pkwy (DO) • 888-332-6363; 407-292-3424 • www.greyhound.com

Car Rental

Alamo
8200 McCoy Rd
• 800-462-5266
• www.alamo.com

Avis
8600 Hangar Blvd
• 800-230-4898
• www.avis.com

Budget
1 Airport Blvd
• 800-527-7000
• www.budget.com

Dollar
9201 Airport Blvd
• 800-800-4000
• www.dollarcar.com

Enterprise
9400 Airport Blvd
• 800-325-8007
• www.enterprise.com

Hertz
1 Airport Blvd
• 800-654-3131
• www.hertz.com

National
5398 Bear Rd • 800-227-7368 • www.national car.com

Thrifty
9302 Airport Rd • 800-847-4389 • www.thrifty.com

Taxis & Private Cars

Mears
324 W. Gore St
•407-422-2222 •www.mearstransportation.com

Airport Orlando Shuttle
•407-797-0717
•airportorlandoshuttle.com

Orlando Airport Van
•866-204-4000 • www.orlandoairportvan.us

Banks

Bank of America
390 N. Orange Ave (DO)
• 407-244-7041

Chase
7674 Dr. Phillips Blvd (WDW) • 407-352-5832

Regions Bank
111 N. Orange Ave (DO)
• 800-734-4667

517 Morse Blvd (WP)
• 800-734-4667

SunTrust
1675 E. Buena Vista Dr (WDW) • 407-828-6103

1000 N. Main St (K)
• 407-870-0022

400 S. Park Ave (WP)
• 800-786-8787

Wells Fargo
7950 Orange Blossom Tr (I-D) • 407-649-5158

Credit Cards

American Express
800-528-4800
• www.american express.com

Streetsmart

Diners Club
800-234-6377 • www.diners-club.com

Discover
800-347-2683 • www.discovercard.com

MasterCard
800-826-2181 • www.mastercard.com

Visa
800-336-8472 • www.visa.com

Hospitals

Celebration Health
400 Celebration Pl (WDW)
• 407-303-4000

Dr. P. Phillips Hospital
9400 Turkey Lake Rd (I-D)
• 407-351-8550

Florida Hospital
601 E. Rollins St
(DO) • 407-303-5600

Orlando Health
1414 Kuhl Ave (DO)
• 321-841-5415

Winter Park Memorial Hospital
200 N. Lakemont Ave (WP)
• 407-646-7000

Walk-In Clinics

Centra Care Walk-In Clinic
12500 S. Apopka Vineland Rd (WDW)
• 407-934-2273

4320 W. Vine St (K)
• 407-390-1888

ExpressCare
2700 Old Winter Garden Rd (DO) • 407-656-2055

Nightlight Pediatrics
7556 W. Sandlake Rd (ID)
• 407-506-0002

WinterPark Family Practice
2950 Aloma Ave (WP)
• 407-679-9222

24-hour Pharmacy

CVS Pharmacy
1205 W. Vine St (K)
• 407-847-5174

7599 W. Sandlake Rd (ID)
• 407-352-1177

Walgreens
2420 E. Colonial Dr (DO)
• 407-894-6781

6201 International Dr (I-D) • 407-345-8402

13502 Apopka Vineland Rd (WDW) • 407-348-2323

Dentists

Advanced Dental Care
12131 S. Apopka Vineland Rd (WDW) • 407-477-5004

Coast Dental
2200 E. Irlo Bronson Memorial Hwy (K) • 407-935-1772

2907 Vineland Rd (K)
• 407-390-1288

Greenburg Dental Associates
4780 S. Kirkman Rd (I-D)
• 407-292-7373

3727 N. Goldenrod Rd (WP)
• 407-671-0001

Help Lines

Central Florida Helpline
407-333-9028

Society for Accessible Travel & Hospitality
212-447-7284

Help Now of Osceola
407-847-8562

Internet Access

Orlando Public Library
101 E. Central Blvd (DO)
• 407-835-7323

South Orange Library
7255 Della Dr
• 407-835-7323

Post Offices

51 E. Jefferson St (DO)
• 407-425-6464

10450 Turkey Lake Rd (I-D)
• 407-351-2492

2600 Michigan Ave (K)
• 407-846-0999

8546 Palm Parkway (WDW)
• 800-275-8777

300 N. New York Ave (WP)
• 407-647-6807

Police

City of Kissimmee Police
8 N. Stewart Ave (K) • 407-847-0176 • Emergency: 911

City of Orlando Police
100 S. Hughey Ave (I-D)
• 407-246-2470
• Emergency: 911

Orange County Sheriff
2500 W. Colonial Dr (DO)
• 407-254-7000
• Emergency: 911

Osceola County Sheriff
2601 E. Irlo Bronson Memorial Hwy (K) • 407-348-1100
• Emergency: 911

Winter Park Police
500 N. Virginia Ave (WP)
• 407-644-1313
• Emergency: 911

Consulates

Germany
100 N. Biscayne Blvd, Ste 2200, Miami • 305-358-0290

Canada
200 S. Biscayne Blvd, Ste 1600, Miami • 305-579-1600

Japan
80 S.W. 8th St, Miami
• 305-530-9090

United Kingdom
200 S. Orange Ave, Ste 2110, Orlando • 407-254-3300

For more on tourist information **See p128**

Left **Fastpass ticket outlet** Center **Souvenirs from SeaWorld®** Right **Disney memorabilia**

TOP 10 Tips on Shopping & Tickets

1 Shopping Hours
Shops in theme parks keep the same hours as the parks. Malls and outlets are usually open from 9 or 10am until 9pm Monday to Saturday and at least noon to 6pm on Sunday. Shops outside the main tourist areas tend to open from 9am to 5pm Monday through Saturday.

2 Sales Tax
With the exception of groceries and some medications, all purchases in Orlando are subject to a 6.5 percent state and local sales tax.

3 Sales
Look for winter-wear bargains from March through April, and summer bargains from August to October as the seasonal stock changes. In August, with the approach of the new school year, there are good buys on kids' clothes. The day after Thanksgiving is the biggest shopping day of the year, with huge pre-Christmas sales attracting hordes of shoppers.

4 Outlets
Outlet stores sell last season's fashions at discounted prices. Shoppers who know the suggested retail prices of the goods they seek will be able to tell what is – and what isn't – a bargain. Some stores promise as much as 75 per cent discount and some actually deliver. Others don't. The big

player is Orlando Premium Outlets, with two giant locations *(see p66)*.

5 Gifts & Souvenirs
Apart from cheap T-shirts, stuffed animals, and baseball caps, Orlando does have some more original souvenirs. These include Florida oranges, alligator meat and leather products, and manatee memorabilia.

6 Shipping Home
If you have bought more souvenirs than you can carry home, why not ship them? Disney and Universal parks, resorts, and shops can make the arrangements, usually via United Parcel Service (UPS). Do-it-yourselfers must take their packages to UPS (call 1-800-742-5877 for the nearest center) or the US Postal Service (1-800-275-8777).

7 Buy Theme Park Tickets Online
Disney (www.disneyworld.com) allows guests to buy tickets online, saving on time waiting in line, but they must be picked up in person. Universal (www.universalorlando.com) allows visitors to print out tickets or pick them from the will-call gate for an additional $2.50 per ticket. SeaWorld®'s online service (www.seaworld.com) lets buyers print out their tickets and, when they arrive at the park, go straight to the turnstiles, where they are verified.

8 Multi-Day & Multi-Park Passes
Disney's Park Hopper and Park Hopper Plus tickets are valid for four to seven days. Both include unlimited entry to the four parks; the Park Hopper Plus tickets also include entry to other Disney attractions. The discounts aren't great, but you save time waiting in line. Universal Studios Florida®, Universal's Islands of Adventure®, Wet'n Wild®, Sea World® Orlando, Aquatica® Water Park, and Busch Gardens® Tampa Bay have joined up to offer the unlimited access, 14-day FlexTicket.

9 Cutting in Line
Disney (FastPass) and Universal and SeaWorld® (Express Access) offer a system that cuts out the long wait for the most popular rides and shows. Just slide your ticket through the turnstile to get an allocated time for your visit. When it's time, simply go to the particular attraction's designated entrance to take your place.

10 Concierge Desks
Most upscale and some moderately priced hotels have concierge desks in the lobby. They're great places to make restaurant reservations or buy tickets for theme parks and other attractions. They don't give discounts, but most do offer the convenience of waiting in a short line as opposed to a long one in the parks.

For more on shopping in Walt Disney World Resort **See p92**

Left **Hotel shuttle bus** Right **Leaflets in a hotel lobby**

TOP10 Tips for the Budget Conscious

1 The Magicard
The Orlando/Orange County CVB's *(see p128)* Magicard offers $500 worth of discounts on accommodation, car rentals, attractions, meals, shopping, and more. It also offers deals that combine rooms with attraction and theme park tickets. Each card is valid for up to six people, and it's free. Allow four weeks for delivery.
- 407-363-5872
- *www.visitorlando.com*

2 Hotel Handouts
Many hotels and motels offer freebies such as continental breakfasts, evening hors d'oeuvres, and newspapers. Their coupon racks are stuffed with two-for-one and other special deals on meals and attractions. For those without a car, most hotels have free or low-fee shuttle services to the parks.

3 Newspaper Coupons
The Sunday travel sections in many major US newspapers lure people to Orlando with offers of coupons, cheap fares, and package deals. Once here, read the Orlando Sentinel (especially Friday's Calendar section), as well as the free papers available on street corners and in hotel lobbies, all of which feature lots of discounts and offers. *See p128.*

4 Rooms with Cooking Facilities
Travelers can save big by booking a room with a kitchen, kitchenette, or even just a microwave and refrigerator. Apart from Walt Disney World properties, most accommodation is close to supermarkets or delicatessens, some of which deliver for a small fee.

5 Pack a Snack & Water
Theme-park prices for refreshments are 30–50 percent higher than what people pay outside the parks. The parks prohibit coolers (containers for keeping food and drink cool), but guests can bring their own bottled water and snacks. Some parks have fountains, but the water in Central Florida does not taste particularly sweet.

6 Eat Big Early & Late
It's often unnecessary to eat three big meals a day, particularly in the hottest months of the year. If you want to skip, or go light on, lunch, you can eat well – and cheaply – before and after your theme-park visit by having a low-priced, all-you-can-eat, buffet breakfast and an early-bird dinner *(see p134)*.

7 Fast Food & Family Restaurants
Orlando is chock-full of fast-food outlets. The city also has an abundance of very well-priced family restaurants *(see pp70–71)*. Most have kids' menus, which can be even cheaper at lunchtime.

8 Red Chair Project
The cultural crowd isn't left out of the discount mix. The city's CVB *(see p128)* regularly has half-price tickets, including those for opera, ballet, music, and theater. The tickets are for same-day performances, and while information is available by phone, the tickets must be picked up in person. 407-872-2382

9 Staying at Disney on the Cheap
People who really want to stay at Disney World, but can't afford the prices, can find the cheapest rates at the All-Star resorts *(see p142)*. Rack rates (those anyone can get without a discount) are extraordinarily reasonable and kids also stay free. But be warned: rooms at these "value" resorts are very cramped.

10 Gas for Renters
Never buy gas for a rental car from the car hire company itself. Some of their offers sound enticing, especially those offering cheaper gas if you buy up front rather than when the car is returned. Most of the time, fuel prices are cheaper – sometimes much cheaper – around town.

Buffet breakfast

TOP10 Tips on Eating & Drinking

1 Disney Restaurant Reservations
Some Disney restaurants use Priority Seating; kind of a FastPass for food. The more upscale ones ask for reservations, sometimes as much as 180 days in advance. Be aware that diners who do not show up are charged anyway. Note that all restaurants inside Disney parks, except Animal Kingdom's Rainforest Café, require park admission.

2 Reservations
Whenever restaurants accept reservations, make them – especially in the main tourist areas of I-Drive, Lake Buena Vista, and along Irlo Bronson Memorial Highway in Kissimmee. Not having a reservation can mean waiting two hours for a table during prime dining time, usually 6–8:30pm. Some restaurants refuse to seat diners who have not reserved in advance and upscale eateries may be unable to accommodate you unless you reserve far ahead.

3 Gratuities
Wait staff expect a tip of at least 15 percent. Those who are particularly helpful may deserve 20 percent; you may want to give just 10 per cent to those who aren't. Some restaurants now add tips to the bill, so check before paying.

4 Smoking
After the laws were passed most hotels and all restaurants are now non-smoking establishments. If you want to smoke while you drink, you have to find a bar where eating is only incidental to drinking. If you aren't sure, just smoke outside.

5 Buffet Breakfast Bargains
There are several modestly priced, all-you-can-eat breakfast buffets around town (especially on I-Drive and in Kissimmee). For a handful of dollars, you can fill your stomach and save money by eating a light lunch or skipping it altogether.

6 Early Birds
Some value restaurants offer cut-rate meals when business is slow, which is usually between 4pm and 6pm, Monday–Friday. These early-bird deals are usually advertised outside and are offered in the free coupon books found in hotel lobbies and tourist attractions. Many of these restaurants also offer 2-for-1 drink specials during these times.

7 Lunch Menus vs Dinner Menus
Many upscale restaurants are not only hard to get in to at dinnertime, but the menus are very expensive. The lunch menu might have fewer options, and portions tend to be a little less generous, but the prices are lower. To save money – and your digestive system – consider eating your main meal at mid-day and eating lighter at night.

8 Special Diets
Some restaurants that don't normally offer meat- and seafood-free options are happy to prepare vegetarian dishes, with some prior warning. Disney restaurants go one step further and provide for a variety of other dietary needs, including kosher, fat- or sugar-free, plus lactose intolerance and allergies. Give 24 hours' notice.
℠ 407-824-2222
(407-939-3463 if staying on Disney property).

9 Happy Hours
Many bars (and restaurants) have happy hours, usually from 4–7pm, when drinks are often two for the price of one. They sometimes serve special hors d'oeuvres as well.

10 Hotel Mini Bars
Put bluntly, these are rip-offs. Years ago, inventive guests drank the good stuff and refilled the bottles with cheap brands. So now the mini bars have a sensor: remove the bottle for 10 seconds and you get charged – a lot – for it.

Left **Sun protection** Right **24-hour pharmacy**

TOP 10 Health Tips

1 Heat, Sun & Insects

Heat and humidity during the summer season (June to mid-September) can cause dehydration, so be sure to drink at least two quarts (two liters) of fluids (preferably water) each day, and wear a wide-brimmed hat and airy clothes. Not only does too much sun result in nasty burns, but it can also cause sun poisoning. Use a sunscreen with a high protection factor. And as much as Disney and Universal want to erase blood-sucking flies and mosquitoes, they can't, so remember to use insect repellent in summer.

2 911

This is the number to call for emergency health matters and for immediate police or fire assistance.

3 Hospitals & First Aid

Ask at your hotel or resort reception for the nearest hospital. Make sure you have some kind of insurance, otherwise hospital costs can be crippling. All of the major parks have first-aid clinics for minor ailments.

4 Ask-A-Pharmacist

Most pharmacists are happy to give you first aid advice, as well as advice regarding how to take medicines. Most pharmacies are not open 24 hours, but pharmacists will usually give advice over the phone so call a Walgreens or a CVS Pharmacy, which are usually open 24 hours. See p131.

5 In-Room Medical Care

House calls are a thing of the past in most US cities, but the tourist areas in Orlando have two services that make house and hotel-room calls. Doctors on Call Service and Centra Care In-Room Services cover most of the areas from Downtown south to Disney and Kissimmee.
 Doctors on Call Service • 407-399-3627 Centra Care In-Room Services • 407-238-2000

6 Centra Care Walk-In Clinics

Centra Care (affiliated with the Florida Hospital) has walk-in clinics scattered throughout Orange, Seminole, and Osceola counties. These clinics can handle minor emergencies (broken limbs, cuts requiring stitches, and fevers), but not life-threatening situations, for which you should call 911.

7 24-Hour Pharmacies

Several drug stores sell over-the-counter and prescription drugs around the clock (see p131). Additional pharmacies, with regular hours, are listed in the Yellow Pages.

8 Dental Referral Service

This nationwide, toll-free service helps people to find the nearest suitable dentist. The telephones are answered 8am–8pm Monday–Friday; the automated answering service informs callers of the website then puts them on hold to speak to an operator. Those who prefer to choose for themselves, or anyone needing 24-hour aid, should use the Yellow Pages (or see p131) 888-343-3440 800-511-8663 • www. dentalreferral.com

9 Poison Control

This 24-hour hotline can and has saved lives. Operators can help deal with a problem, summon rescuers, and answer questions. But, don't overlook 911 for any emergency situation. 800-222-1222.

10 Visit Florida

While it shouldn't be used for emergencies, Florida's official tourism marketing corporation can provide basic information about medical services and assistance throughout the state. It also has a range of other services, including assistance with lost credit cards and documents, help with accidents, directions, and more. Operators can help in more than 150 languages. 850-488-5607 • www.visitflorida.org

Left **ATM machine** Right **Quarters (25¢) & pennies (1¢)**

🔟 Communications & Money Tips

1 Making Phone Calls

Orlando's numbers have 10 digits – the area code (Central Florida's are 407 and 321), plus the seven-digit number. If calling a number with a different area (or toll-free) code, dial 1 before the code and phone number. To make calls overseas, consider buying a phone card.

2 Internet Access

Many coffee shops, restaurants, and office copy stores *(see p131)* offer free Wi-Fi access. Public libraries and the airport provide free access to the Internet.

3 Languages

Disney, Universal, and larger hotels have multilingual staff who speak Spanish, French, German, and, in some cases, Dutch, Japanese, and other languages. They also have information printed in these languages. The Orlando/ Orange County Convention & Visitors Bureau and USA Tourist have multilingual websites.
🔊 www.visitorlando.com
🔊 www.usatourist.com

4 Post Offices

The United States Postal Service (USPS) *(see p131)* has 11 post offices in the Orlando area. Opening hours vary, but they are usually 9am to 5pm weekdays, although some open Saturday mornings as well. Drugstores and hotels often sell stamps, but they are slightly more expensive than those sold at post offices. Mailboxes, which are blue, are on most main streets and in hotels. Most major hotels also have daily collection services.

5 Credit Cards & Traveler's Checks

Most hotels, restaurants, attractions, and shops accept American Express, Discover, MasterCard, and Visa credit cards. Some also take Diners Club, Carte Blanche, and JCB cards. US dollar denominations of American Express, Thomas Cook, and Visa traveler's checks are widely accepted with ID.

6 Currency & Exchanges

Dollar notes come in $1, $5, $10, $20, $50, and $100 bills. Coins in circulation are of 1 cent, 5 cents (a nickel), 10 cents (a dime), and 25 cents (a quarter) value. One-dollar and 50 cent coins exist but are very rare. Currency exchanges are based at all the airports, major branches of banks, and near guest services or guest relations in all major theme parks.

7 ATMs

Automatic Teller Machines (ATMs) are located at almost all bank branches, in all major theme parks, major shopping malls, some hotels, and at airports. Most also accept withdrawals on American Express, MasterCard, and Visa credit cards. There is a $1.50 to $3 advance charge for cards not affiliated to that particular bank. It's often cheaper to use a debit card, but not all debit systems are supported by US banks; check the symbols on the ATM to see if yours is one that is accepted.

8 Bank Opening Hours

Most Central Florida banks are open 9am to 4pm weekdays (to 6pm on Friday). A few branches also open Saturday mornings. Most have ATMs with 24-hour access.

9 Western Union

International money transfers can be sent to more than 101,000 Western Union agents and offices in 187 countries. They can also arrange international telegrams.
🔊 1-800-325-6000

10 Taxes

The USA doesn't have a national sales tax. Instead, individual states and counties set the rate of sales tax. Florida levies a 6 percent sales tax (6.5 percent in Orlando) on everything except groceries and certain medicines. Hotels also add an extra 3 to 5 percent bed tax *(see p141)*.

Left **Valuables** Center **Orange County Sheriff's car** Right **Residential speed limit**

🔟 Safety Tips

1 On the Coast
Florida's beaches are usually well supervised by lifeguards, but still keep a close eye on young children and stick to areas where you can see the lifeguards. The same goes for rivers and pools.

2 Non-Emergency Numbers
Outside city limits, county sheriff's offices (see p131) are the primary police agencies: in Central Florida they are in Orange County, Osceola County, and Seminole County. For traffic and highway-related matters, call the Florida Fish and Wildlife Commission. For coastal issues, see the Florida Marine Patrol. ✎ *Florida Highway Patrol • 407-897-5959* ✎ *Fish and Wildlife Commission • 352-732-1225*

3 Hurricanes
The coast is usually hit hardest by hurricanes, but Central Florida is also affected. Hurricane season is from August to November. If caught in one, stay inside, away from windows, and have water, canned food, and a flashlight to hand. For more tips and up-to-date forecasts, see the National Hurricane Center. ✎ *www.nhc.noaa.gov*

4 General Safety
Always keep car and hotel-room doors locked. Before driving, ask the rental-car company, your hotel's front-desk staff, or Visit Florida, the Florida tourism marketing corporation (see p135) for the safest and most direct route to your destination. Don't let strangers change your currency, and when paying for anything, check you've been given the correct change before leaving the premises.

5 Valuables
Smart travelers leave valuables at home. If you do bring watches, jewelry, or other items of value, keep them in a hotel safe. The safes in hotel rooms should only be used for less valuable items. It's also advisable to carry credit cards or traveler's checks rather than large amounts of cash.

6 Stay in Populated, Well-Lit Areas
Orlando doesn't have the same crime rate as many cities, but it has its share of thieves who prey on the unsuspecting. At night, avoid badly lit areas (especially Downtown's westside, south of Colonial Drive), and at all times be wary of pickpockets.

7 Lost Children
Nothing frightens a parent or guardian more than turning away for a moment only to find their child gone. It happens every day in Orlando's theme parks. To help staff reunite familes, children under seven should wear tags with their name, hotel, and a contact number on it. When any member of your group gets lost, find a park employee for assistance.

8 Seat Belts
Florida law requires seat belts to be worn by the driver and all passengers. Children five years and under need a federally approved child restraint: for those under three years the restraint must be a child seat; children four through five years can use a child seat or a seat belt. A fine of at least $50 will be made for non-compliance.

9 Drinking & Driving
In a word: Don't. Florida strictly enforces this law. Violators risk time in jail if convicted of a drink-driving offense. Have a designated driver in the group, skip alcohol for the night, use public transport, or take taxis. Police are known to survey bars to see who is drinking, then wait outside until drinkers get in a car to drive off, when they are tested.

10 Speed Limits
Speed limits on interstates, toll roads, and major highways range from 55 to 70 mph (88–112 kmph). On smaller highways, the limit is 45 mph (72 kmph), and in residential areas, it's 25 to 35 mph (40–56 kmph). Fines begin at $160, doubling if it's in a school or construction zone.

Left **Mobility products** Center **Disabled parking facility** Right **Mature travelers**

🔟 Tips for Seniors & Disabled People

1 Orlando for Mature Travelers

VisitOrlando.com has plenty of suggestions for older travelers who prefer to balance theme park fun with more relaxing cultural pursuits.
◈ 407-363-5872 • www. visitorlando.com

2 AARP

The AARP (American Association of Retired Persons) is America's most vocal group for seniors, but it doesn't forget there's room for fun. The website's travel articles are available to the public, but only members find out about AARP's travel deals and discounts. Membership costs are minimal but require a US address.
◈ 1-202-434-2277 • www. aarp.org

3 Road Scholar

This educational travel organization sends people 55 and over on courses (usually for a week) all over the world. The choice of courses in Orlando is astounding, from travel photography to politics and philosophy. Stay at retreats, hotels, or campsites. ◈ 1-800-454-5768
• www.roadscholar.org

4 Disney Grandkids & You Getaway

Knowing that a lot of seniors come to Orlando with their grandkids, Disney occasionally offers discounted packages. Most include three nights in a Disney hotel,

multiple-day tickets to the parks, and a range of goodies for the kids, such as dolls and autograph books. ◈ 407-934-7639
• www.disneyworld.com

5 Accessible Mini Van Rentals

This service offers accessible van rentals by the day, week, or month. Vehicles include rear- and side-entry vans, and minivans with ramps or electric lifts. ◈ 6307 Hansel Ave, Orlando • 407-438-8010
• www.accessibleminivan rentals.com

6 Walker Medical & Mobility Products

The local franchise for Walker Medical & Mobility Products rents wheelchairs and three-wheel rechargeable electric scooters, including ones for people weighing more than 375 lbs (170 kg). They all fit into Disney's transport vehicles and can be taken apart to fit into cars. The company delivers to local hotels and houses. ◈ 888-726-6837
• www.walkermobility.com

7 Disney for Disabled Guests

The free *Guidebook for Guests with Disabilities* details special needs services, including: accessibility in parks; Braille directory locations; special-needs parking; wheelchair and electric-cart rentals; audio tours; and translator units for the deaf. They are available at Guest Services

in all the theme parks or at Disney hotels' front desks. ◈ 407-824-4321
• www.disneyworld.com

8 Universal for Disabled Guests

Universal's parks and hotels have the following services: audio guides; wheelchair and scooter rentals; and telecommunications devices for the deaf. A free booklet is available from Guest Relations at park entrances and resort front desks. Call to have the brochure sent to you in advance, or check it out online.
◈ 407-363-8000 • www. universalorlando.com

9 SeaWorld® for Disabled Guests

SeaWorld® provides a Braille guide, plus a written synopsis of its shows and telecommunications devices for the hearing impaired. Most of its rides and shows are accessible. It rents wheelchairs and scooters. A small guidebook is available at Guest Relations. ◈ 407-351-3600
• www.seaworld.com

10 Society for Accessible Travel & Hospitality

Members pay an annual subscription for access to a range of services, but non-members can get information on travel for the disabled (including specific hotels and attractions) for a small fee. ◈ 1-212-447-7284
• www.sath.org

Left **Getting wet** Center **Kids' menu** Right **SeaWorld®** stroller rental

TOP 10 Tips for Families

1 Name Tags & Reunion Places

It's very easy to get lost in crowded theme parks. If that happens, find a park employee (they're usually in uniform) and ask for help. Kids seven and under should wear tags bearing their name, hotel, and a contact number. Older kids and adults should pick a place inside the park to meet if they become separated.

2 Parent-Swaps

Height restrictions (see below) mean that some younger children may not be able to go on certain rides. The theme parks usually have a program that lets one parent ride while the other then should wear tags bearing their name, hotel, and a contact number. Older kids and adults should pick a place inside the park to meet if they become separated.

Then the second parent can go on the ride: it might not be so much fun riding by yourself but at least you don't have to wait in line again.

3 Stroller Rental & Baby Care

All the major theme parks offer stroller rental. There are also excellent nursing facilities, often with free formula provided. Diaper changing tables can be found in women's and some men's restrooms. Orlando is very family-friendly so finding facilities is not a problem.

4 Breaks

Theme parks are tiring at any time of year, but excessively so in summer, when even standing in line can be exhausting. Plan regular breaks at air-conditioned venues (best visited around midday, when it's hottest outside), or "splash areas" (see below).

5 Refreshments

Bring snacks for energy and don't forget water. The parks have a few drinking fountains, but bottled water is very expensive.

6 Getting Wet & Not Getting Wet

Take a change of clothes to the theme parks, if not for yourself then for the children. Apart from water rides where you might expect to get wet, kids enjoy running through "splash areas" to cool off, and drying off naturally might not be possible. A rain poncho is smart year round, since Florida has rainy spells in both summer and winter.

7 Theme Park Ride Restrictions

Disney parks tend to have few health and height restrictions, although Disney Hollywood Studios® is a little limiting. Universal's parks can be more restrictive for younger kids, especially Islands of Adventure® (with warnings on most of the major rides), but like Universal Studios, it has a dedicated kids' area. SeaWorld® has height restrictions on a couple of rides, while at Discovery Cove®, you must be at least six years old to swim with the dolphins. Non-swimmers can still join in, but obviously can't enjoy the full experience.

8 Children's Menus

Most of the more expensive and dressy restaurants discourage young diners either by failing to provide children's menus or with outright bans on anyone under 17 years of age. However, most restaurants have some kind of kids' menu, usually in the $4 to $6 range. Some also provide distractions such as crayons and coloring-in placemats.

9 Character Meals

Disney lures families with children to a dozen of their restaurants to charge exorbitant prices for eating breakfast, lunch, or dinner with humans dressed in Disney character costumes. Universal also has one "character" restaurant, and there are some similar set-ups outside of theme parks. See p71.

10 Kids Stay Free

Orlando is Kidsville. The little ones don't pay, but they're the reason adults do. Smart hoteliers let kids stay free. Most rooms have beds for four, so even if there are only two in the party, the extra beds are part of the deal.

Left **Rush hour on I-4** Right **Merritt Island National Wildlife Refuge**

🔟 Things to Avoid

1 Park Visits When School's Out
All the parks are packed during school breaks (late Jun–late Aug; late Dec–early Jan; mid-Feb, and Easter), since that's when families hit the parks with their kids. Summer is the worst, since not only is it crowded, but it's also brutally hot. The least crowded months are November plus early and late February.

2 Theme Park Isolation
Don't spend every waking minute in Orlando's theme parks, because burn-out is inevitable. Make sure you take time to see Central Florida's natural attractions *(see pp82–5)*, smaller attractions *(see pp44–5)*, and museums *(see pp60–61)*.

3 Early Arrivals
It might seem smart to hit the theme parks as soon as they open, but it is not always the best plan. Kids who arrive early tend to collapse by 2pm and are a mess the rest of the day. Instead, take it easy in the morning and head for the parks in late afternoons and evenings. Temperatures are cooler and the parks take on a magical glow under the lights.

4 Inflexibility
Relax. It's a vacation. There are no prizes for those who joylessly cram

every single ride at their chosen theme park into one day. Make plans, but be flexible. Don't attempt to do everything on your list, and maybe save a few things for the next visit.

5 Big Meals In-Park
In general, theme-park food is bland and overpriced, so don't waste your main meal of the day on it. Instead, at Universal, check out the eateries on CityWalk® *(see p105)*; while at Disney, visit one of the excellent resort dining options, where you'll find that high-end restaurants offer great value. Parks allow same-day reentry on single tickets – every ticket-holder gets a fingerprint scan for reentry.

6 Free and Discount Tickets
There are a lot of offers floating around Orlando that sound too good to be true. If someone promises free or heavily discounted tickets, ask "What's the catch?", especially if they're promising a Disney ticket. Most are timeshare salespeople trying to get you to "buy" a week's holiday for the next 20 years. In some cases they have legitimate tickets, but most of the time you have to endure hours of sales pitches. Usually, such properties are overpriced.

7 Wearing Skimpy Bathing Suits at Water Parks
Women should consider one-piece suits at water parks since most of the best rides can quickly rip off a bikini top. Bare feet are not a good idea, since the ground can get very hot – take a pair of flip-flops or water shoes.

8 Public Transport
Lynx buses might appear to be everywhere, but don't set your schedule by them, especially for longer trips. They stop frequently and are notoriously slow, but they do offer inexpensive transportation to and from the airport.

9 Downtown's Westside
The area of Downtown south of Colonial Drive and west of I-4 is not a particularly safe place to wander around. Avoid it. But if you are going to a destination here, including the Greyhound Bus station, call a cab.

10 Rush Hour on I-4
Sometimes called "Orlando's Parking Lot", I-4 can get very congested, particularly during evening rush hour (3–6:30pm), as attraction employees head home. Disney-generated traffic on I-4, between Lake Buena Vista and US Hwy 192, has a life of its own. Traffic jams there can occur around the clock.

Left **Family-friendly motel** Right **View from hotel room**

🔝10 Accommodation Tips

1 Bed & Sales Taxes
Hotels have an assortment of hidden add-ons that can come as a surprise when you get the bill. Charges for the mini-bar and pay-per-view movies are always inflated. But the sales tax *(see p132)* and bed tax can really add to the bill. Orange County, including the theme parks, I–Drive, and downtown Orlando, adds 6 percent bed tax; Osceola County, which includes Kissimmee, adds 6 percent; and Seminole County, which includes Sanford *(see p85)*, adds a 5 percent tax. Don't forget to factor in these extras when determining your budget.

2 Rack Rates
These are the rates no one should agree to pay for a room! They're the walk-in-and-ask rates anyone can get without a coupon or package, and without asking for a discount or special deal. They're used in this book to provide a guide price, but don't settle for them. Insist on a better deal – it is almost always possible. Always ask if there is an additional resort charge to avoid a surprise charge at the checkout.

3 Rooms with a View
Many properties charge more for a room that has a view of anything other than the parking lot or the building next door. Before you pay, consider how much time you will want to spend in your room.

4 The Pros of Staying with Mickey
The main benefits are proximity to the parks, access to the free Disney transportation system *(see p127)*, preferred tee times at Disney golf courses *(see pp54–5)*, extra hours in the parks, and an easy way to break up the day by returning to base for a midday nap or swim.

5 The Cons of Staying with Mickey
The main drawback is the cost. Rates at Disney World® Resorts are about 30 per cent more than comparable accommodation on the outside.

6 Types of Accommodation
Orlando has more than 117,000 hotel rooms. Most tend to be functional budget options, but there are plenty of upscale choices, too, from lavish resorts to one-off B&Bs and boutique hotels.

7 Booking Services
In addition to making independent reservations or dealing directly with Disney or Universal resorts, vacationers can use reservations networks to book rooms. Central Reservation Service (CRS), Orlando. com, and Kayak.com are three of the more popular ones. ⊗ *Walt Disney World* • 407-828-8101 • www.disneyworld.com ⊗ *Universal* • 407-224-7000 • www.universal orlando.com ⊗ *CRS* • 407-740-6442 • www.crshotels.com ⊗ *Orlando.com* • 800-675-2636 • www.orlando.com ⊗ *Kayak* • www.kayak.com

8 Land-Sea Options
A different approach is to take a seven-day land-sea package that includes a stay at any one or more Disney resorts plus a Caribbean cruise. ⊗ *Disney Cruise Line* • 800-951-3532 • www.disneycruise.com

9 Family-Friendly Motels
Most Orlando properties go the extra mile to make sure kids are treated like royalty. In fact, most let kids under 17 stay free with accompanying adults. Nickelodeon Suites Resort *(see p145)* and Holiday Inn Resort *(see p145)* offer more than the usual child-friendly amenities.

10 In-Room Calls
Don't use the in-room phone without knowing the billing policy. Some hotels offer free local calls; others charge steep rates. Some impose a $1-plus service charge whenever the phone is used (including for toll-free numbers), in addition to long-distance rates.

➡ *For accommodation listings See pp142–9*

141

Portofino Bay Hotel, a replica of a real village in Italy

TOP10 Disney & Universal Resorts

1 Disney's Grand Floridian Resort & Spa

Disney's top hotel is an opulent, early 20th-century New England-style resort. Expect a ragtime mood and intimate rooms that promise romance and great views. The resort also has a full spa, health club, and tennis courts. ✆ 4401 Floridian Way • Map F1 • 407-824-3000 • www.disneyworld.com • $$$$

2 Disney's Board-Walk Inn & Villas

This re-created 1940s seaside village is Disney's smallest deluxe hotel. The rooms are delightfully quaint; if you want more space, villas are available too. It is ideally located for all the facilities and buzz of the BoardWalk. ✆ 2101 N. Epcot Resorts Blvd • Map G2 • 407-939-5100; www.disneyworld.com • $$$$

3 Portofino Bay Hotel

This Universal resort is a replica of Italy's Portofino village, right down to the boats and "fishermen" in the harbor. The rooms are spacious and feature luxe bed linen. The gelati (ice cream) machines by the pool are another nice touch. Guests get to skip the line for rides and shows at Universal's parks. ✆ 5601 Universal Blvd • Map T1 • 407-503-1000 • www.universalorlando.com • $$$$

4 Walt Disney World Dolphin

This resort is on Disney property and offers some Disney perks, such as use of the free transportation system (see p127). The 27-floor pyramid contains oversize sculptures, a waterfall, and more than 1,500 suites and rooms. ✆ 1500 Epcot Resorts Blvd • Map G2 • 407-934-4000 • www.swandolphin.com • $$$

5 Walt Disney World Swan

With two 46-ft (14-m) swans gracing its roof, this hotel is hard to miss. The beach-themed rooms are a little smaller than at its sister hotel, the Dolphin, but Swan guests share some of the facilities and perks of the Dolphin, including a spa. ✆ 1200 Epcot Resorts Blvd • Map G2 • 407-934-3000 • www.swandolphin.com • $$$

6 Disney's Yacht Club Resort

The theme here is New England yacht club. Some of the 630 nautical-style rooms have views over a lake. Guests can walk to Epcot® in about 10 minutes. ✆ 1700 Epcot Resorts Blvd • Map G2 • 407-934-7000 • www.disneyworld.com • $$$$

7 Disney's Wilderness Lodge

Live oaks and tall pines surround this lovely wooded resort, modeled on the Yosemite Lodge at Yosemite National Park. Some rooms overlook woodlands; the villas are roomy and come with kitchens. ✆ 901 W. Timberline Dr • Map F1 • 407-824-3200 • www.disneyworld.com • $$$$

8 Disney's Port Orleans Resort

You can opt to stay in the French Quarter's colonial houses with iron balconies or in the Riverside's southern-style mansions. Gardeners love the landscaping, and shoppers like the location. ✆ 2201 Orleans Dr • Map F2 • 407-934-5000 • www.disneyworld.com • $$$

9 Hard Rock Hotel

This Universal resort boasts Mission-style architecture and a rock 'n' roll theme. Rooms are attractive and comfortable; the best views are from those facing the lake. Guests get to skip the lines for rides and shows at Universal's parks. ✆ 5000 Universal Blvd • Map T1 • 407-503-7625 • www.universalorlando.com • $$$$

10 Disney's Value Resorts

The All-Star Movies, All-Star Music, and All-Star Sports resorts have relatively small rooms, but rates here are the cheapest in Walt Disney World Resort. ✆ 407-934-7639 • Map G1 • www.disneyworld.com • $$

Unless indicated, all hotels have DA, A/C, pool, parking, and kids' accommodations, and accept credit cards

Price Categories

For a standard, double room per night (with breakfast if included), taxes and extra charges.

$	under $90
$$	$90–180
$$$	$180–250
$$$$	over $250

Villas of Grand Cypress

TOP 10 Luxury Hotels

1 Hyatt Regency Grand Cypress

This vast resort is one of Orlando's most amazing places to stay. The 18-story atrium has inner and outer glass elevators with great views, some rooms have whirlpool baths, and the resort boasts a golf course, tennis courts (see p56), a beach, and plenty of nature, including a lake and waterfalls. ◈ 1 Grand Cypress Blvd • Map F2 • 407-239-1234 • www.grandcypress.hyatt.com • $$$$

2 Buena Vista Palace Hotel and Spa

The classy rooms at this, the largest Lake Buena Vista hotel, have either balconies with lake views or patios. Hypo-allergenic evergreen rooms have air and water filter systems. This spacious and luxurious hotel has rooms, which offer great views of the nightly Epcot® fireworks from the private balconies. ◈ 1900 Buena Vista Dr • Map F2 • 407-827-2727 • www.buenavistapalace.com • $$$

3 Villas of Grand Cypress

The Hyatt's sister property offers condos and town houses, plus some suites. Some accommodations have Roman tubs and patios. Amenities include a golf course, tennis courts, bike trails, and fishing. ◈ 1 N. Jacaranda • Map F2 • 800-835-7377 • www.grandcypress.com • $$$$

4 Gaylord Palms Resort

Located on acres of beautiful gardens, this resort hosts five restaurants, two pools, two bars and three separate Florida-style residences. There's a full-service spa and childcare center, and it's well located for theme parks. ◈ 6000 W. Osceola Pkwy • Map G2 • 407-586-2000 • www.gaylordhotels.com • $$$

5 Renaissance Orlando at SeaWorld®

Both the amenity-filled rooms and their marble bathrooms in this snazzy hotel are massive. Even the atrium, filled with aquariums, waterfalls, and palm trees, is 10 stories high. ◈ 6677 Sea Harbor Dr • Map T5 • 407-351-5555 • www.renaissancehotels.com • $$$$

6 Peabody Orlando

This hotel boasts an elegant feel, friendly staff, and a great location for I-Drive attractions. Home of the Peabody Ducks (see p46), it has a rooftop tennis court, as well as a health center. ◈ 9801 International Dr • Map T4 • 407-352-4000 • www.peabody-orlando.com • $$$$

7 Marriott's Orlando World Center

The 2,000 rooms at this 28-story tower tend to be a bit smaller than others in this price category, but they come with plenty of in-room features. The resort boasts a wide array of facilities including a spa and the biggest pool in town. ◈ 8701 World Center Dr • Map G2 • 407-239-4200 • www.marriott-hotels.com • $$$

8 Grand Bohemian

Soft-as-clouds beds are one of this elegant downtown hotel's greatest selling points. Rooms are modern, and public areas display rare artworks. ◈ 325 S. Orange Ave • Map P3 • 407-313-9000 • www.grandbohemianhotel.com • $$$$

9 Waldorf Astoria

This elegant hotel sits among 482 acres (195 ha) of land and features elegantly furnished rooms, a championship golf course, and bars and restaurants that mirror the hotel's original New York establishments. ◈ 14200 Bonnet Creek Resort Lane • Map G2 • 407-597-5500 • www.waldorfastoriaorlando.com • $$$$

10 Disney's Animal Kingdom® Lodge

This Disney resort resembles a South African game lodge in a semi-circular kraal (compound). Rooms have an African theme and some have views of a wildlife-filled tropical savanna. ◈ 2901 Osceola Pkwy • Map G1 • 407-938-3000 • www.disneyworld.com • $$$$

Left **Doubletree by Hilton Guest Suites** Right **Holiday Inn Walt Disney**

Mid-Price Hotels (A-G)

1 Best Western Lake Buena Vista Resort Hotel

All rooms have balconies at this official Disney hotel; some of them overlook beautiful gardens bordering the lake. There's free transportation to Disney's major parks, and it's within walking distance of Downtown Disney. ✆ *2000 Hotel Plaza Blvd • Map F2 • 407-828-2424 • www.lakebuenavista resorthotel.com • $$*

2 Caribbean Beach Resort

Disney's largest hotel (with 2,112 rooms) is split into five "villages": Aruba, Trinidad, Martinique, Barbados, and Jamaica, each with its own pool and sandy beach. The rooms are on the small side but are good value. ✆ *900 Cayman Way • Map G2 • 407-934-3400 • www. disneyworld.com • $$$*

3 Bohemian Hotel Celebration

The elegant lakefront rooms at this three-story, timber-framed resort offer a tranquil water-and-woodlands view. Facilities include an outdoor pool with Jacuzzi, a fitness center, and nature trails. There's an 18-hole golf course *(see p54)* too. ✆ *700 Bloom St • Map G2 • 407-566-6000 • www. celebrationhotel.com • $$$*

4 Courtyard at Lake Lucerne

Downtown's best B&B has four period buildings, from the Victorian Norment-Parry Inn to the Art Deco Wellborn Suites, which has apartments and a honeymoon suite. ✆ *211 N. Lucerne Circle E • Map P3 • 407-648-5188 • www. orlandohistoricinn.com • No pool • $$*

5 Courtyard by Marriott, Lake Buena Vista Centre

This mid-priced hotel has two outdoor heated swimming pools, a games room, and a Pizza Hut restaurant on site. It is well located for theme parks. ✆ *8501 Palm Pkwy • Map F3 • 407-239-6900 • www.courtyard.com • $$*

6 Extended Stay Deluxe Orlando Convention Center

Some of the 137 suites have wheelchair access, others are tailored to the hearing impaired. There's a heated pool, barbecues, and a Jacuzzi, and it's on the I-Ride Trolley circuit and provides a free shuttle to Disney. ✆ *8750 Universal Blvd • Map E3 • 407-903-1500 • www. extendedstay.com •$$*

7 The Holiday Inn Resort Orlando – The Castle

The towering spires of this themed hotel make it look like a fairytale castle – if castles came in pink and blue, that is. Its 216 rooms and seven suites come with big-screen TVs and Sony Playstations. The resort has a roof terrace, a fitness center, and two restaurants. ✆ *8629 International Dr • Map T3 • 407-345-1511 • www.thecastle orlando.com • $$*

8 Doubletree by Hilton Guest Suites

After being welcomed with home-made cookies, head to your cozy one- or two-bedroomed suite at this official Disney hotel. With a landscaped pool and a spa, you can't fail to relax. ✆ *2305 Hotel Plaza Blvd • Map F2 • 407-934-1000 • www. doubletreeguestsuites.com • $$*

9 Doubletree by Hilton Universal Orlando

A $16 million renovation helped convert this former convention hotel into one that woos travelers who want to be near the Universal parks. The hotel's two towers house 742 modern rooms and suites; those on the west side overlook the parks and CityWalk. ✆ *5780 Major Blvd • Map U1 • 407-351-1000 • www.doubletreeorlando. com • $$*

10 Caribe Royale

This hotel has well-appointed one-bedroom suites on 53 acres (21 ha), with shuttles to Downtown Disney and theme parks. ✆ *8101 World Center Dr • Map G3 • 407-238-8000 • www.thecaribe orlando.com • $$$*

Unless indicated, all hotels have DA, smoking rooms, A/C, pool, parking and kids' accommodation, and accept credit cards.

Price Categories

For a standard, double room per night (with breakfast if included), taxes and extra charges.

$	under $90
$$	$90–180
$$$	$180–250
$$$$	over $250

Nickelodeon Suites Resort

⑩ Mid-Price Hotels (H-Z)

1 Nickelodeon Suites Resort

Children rule in this resort, which has Kidsuites (sleeping up to seven) with big-screen TVs. Other types of suite include Cinemasuites, with even bigger TVs. Activities offered range from karaoke to ping-pong, and there are also two water parks. ✆ 14500 Continental Gateway • Map G3 • 407-387-5437 • www.nickhotel.com • $$$

2 Holiday Inn Lake Buena Vista Resort

If keeping the kids happy is top priority, this hotel is a good bet. Apart from the themed, two-roomed Kidsuites, there's a free activities program for 3–12-year-olds. Children can watch movies from the pool, and kids eat free. ✆ 13351 Apopka-Vineland Rd • Map G3 • 407-239-4500 • www.hiresortlbv.com • $$

3 Holiday Inn Walt Disney

This comfortable hotel makes for a good choice on the Hotel Plaza strip. The glass elevator scales the 14-story, plant-filled atrium and makes for a very exciting ride. The hotel provides a free Disney shuttle, free Wi-Fi and does not charge any resort fee. ✆ 1805 Hotel Plaza Blvd • Map F2 • 407-828-8888 • www.hiorlando.com • $$

4 Quality Suites Orlando

These modern luxury suites in neutral tones, with spacious living rooms and kitchens, can sleep up to six. Free coffee and tea is provided in the lobby apart from a free shuttle to the Disney parks. Rates include breakfast. ✆ 8200 Palm Pkwy • Map F2 • 407-465-8200 • www.qualitysuites-lvb.com • No DA • $$

5 Hotel Royal Plaza

Some of the spacious rooms at this hotel have whirlpools; pool-side ones have balconies or patios. The pool is heated, and there's a Jacuzzi, fitness center, and four lit tennis courts. ✆ 1905 Hotel Plaza Blvd • Map F2 • 407-828-2828 • www.royalplaza.com • $$$

6 World Gate Resort

Catering to business travelers and families, the rooms offer work stations, refrigerators, Internet access, and lush linens. Price, location, and service make it attractive. ✆ 3011 Maingate Lane • Map G2 • 407-396-1400 • www.worldgateresorts.com • $$

7 Heron Cay Lakeview B&B

This Victorian-style hotel situated within a large garden overlooks Lake Dora. The Queen Victoria suite, with its crimson furnishings and four-poster bed, is the most inviting of the six rooms. Gourmet breakfasts can include spinach strata and potato pancakes. ✆ 495 Old Hwy 441 • Off map • 352-383-4050 • www.heroncay.com • $$$

8 Springhill Suites

This pleasant suite hotel located in the Marriott Village is close to Disney. All the suites have a king-size or two double beds, plus separate living and cooking areas. ✆ 8601 Vineland Ave • Map G3 • 407-938-9001 • www.marriott.com • $–$$

9 Thurston House

Built in 1885, and set in woodland, just minutes north of Orlando, this charming B&B offers a quiet retreat, popular with adults. The four rooms, with queen-size beds, overlook Lake Eulalia. It's smoke-free and has no pool, but the home-away-from-home atmosphere is a winner. ✆ 851 Lake Ave • Map K3 • 407-539-1911 • www.thurstonhouse.com • No DA • $$

10 Liki Tiki Village

Just 7 miles (11 km) from the south gate of Disney, Liki Tiki is a luxurious complex offering furnished condos. With a vast water park on site, the kids may never leave for the parks. ✆ 17777 Bali Blvd, Winter Garden • Off map • 407-856-7190 • www.likitiki.com • $$

Left **Rosen Inn International** Right **Quality Inn sign**

🔟 Inexpensive Hotels (A-H)

1 Best Western Mount Vernon Inn

Located some 20 miles (32 km) north of Disney World, this is a cozy, colonial-style motel, with friendly staff. There's a city park nearby, and a charming Winter Park is minutes away. 🗐 *110 S. Orlando Ave • Map L3 • 407-647-1166 • www.bestwestern.com • $*

2 Clarion Inn Lake Buena Vista

Well located for the theme parks, this hotel offers a free shuttle service for Walt Disney World®, Universal Studios®, and Seaworld®. There are two swimming pools and a mini-market deli for buying snacks. Kids stay and eat for free at the on-site restaurant. 🗐 *8442 Palm Pkwy • Map F3 • 407-996-7300 • www.clarionlbv.com • $*

3 Howard Johnson Inn Maingate East

Rooms at this inn are sparse and small but comfortable and well-equipped . Ask for a room at the rear to escape the noise of traffic. One child eats free with each paying adult in the restaurant. Efficiencies (small serviced apartments) are available. 🗐 *6051 W. Irlo Bronson Memorial Hwy • Map G2 • 407-396-1748 • www.hojomge.com • $*

4 Rosen Inn

The Rosen Inn's 315 rooms, renovated in 2013, all have double or king beds, refrigerators, and microwaves. There is a pool as well as several restaurants on site. Guests can take the free shuttle service to Universal® Orlando or SeaWorld® Orlando, or use the I-Drive Trolley stop in front of the hotel. 🗐 *6327 International Dr • Map T3 • 800-999-6327 • www.roseninn6327.com • $*

5 Drury Inn & Suites

Located conveniently near the theme parks, this hotel provides clean rooms at a bargain price. Facilities here include a fitness center, Wi-Fi, free breakfast and light supper. 🗐 *7301 Sand Lake Rd • Map T3 • 407-354-1101 • www.drury hotels.com • No smoking rooms • $$*

6 Days Inn Convention Center

This branch of the Days Inn chain boasts a fitness centre, a sundeck, and an outdoor pool. The hotel is surrounded by landscaped grounds and has a pancake restaurant and playground. Transport service is provided. 🗐 *9990 International Dr • Map T5 • 407-352-8700 • www.days inn.com • $*

7 Maingate Lakeside Resort

Located just 2 miles (1km) from Disneyworld, the hotel offers a free shuttle service to many theme parks. There are also three restaurants and three pools within its 24 landscaped acres. Rooms are bright and spacious, offering good value for money. 🗐 *7769 W. Highway 192 • Map G2 • 407-396-2222 • www.maingatelakeside resort.com • $*

8 Fairfield Inn & Suites Orlando Lake Buena Vista

Part of the landscaped Marriott Village, this is located near Disney. The facilities on offer include luxury bedding, a mini-fridge, free Wi-Fi, fitness center, and a pool. 🗐 *8615 Vineland Ave • Map G3 • 407-938-9001 • www.marriott.com • No smoking rooms • $$*

9 Galleria Palms Hotel & Suites

This hotel has a better feel than most establishments in this price bracket. Rooms are smallish but sleep up to four. There's a free Disney shuttle, and rates include breakfast, free internet access, and free local phone calls. 🗐 *3000 Maingate Lane • Map G2 • 407-396-6300 • www.galleria kissimmeehotel.com • $$*

10 Coco Key

If water parks delight you then this family-friendly, pool-centric resort is a great option. A canopy over the kids' pool, high-speed slides for the older ones, free Wi-Fi, and fitness center are among the highlights here. 🗐 *7400 International Dr • Map T2 • 407-351-2626 • www.cocokeyorlando.com • No smoking rooms • $$*

Unless indicated, all hotels have DA, smoking rooms, A/C, pool, parking and kids' accommodation, and accept credit cards.

Left **Best Western Mount Vernon Inn**

Price Categories

For a standard, double room per night (with breakfast if included), taxes and extra charges.	**$** under $90 **$$** $90–180 **$$$** $180–250 **$$$$** over $250

🔟 Inexpensive Hotels (I-Z)

1 Rosen Inn International

With its convenient location, quality service, and top-notch amenities, this hotel is a pretty good bargain. Kids can eat for free. ✆ *7600 International Dr • Map T3 • 407-996-1600 • http:// roseninn7600.com• No smoking rooms • $$*

2 Parc Corniche Suites

Conveniently located midway between Walt Disney World® and Universal Studios®, Parc Corniche is surrounded by golf course fairways and pines. It offers well-equipped suites at reasonable prices. ✆ *6300 Parc Corniche Dr • Map T6 • 407-239-7100 • www. parccorniche.com • No smoking rooms • $*

3 Comfort Suites Universal Studios

This hotel is just a few minutes from I-Drive, Wet 'n Wild®, and Universal Studios Florida®. Rooms have refrigerators, microwaves, and free Wi-Fi, and breakfast is included. ✆ *5617 Major Blvd • Map U1 • 407-363-1967 • www. comfortsuites.com • $*

4 Enclave Suites at Orlando

The Enclave Suites are close to the major theme parks. Family-friendly features include swimming pools, children's play areas, and several on-site dining options,

including Pizza Hut. ✆ *6165 Carrier Dr • Map T2 • 800-457-0077 • www. enclavesuites.com • $$*

5 Ramada Convention Center I-Drive

The rooms are a step above most in this price category, and the majority are situated away from the noise of I-Drive traffic. The motel is located between SeaWorld® and the Universal parks, and it's on the I-Ride Trolley circuit (see p127). Rates include breakfast. ✆ *8342 Jamaican Ct • Map T3 • 407-363-1944 • www. ramada.com • $*

6 Rosen Inn at Pointe Orlando

This is a good-value hotel given its location on I-Drive, just opposite Pointe Orlando. The standard rooms are really quite small, so if space is an issue, opt for a semi-suite. Three pools, two games rooms, and a 24-hour deli are among the on site amenities. ✆ *9000 International Dr • Map T4 • 407-996-8585 • www. rosen inn9000.com • $*

7 La Quinta Inn & Suites UCF

This hotel, near the University of Central Florida, is for guests who want an east Orlando location. Rooms are comfortable, and rates include breakfast, local phone calls, Internet access, and weekday

newspapers. ✆ *11805 Research Pkwy • Off map • 407-737-6075 • www.lq. com • $$*

8 Ramada Orlando International Drive Lakefront

Close to Universal and Wet 'n Wild®. Rooms have lake views, and there's free Wi-Fi and shuttles to Disney. Facilities include basketball and tennis courts. No resort fee. ✆ *6500 International Dr • Map T3 • 407-345-5340 • www.ramada. com • $$*

9 Palms Hotel & Villas

This condo-style hotel is well located for Walt Disney World® Resort and offers a free shuttle service to the Disney theme parks. There is a complimentary breakfast and free Wi-Fi. ✆ *3100 Parkway Blvd • Map G2 • 407-396-8484 • www. thepalmshoteland villas. com • $$*

10 Royal Celebration Inn

Situated on Lake Cecile, this motel is 5 miles (8 km) from Mickey's place. The rooms are a bit cramped, but they offer free continental breakfast and shuttles to Disney. The inn has a lakeside beach, with jet skis and water-skiing. ✆ *4944 W. Irlo Bronson Mem. Hwy • Map H3 • 407-396-4455 • www.royalcelebration orlando.com • $*

For ways to have fun on the cheap **See pp46–7**

Left **Sheraton's Vistana Resort** Right **Beach Tree Villas**

Condo & Timeshare Rentals

1 Disney Vacation Club

The same upscale Disney units that are sold as timeshares are also available for rental. Properties are located on land owned by Disney, including Old Key West Resort, Animal Kingdom Lodge, and Boardwalk Villas. ✎ 800-800-9100 • Map F2, G2 & F1 • www.dvcresorts.com • $$$$

2 Sheraton's Vistana Resort

This resort offers modern one- and two-bedroom villas and town houses, packed with home comforts, that can be rented by the week. The tennis facilities are excellent, with both clay and all-weather courts. ✎ 8800 Vistana Center Dr • Map G2 • 407-239-3100 • www.starwood.com/sheraton • $$$

3 Summer Bay Resort

Accommodation at Summer Bay ranges from one-bedroom condos to three-bedroom villas; all have washers and dryers. The property has a clubhouse and offers jet-skiing, waterskiing, and canoeing on several lakes. ✎ 17805 W. Irlo Bronson Memorial Hwy\• Map G1 • 877-782-9387 • www.summerbayresort.com • $$

4 Liki Tiki Village

This lush Polynesian-themed resort has one- and two-bedroom condos with fully equipped kitchens, large TVs, whirlpool tubs, and washers and dryers. The resort itself offers poolside dining, a kids' water park, tennis, mini golf, and many other diversions. ✎ 17777 Bali Blvd, Kissimmee • Off map • 888-697-7152 • www.liki tiki.com • $$

5 Marriott Vacation Club International

Marriott's timeshare program covers five Orlando locations. The apartments and villas can also be rented by the week. Some of the villas have patios or porches, and facilities include activity programs, fitness centers, golf-course privileges, tennis courts, clubhouses, and saunas. ✎ 800-845-5279 • www.vacationclub.com • $$$

6 Holiday Villas

For generous living space, Holiday Villas offers two- and three-bedroom condos that can sleep up to eight, on eight different properties near Disney. Each comes with a washer and dryer. ✎ 4201 Vineland Rd • 800-344-3959 • www.holiday villas.com • $$

7 Blue Tree Resort

Blue Tree's elegant and spacious one- and two-bedroom villas are well-located for Disney attractions. The resort has four pools, two tennis courts, a volleyball court, and a playground. Rates are available with or without housekeeping services. ✎ 12007 Cypress Run Rd • Map F3 • 407-238-6000 • www.bluetree-orlando.com • $$

8 Orlando Breeze Resort

This resort, with its two and three-bedroom villas, is a real home-away-from-home for timeshare owners. It lacks the crowds and tourist frenzy of the mainstream areas. ✎ 121 Emerald Loop • Off map • 1-800-613-0310 • www.silverleafresorts.com • Smoke free • $$

9 Island One Resorts

There are four themed resorts to choose from, offering roomy one- to three-bedroom condos and villas. Facilities vary, but range from whirlpools to nature trails, and they sell discount attraction tickets. ✎ 8680 Commodity Circle • 407-859-8900 • www.islandone.com • $$

10 Beach Tree Villas

Great for families, the Beach Tree has two- to four-bedroom homes, the larger of which have private pools. There's an on-site recreation center, sauna, and a tennis court, but rates don't include an extra cleaning fee. Villas have a four-night minimum stay; houses have a five-night minimum. ✎ 2545 Chatham Circle • Map G3 • 407-396-7416 • www.beachtreevillas.com • Smoke free • $$

Price Categories

For a standard, double room per night (with breakfast if included), taxes and extra charges.

$	under $90
$$	$90–180
$$$	$180–250
$$$$	over $250

Left **Orlando Southwest Fort Summit KOA**

Close to Nature

1 Fort Wilderness Resort & Campground

Vast tracts of cypress and pine trees, fish-filled lakes, and fresh air envelop this Disney resort. It has 783 camp sites plus 409 cabins, which sleep up to six and have kitchens (the newer ones also have sun decks). Canoeing and horseback riding are two of the many outdoor activities on offer. ⌖ 4510 N. Fort Wilderness Trail • Map F1 • 407-824-2900 • www. disneyworld.com • $$$$

2 Disney's Saratoga Springs Resort & Spa

Choose from one-bedroom bungalows, two-bedroom town houses, fairway villas next to Disney golf courses, or three-bedroom Treehouse Villas 10 ft (3 m) off the ground. Most include daily housekeeping and there are lots of recreation choices. ⌖ 1960 Broadway • 407-827-1100 • www.disneyworld.com • $$$$

3 Southport Park Campground & Marina

This relaxing park is in 25-acres (10 ha) of lakeside woods. While away time by fishing, wandering among the wildlife (such as deer and eagles), or taking an airboat trip. There are RV and tent sites with full hook-ups. ⌖ 2001 E. Southport Rd • Off map • 407-933-5822 • www. southportpark.com • $

4 Floridian RV Resort

This woodsy retreat near East Lake Tohopekaliga has full hook-ups for RVs, two clubhouses, a playground, tennis courts, and a volley-ball court. There are plenty of leisure activities in the area, such as airboat rides and parasailing. ⌖ 5150 Boggy Creek Rd • Off map • 407-892-5171 • www. florida-rv-parks.com • $

5 Kissimmee/ Orlando KOA

A great place to camp if you want to be close to Walt Disney World and SeaWorld®. There are RV sites, camp sites, and cabins. The RV sites can have cable TV and modem dataport connected for an extra charge. ⌖ 2644 Happy Camper Pl • 407-396-2400 • www.koa.com • $

6 Clerbrook Golf & RV Resort

This large site, popular with golfers, offers 1,250 RV hook-ups, non-smoking villas, as well as amenities including a driving range, four whirlpools, a library, and a beauty salon. ⌖ 20005 Hwy 27 • Off map • 352-394-5513 • www.florida-rv-parks.com • $

7 Cypress Cove Nudist Resort

Unself-conscious couples and families with American Association for Nude Recreation or Cypress Cove resort membership, can stay in villas, rooms, and RV sites here. ⌖ 4425 Pleasant Hill Rd • Off map • 407-933-5870 • www. cypresscoveresort.com • $$

8 Orlando Southwest Fort Summit KOA

This resort offers full hook-ups for RVs, as well as small timber cabins and pitches for tents. There's a store, laundromats, and internet access. ⌖ 2525 Frontage Rd • Off map • 863-424-1880 • www.fort summit.com • $

9 Circle F. Dude Ranch Camp

This kids' summer camp is also a family retreat on selected weekends between November and May. Hay rides, horseback riding, lake swimming, and sailing are some of the activities on offer. Weekend rates include five meals. ⌖ Hwy 60 & Dude Ranch Rd • Off map • 863-676-4113 • www.circlefdude ranchcamp.com • smoke-free • No DA • $$

10 Orlando Winter Garden RV Resort

Pines and ponds are all around this RV resort, about a 30-minute drive from Disney World. It boasts lots of facilities such as laundry, games room, dances, bingo, and barbecues. Popular with an older crowd. ⌖ 13905 W. Colonial Dr • Map C1 • 407-656-1415 • www. wintergardenrv.com • $

General Index

180 Grey Goose Lounge 116
1900 Park Fare 71
2001 Ski Odyssey 36
4Rivers Smokehouse 123

A

AARP (American Association of Retired Persons) 138
Accessible Mini Van Rentals 138
Adobe Gila's 75, 104
Advanced Dental Care 131
Air Florida Helicopters 100
air travel 126
airports 126, 130
Akershus 95
Alamo 130
Albin Polasek Museum and Sculpture Gardens 61, 119
A'Lure 29
Amazing Adventures of Spider-Man® 20, 23, 42
American Adventure 14–15
American Automobile Association (AAA) 130
American Express 130
American Ghost Adventures 112, 113
Amtrak train stations 130
Animal Kingdom Lodge 143
animals
  Animal Actors on Location 26
  Arabian Nights 80
  Canaveral National Seashore 52
  Center for Birds of Prey 47, 120
  Central Florida Zoo 85
  Crystal River Swim & Snorkel Manatee Tour 85
  Disney's Animal Kingdom Park 6, 18–19, 89
  Florida Aquarium 82
  Fort Wilderness Petting Farm 47
  Gatorland 107, 109
  Green Meadows Petting Farm 107
  Jungleland Zoo 45
  Lake Kissimmee State Park 52

animals (cont.)
  Lake Louisa State Park 52
  Lowry Park Zoo 82
  Merritt Island National Wildlife Refuge 52
  SeaWorld® Orlando 7, 28–31, 97, 129
  swim with the manatees 83
  Tosohatchee State Reserve 53
  Wekiva Springs State Park 52
Anime Festival Orlando 65
Antarctica: Empire of the Penguin 29
Anthony, Susan B. 15
Apollo/Saturn V Center 39
Aquarium, Florida 82
Aquatica 49
Arabian Nights 80
Armstrong, Neil 40, 41
Arnold Palmer Invitational 57
Around the World at Epcot 129
Art of Disney 92
Artist Point 94
Ask-A-Pharmacist 135
Astronaut Encounter 38
Atlanta Braves Spring Training 57
Atlantic Dance Hall 75, 93
Atlantis 38
ATMs 136
Avis 130
Azteca's Mexican 111

B

baby care 139
Backstage at the Rosen Plaza 75
Backstage Magic 129
Bahama Breeze 105
Baja Burrito Kitchen 71
Bands Brew & BBQ 65
Bank of America 130
banks 130, 136
The Bar at California Grill 72
Bar-B-Q Bar 73
bars 72–3
  Downtown Orlando 116
  happy hours 134
  International Drive 104

bars (cont.)
  Walt Disney World® Resort and Lake Buena Vista 93
  Winter Park, Maitland and Eatonville 122
baseball 57
basketball 57
Be Our Guest 94
Beach Tree Villas 148
Beacham Theatre 76, 116
beaches
  Cocoa Beach 84
  Daytona Beach 84
  Gulf beaches 83
  New Smyrna Beach 84
  safety 137
Beauty & the Beast Live on Stage! 17
bed tax 141
Beetlejuice's Rock 'n Roll Graveyard Revue 26
behind-the-scenes tours 129
Berber Oasis 92
Best Value Hawaiian Inn 146
Best Western Lake Buena Vista Resort Hotel 144
Best Western Mount Vernon Inn 146
Big Thunder Mountain Railroad 8
Big Tree Park 53
Bill Frederick Park at Turkey Lake 53
Birds of Prey Center 47, 120
Birdwalk Aviary 37
Black Angus Restaurant 111
Black Hole 34
The Blast 35
Blizzard Beach 48, 89
Blue Horizons 30
Blue Martini 74
Blue Skies Balloon Festival 64
Blue Tree Resort 148
Blues Bar at House of Blues 74–5
Blues Brothers 26
boating 56
Bob Marley – A Tribute to Freedom 104
Boggy Creek Airboat Rides 110

Boggy Creek Parasail Rides 110
The Boheme 69, 117
Boma – Flavors of Africa 70
The Bomb Bay 34
The Boneyard 19
Bongo's Cuban Café 75, 93
The Bösendorfer Lounge 73, 74, 115, 116
Botanical Gardens 36
Botanical Gardens Cruise 36
Brain Wash 35
breakfast 134
Briar Patch 121, 123
The Brink 78
Brio Tuscan Grille 121, 122, 123
brochures 128
Brooks Brothers Outlet 101
Bubba Tub 35
Bubba's Bar-B-Q & Chicken 36
Budget (car rental) 130
budget travel 46–7, 133
Buena Vista Palace 58, 143
Buena Vista Watersports 49
Busch Gardens 82
buses 126, 127, 140
Buzz Lightyear's Space Ranger Spin 9

C
Café Annie 117
Café de France 123
Café Tu Tu Tango 70, 105
cafés
 Downtown Orlando 117
 Winter Park, Maitland and Eatonville 123
Caladesi State Park 83
California Grill 68, 72, 94
Calling All Animals 37
Camp Jurassic 22
Canada
 Consulate 131
 US entry requirements 126
 World Showcase Pavilion 14
Canaveral National Seashore 52
Cape Canaveral: Then & Now Tour 38
Cape May Café 71
Capital One Florida Citrus Bowl 57

Capone's Dinner & Show 81
Caribbean Beach Resort 144
Caro-Seuss-El 22, 43
Carpenter, Scott 40
cars
 car rental 127, 130, 133
 drinking and driving 137
 safety 137
 seat belts 137
 speed limits 137
Cask & Larder 123
The Cat in the Hat 21, 43
Celebration 107
Celebration Golf Club 54
Celebration Health 131
Celebration Hotel 144
Celebration Town Tavern 111
Center for Birds of Prey 47, 120
Centra Care Walk-In Medical Care 131, 135
Central Florida Fair 64
Central Florida Helpline 131
Central Florida Zoo & Botanical Gardens 85
Centro Ybor 82
Century Walk-In Medical Center 131
Ceviche Tapas Bar & Restaurant 117
Chalet Suzanne 36
Champions Gate 54–5
Charles Hosmer Morse Museum of American Art 60, 119, 121
Charley's Steak House 111
Chase Bank 130
Chef John's Place 111
Chef Mickey's 71
Chefs de France 95
children
 in hotels 139
 lost 137, 139
 in restaurants 139
Children's Miracle Network Classic 57
Chili's Grill & Bar 71, 105
China, World Showcase Pavilion 14
Chip 'n' Dale's Campfire Sing-A-Long 93
Church Street 114, 116
Cinderella Castle 10

Cinderella's Royal Table 71, 95
Circle F. Dude Ranch Camp 149
Circus McGurkus 71
Cirque du Soleil 89, 93
City of Kissimmee Police 131
City of Orlando Police 131
Citysearch 130
CityWalk® & Portofino Bay Ride 47
Clerbrook Golf & RV Resort 149
climate 126
clinics, walk-in 131, 135
clothing 139, 140
clubs 76–7
 Downtown Orlando® 116
 International Drive area 104
 Walt Disney World® Resort and Lake Buena Vista 93
Coach Factory Store 101
Coast Dental 131
Coco Key 146
Cocoa Beach 84
Colonial Lanes 115
Columbia Restaurant Celebration 94
Comfort Inn Lake Buena Vista 146
Comfort Suites Universal Studios 147
communications 136
concierge desks, hotels 132
condo and timeshare rentals 148
consolidators 126
consulates 131
cooking facilities 133
Cooper, Gordon 40
Copper Rocket Pub 122
Coral Reef Restaurant 70, 95
Cornell Fine Arts Museum 60–1, 119, 121
Country Bear Jamboree 11
The Courtesy 73
Courtyard at Lake Lucerne 144
Courtyard by Marriott – Lake Buena Vista Centre 144
Cowboys Orlando 72, 116
credit cards 130–1, 136

Cricketers Arms Pub 104
crime 137
The Crystal Palace 71
Crystal River Manatee
    Swim & Snorkel Tour 85
Cuba Libre 105
cultural venues and
    organizations 62–3
Cunningham, Earl 61
Curious George Goes To
    Town 26
currency and exchanges 136
CVS Pharmacy 131
cycling 56
Cypress Cove Nudist
    Resort 149
Cypress Junction 37
Cypress Roots 37

D

A Day in the Park with
    Barney 26
day trips 82–5
Days Inn Convention
    Center 146
Daytona Beach 84
Dental Referral Service 135
dentists 131, 135
Despicable Me 25
Dexter's of Thornton Park
    73, 117
Dexter's Winter Park 122
Diners Club 130
dinner shows 80–1
DINOSAUR 19
disabled travelers 138
Disaster! 25
Disco H2O 34
discounts 132, 133, 140
Discover 130
Discovery Cove 48, 97
Disney
    Art of Disney 92
    behind-the-scenes tours
        129
    Blizzard Beach 48, 89
    budget travel 133
    Celebration 107
    dining with Disney
        characters 71
    disabled guests 138
    Disney Hollywood
        Studios® 6, 16–17, 89
    Disney Institute Spa
        58–9
    Disney Vacation Club 148
    Disney World Festival of
        the Masters 65

Disney (cont.)
    Disneyana Convention
        65
    DisneyQuest 90, 93
    Disney's Animal
        Kingdom® Park 6, 18–19,
        89
    Disney's BoardWalk
        46, 93
    Disney's Board-Walk Inn
        & Villas 142
    Disney's Grand Floridian
        Resort & Spa 142
    Disney's Grandkids &
        You Getaway 138
    Disney's Lake Buena
        Vista 55
    Disney's Magnolia 54
    Disney's Osprey Ridge
        54
    Disney's Palm 55
    Disney's Port Orleans
        Resort 142
    Disney's Value Resorts
        142
    Disney's Wilderness
        Lodge 142
    Disney's Yacht Club
        Resort 142
    Downtown Disney® 46,
        67, 93
    Epcot® 6, 12–15, 89
    Hoop-Dee-Do Musical
        Revue 80, 93
    hotels 141
    Magic Kingdom® Park
        6, 8–11, 89
    resorts 142
    restaurants 134, 139
    River Country 48–9,
        89
    Sammy Duvall's
        Watersports Centres 49
    transportation system
        127
    Typhoon Lagoon 48, 89
    Walt Disney World
        Dolphin 142
    Walt Disney World
        Marathon 57
    Walt Disney World®
        Resort and Lake Buena
        Vista 88–95
    Walt Disney World Swan
        142
    World of Disney 92
Disney, Walt 90
Diver's Outlet 101

Doctor Doom's Fearfall
    20, 42–3
doctors 135
Dollar 130
Dolphin Cove 28
Dolphin Nursery 30
Doubletree Guest Suites
    144
Doubletree Universal
    Orlando 144
Downtown Disney® 46, 67,
    93
Downtown Orlando®
    112–17
    map 112
    nightspots 116
    restaurants and cafés 117
Downtown's Westside 140
Dragon Challenge 21, 23,
    42
driving in Orlando 127
Drury Inn 146
Dudley Do-Right's Ripsaw
    Falls 21, 43
Duvall, Sammy 49
Dye, Pete 54

E

Eagle Pines 54
Early Space Exploration 39
East Lake Fish Camp 110
Edwin Watts Golf National
    Clearance Center 101
Eighth Voyage of Sinbad
    22
Elderhostel 138
Ellen's Energy Adventure 12
emergencies 135
Emeril's 68
Emeril's Tchoup Chop 94
Enclave Suites Orlando 147
Enterprise 130
Enzian Theater 62, 121
Eó Inn 59, 144
Eola, Lake 47, 52, 114
Eola Wine Co 122
Epcot® 6, 12–15, 89
Epcot® International
    Flower & Garden
    Festival 65
Epcot® International Food
    & Wine Festival 65
ESPN Club 93
ESPN Wide World of
    Sports 56, 88, 91
ESTA (Electronic System
    for Travel Authorization)
    126

E.T. Adventure 26, 43
ExpressCare 131
Extended Stay Deluxe Orlando Convention Center 144
Extreme Jet Ski 110
Everglades (restaurant) 105

F

Fairfield Inn & Suites Lake Buena Vista Orlando 146
Falcon's Fire Golf Club 55, 110
families, tips for 139
Family Magic Tour 129
family restaurants 133
Fantasia Gardens 90–1
Fantasmic! 16
Fantastic World of Hanna-Barbera 25
fast food 133
Fear Factor Live 26
Festival of the Lion King 18
festivals and events 64–5
Fiddler's Green 72, 122, 123
Fievel's Playground 26
film studios
  Disney Hollywood Studios® 6, 16–17, 89
  Universal Studios® Florida 7, 24–7, 97
Finding Nemo – The Musical 19
Fiorella's Cucina Toscana 69, 105
fire services 135
Firestone Live 76, 116
fireworks, Epcot® 15
fishing 57
  deep sea fishing 83
  East Lake Fish Camp 110
Flea World 67
Flight of the Hippogriff 21, 43
Florida Aquarium 82
Florida Film Festival 65
Florida Hospital 131
Florida International Museum 82
Florida Mall 66
Florida Southern College 83
Floridian RV Resort 149
The Flyer 35

football 57
Forever Florida – Florida Eco-Safaris 108
Fort Wilderness Petting Farm 47
Fort Wilderness Resort & Campground 149
Fortnightly Inn 144
Four Points by Sheraton Orlando Studio City 100
France, World Showcase Pavilion 15
Franklin, Benjamin 14
Fun-Spot America 44, 97
Fun With Jetskis 110

G

Galleria Palms Hotel & Suites 146
gardens see parks
gasoline 133
Gatorland 44, 107, 109
gay and lesbian nightlife 78–9
Gay Days 65
Gaylord Palms Resort 143
German Consulate 131
Germany, World Showcase Pavilion 15
gifts and souvenirs 132
Glenn, John 39, 40, 41
golf 54–5
  Bay Hill Classic 57
  Falcon's Fire Golf Club 110
  Fantasia Gardens & Winter Summerland Miniature Golf 90–1
  Kissimmee Golf Driving Range 110
  National Car Rental Golf Classic 57
Graffiti Junction American Burger Bar 117
Grand Bohemian 143
Grand Cypress Golf Club 54
Grand Floridian Senses Spa & Health Club 58
gratuities 134
Green Eggs and Ham Café 20
Green Meadows Petting Farm 107
Greenburg Dental Associates 131
Greyhound bus terminals 126, 130
Grinchmas 65

Grissom, Gus 41
The Groove 77, 104
Gulf beaches 83

H

Hall of Presidents 11
Halloween Horror Nights 65
Hanks 79
Hannibal's on the Square 122
happy hours 134
Hard Rock Hotel 142
Hard Rock Live 74, 76, 104
Harley-Davidson 92
Harry P. Leu Gardens 113
Harry Potter and the Forbidden Journey™ 21
Haunted Mansion 11
hayrides 57
health 135
heat 135
help lines 131
Help Now of Osceola 131
Heron Cay Lakeview B&B 145
Hertz 130
hidden Mickoys 91
High in the Sky Seuss Trolley Train Ride! 22
Hillstone 122, 125
Hire, Kathryn P. 41
Historic Bok Sanctuary 83
HOB Blues Bar 46
Holiday Inn Resort – Lake Buena Vista 145
Holiday Inn Resort Orlando – The Castle 144
Holiday Inn Resort Walt Disney 145
Holiday Villas 148
Hollywood Brown Derby 95
Hollywood Rip Ride Rockit® 25, 43
Holocaust Memorial Resource & Education Center 61
The Holy Land Experience 44, 98
Hoop-Dee-Do Musical Revue 80, 93
horseback riding 56, 110
Horse World Riding Stables 110

hospitals 131, 135
Hotel Royal Plaza 145
hotels 141–7
  budget travel 133
  children in 139
  concierge desks 132
  cooking facilities 133
  Disney and Universal resorts 142
  inexpensive hotels 146–7
  luxury hotels 143
  mid-price hotels 144–5
  mini bars 134
  safes 137
  shuttle buses 127
House of Blues 74, 93
House of Good Fortune 92
Howard Johnson Inn Maingate East 146
Howl at the Moon 104, 116
Hoypoloi Gallery 92
Hurston, Zora Neale 61, 120
Hyatt Regency Grand Cypress 143

I
I-Ride Trolley 99, 127
Ice Bar 100
The Ice Factory 110
If I Ran the Zoo 22
iFLY Orlando 45, 100
IMAX Theaters 39
Incredible Hulk Coaster® 20, 23, 42
Indiana Jones™ Epic Stunt Spectacular 16
Inness, George 60
Innovations East 12
Innovations West 12
insects 135
Inside Central Florida 130
International Drive area 96–105
  bars, clubs and entertainment 104
  eye-openers 100
  map 96
  restaurants 105
  stores and outlet centers 101
International Space Station Center 39
Internet 126, 131
Internet cafés 136
Island One Resorts 148

Islands in the Sky 37
Islands of Adventure 6, 20–3, 97
It's a Small World 10–11
It's Tough to Be a Bug! 19
Ivanhoe Row 67

J
Japan Consulate 131
Japan, World Showcase Pavilion 15
Jiko – The Cooking Place 94
Jimmy Buffet's Margaritaville 104
Jones, Robert Trent Sr. and Jr. 54
Journey to Atlantis 28
Journey to Imagination with Figment 11
Junior Belle Program 36
Jupiter C rocket 40
Jurassic Park Discovery Center 22
Jurassic Park River Adventure® 20

K
K Restaurant & Wine Bar 117
Kali River Rapids 18
Kennedy Space Center 7, 38–41, 84
Kenneth Cole 101
Keys to the Kingdom 129
Kilimanjaro Safaris® 18
Kings Bowl 100
Kissimmee 106–11
  leisure pursuits and activities 110
  map 106
  restaurants 111
Kissimmee/Orlando KOA 149
Kissimmee/St. Cloud Convention & Visitors Bureau 128
Kraken® 28, 43

L
La Quinta Inn & Suites UCF 147
Lake Buena Vista see Walt Disney World® Resort and Lake Buena Vista
Lake Buena Vista Golf Course 55

Lake Eola Park 47, 52, 114
Lake Kissimmee State Park 52
Lake Louisa State Park 52
Lakefront Park 48, 108
land-sea options 141
laser shows, Epcot 15
Latin Quarter 104
Lazy River 35
LEGO Imagination Center 92
Lesbian, Gay, Bisexual & Transgender Community Services of Central Florida 128
Liberty Tree Tavern 71, 95
Liki Tiki Village 145, 148
limousines 127
Little Saigon 117
live music venues 74–5, 93
Living with the Land 13
Lloyd, Christopher 24
Logan's Roadhouse 111
Lowry Park Zoo 82
Lucas, George 8
Lucky Leprechaun 72, 104
Luma on Park 123
lunch menus 134
Lynx buses 127, 140

M
Mach 5 35
Mad Cow Theatre 63
Magic Carpets of Aladdin 10
Magic Kingdom Park 6, 8–11, 89
  behind-the-scenes tours 129
Magicard 133
Magnolia 54
Maharajah Jungle Trek 19
Maingate Lakeside Resort 146
Maitland see Winter Park, Maitland and Eatonville
Maitland Art Center 120
Maitland Historical & Telephone Museums 61
Makinson Aquatic Center 49
Mamet, David 62
manatees
  Crystal River manatee tour 85
  swim with the manatees 83
Mandara Spa 58

Manta 29
Manta Aquarium 30
Many Adventures of
    Winnie the Pooh 9, 43
marathon 57
Mardi Gras at Universal 65
Marriott Vacation Club
    International 148
Marriott's Orlando World
    Center 143
Massageworks Salon &
    Day Spa 59
MasterCard 130
mature travelers 138
Me Ship, The Olive 22
Medieval Times 80
Mellow Mushroom Beer
    Bar 122
Men in Black™ Alien
    Attack™ 24
Mennello Museum of
    American Folk Art 61,
    113, 115
Mercury Atlas rocket 40
Mercury Redstone rocket
    40
Merritt Island National
    Wildlife Refuge 7, 36–7,
    52, 85
Mexico, World Showcase
    Pavilion 15
Mickey Mouse
    hidden Mickeys 91
    Mickey's Backyard BBQ
    71
    Mickey's Mart 92
    Mickey's PhilharMagic 11
    Mickey's Very Merry
    Christmas Party 65
Millay, George 34
Miller's Winter Park Ale
    House 122
Milne, A.A. 9
mini bars 134
Mission: SPACE 13
Mitsukoshi Department
    Store 92
money 136
Monkey Bar 76–7
Monroe, Marilyn 27
Moon Rock Café 38
Moore, Henry 61
Monsters Inc. Laugh Floor
    11
Morocco, World Showcase
    Pavilion 14
motels 141
motor racing 57

Mount Dora 85
Muppet™Vision 3-D 16
museums 60–1
    Albin Polasek Museum
    and Sculpture Gardens
    61, 119
    Charles Hosmer Morse
    Museum of American
    Art 60, 119, 121
    Cornell Fine Arts
    Museum 60–1, 119, 121
    Flying Tigers Warbird
    Restoration Museum
    61, 108–9
    Henry B. Plant Museum
    82
    Maitland Historical &
    Telephone Museums 61
    Mennello Museum of
    American Folk Art 61,
    113, 115
    Orange County Regional
    History Center 60, 113,
    115
    Orlando Museum of Art
    (OMA) 60, 113, 115
    Orlando Science Center
    60, 113
    Osceola County Pioneer
    Village & Museum 107
    Waterhouse Residence &
    Carpentry Museum 120
    Zora Neale Hurston
    National Museum of
    Fine Arts 61, 120
music venues 74–5
    Walt Disney World®
    Resort and Lake Buena
    Vista 93
Mystic Fountain 22

N
Napa (restaurant) 69
Napasorn Thai Restaurant
    117
NASA 38–41
National (car rental) 130
National Car Rental Golf
    Classic 57
NBA City 105
nèu Lotus Spa 58
The New Phoenix 78
New Smyrna Beach 84
News Channel 13 128
newspapers 133
Nickelodeon Suites Resort
    145
Nicklaus, Jack 54

Night of Joy 65
Nightlight Pediatrics 131
Nike Factory Store 101
Norman, Greg 54–5
Norman's 68
Norway, World Showcase
    Pavilion 15
NV Lounge 116

O
Off 5th 101
O'Keefe, Georgia 60
Old Town 108, 109
One Fish, Two Fish,
    Red Fish, Blue Fish™ 22
One Ocean™ 28
opening hours
    shops 132
    banks 136
Orange County National
    – Panther Lake 55
Orange County Regional
    History Center 60, 113, 115
Orange County Sheriff 131
Orlando Ballet 63
Orlando Breeze Resort 148
Orlando City Soccer 57
Orlando Dive and Snorkel
    Tours 48–9
Orlando Executive Airport
    (ORL) 126, 130
Orlando International
    Airport (MCO) 126, 130
Orlando International
    Fringe Festival 63, 64
Orlando Kissimmee KOA
    Kampground 149
Orlando Magic 57
Orlando Museum of Art
    (OMA) 60, 113, 115
Orlando Opera Company 63
Orlando/Orange County
    Convention & Visitors
    Bureau 128, 130
Orlando Philharmonic 63
Orlando Predators 57
Orlando Public Library 131
Orlando Repertory Theatre
    62
Orlando Sanford Airport
    (SFB) 126, 130
Orlando Science Center
    60, 113
Orlando Sentinel 128
Orlando Shakespeare
    Theater 62
Orlando Southwest Fort
    Summit KOA 149

Orlando Speedworld Speedway 47
Orlando-UCF Shakespeare Festival 62, 64
Orlando Weekly 128
Orlando Weekly Calendar 130
Orlando Winter Garden RV Resort 149
Osceola Center for the Arts 63, 110
Osceola County Historical Museum and Pioneer Center 107
Osceola County Sheriff 131
Oshkosh B'Gosh 101
Osprey Ridge 54
Outback Steakhouse 70
outdoor activities 56–7
  Kissimmee 110
outlet stores 132
  International Drive area 101
Outta Control Magic Comedy Dinner Show 81

P
Pacific Point Preserve 29
Pacino's Italian Ristorante 109, 111
packagers 126
The Palm 105
Palmer, Arnold 57
Palms Hotel & Villas 147
Panera Bread 71
Pangani Forest Exploration Trail 18
Panther Lake 55
Panullo's Italian Restaurant 123
parades, Magic Kingdom® 11
Parc Corniche Suites 147
Park Avenue 66, 119, 121
Park Inn 146
Park Plaza Gardens 69, 122, 123
parks, gardens and preserves 52–3
  Big Tree Park 53
  Canaveral National Seashore 52
  Cypress Gardens 7, 36–7
  Gardens of the World 129
  Harry P. Leu Gardens 113
  Lake Eola Park 47, 52, 114
  Lake Kissimmee State Park 52

parks, gardens and preserves (cont.)
  Lake Louisa State Park 52
  Merritt Island National Wildlife Refuge 52
  Ralph V. Chisolm Park 53
  Tosohatchee State Reserve 53
  Turkey Lake Park 53
  Wekiva Springs State Park 52
  Wheatley Park 53
Parliament House Resort 78
passports 126
The Peabody Ducks 46, 98
Peabody Orlando 143
The Peacock Room 78–9
Pegasus rocket 40
Peter Pan's Flight 8, 43
Pets Ahoy 30
pharmacies, 24-hour 131, 135
Pine 22 117
Pirate's Cove Adventure Golf 100
Pirates of the Caribbean 9
Pirates Dinner Adventure 80–81
Pointe Orlando 67
poison control 135
Polasek, Albin 61, 119
police 131, 135, 137
Portobello Yacht Club Restaurant 94
Portofino Bay Hotel 58, 142
Portofino Bay Ride 47
Poseidon Spa 59
Poseidon's Fury 21
post offices 131, 136
Primo 68
Prince Charming Regal Carousel 9, 43
Pro Bass Shops Outdoor World 101
Pteranodon Flyers 20, 43
Puerto Rico's Café 111
Pulse 79

Q
Quality Inn International 147
Quality Suites Orlando 145

R
radio 128
Rainforest Café 70, 95
Ralph V. Chisolm Park 53

Ramada Convention Center I-Drive 147
Ramada Orlando I-Drive Lakefront 147
Rauschenberg, Robert 60
recreational vehicle (RV) sites 149
Red Chair Project 133
Red Coconut Club 104
Relâche Spa 58
Regions Bank 130
Renaissance Orlando at SeaWorld® 58, 143
Renningers Antique & Flea Markets 67
Renningers Antique Extravaganzas 64
Reptile World Serpentarium 45, 108
Restaurant Marrakesh 70
Restaurantosaurus 18, 71
restaurants 134
  budget travel 133
  children in 139
  Downtown Orlando 117
  family restaurants 70–1
  high-end restaurants 68–9
  International Dr area 105
  Kissimmee 111
  in theme parks 140
  Walt Disney World® Resort and Lake Buena Vista 94–5
  Winter Park, Maitland and Eatonville 123
Revenge of the Mummy 25
Revolution Nightclub 76, 78
Richard Petty Driving Experience 90
Ripley's Believe It or Not®! Odditorium 44, 98, 100
Ritz-Carlton Spa 59
Riverside Romance 85
roads 127
Rock 'n' Roller Coaster 16, 42
Rocket Garden 39
rockets 40
rodeo
  Kissimmee Rodeo 109
  Silver Spurs Rodeo 57
Rok Room 77
Romano's Macaroni Grill 70
Roosevelt, Franklin Delano 7
Rose & Crown Pub & Dining Room 95
Rosen Inn at Pointe Orlando 147
Rosenthal, Marvin J. 98

Rosselli, Cosimo 61
Roxy 77
Roy's 105
Royal Celebration Inn 147
rush hours 140

S
safety 137
SAK Comedy Lab 62
sales 132
sales tax 132, 136, 141
Salvador Dali Museum 83
Samba Room 77
Sammy Duvall's
    Watersports Centres 49
San Angel Inn 95
Sanaa 94
Saturn 1B 40
Saturn V rocket 40
Savoy Orlando 79
The Seas with Nemo &
    Friends 12
Seasons 52 105
Seven Dwarfs Mine Train 9
Scenic/Eco Lake Tours 129
Schirra, Wally 40
Sci-Fi Dine-In Theater 16
SeaWorld® Adventure
    Camp 129
SeaWorld Orlando 7,
    28–31, 97
    behind-the-scenes tours
    129
    disabled guests 138
senior travelers 138
Shamu Rocks 30
Shamu's Happy Harbor 30
Shark Encounter 29
Sharks Underwater Grill 28
Shepard, Alan B. 40, 41
Sheraton's Vistana Resort
    148
shipping home 132
Shipyard Emporium 122
shopping 66–7, 132
    International Drive area
    100–1
    Walt Disney World®
    Resort and Lake Buena
    Vista 92
Shrek 4-D 24
Shuttle buses 127
Shuttle Launch Experience
    38
Silver Spurs Rodeo 46, 57,
    109
The Simpsons Ride 24
Sky 60 (bar) 73, 116

Sky Tower 30, 116
Sleuth's Mystery Dinner
    Show 81
smoking, in restaurants
    134
snacks 133
Soarin 13
Snow White's Scary
    Adventure 10
The Social 74, 77, 115, 116
Society for Accessible Travel
    & Hospitality 131, 138
South Orange Library 131
Southern Cassadaga
    Spiritualist Camp 84–5
Southern Freeze 37
souvenirs 132
Spa at Disney's Saratoga
    Springs Resort 58
Spa at Omni Orlando
    Resort 59
Spa at the Buena Vista
    Palace 58
space
    Kennedy Space Center
    7, 38–41, 84
Space Mountain 8
Space Shuttle 41
spacecraft launches 38
Spaceship Earth 13
spas 58–9
special diets 134
speed limits 137
Speedweek 57
Spielberg, Steven 23, 26
Spirit of Aloha Dinner
    Show 80
Splash Mountain 8, 42
sports 56–7
    Disney's Wide World of
    Sports 91
    Kissimmee 110
Springhill Suites 145
Star Tours 17
state parks 52–3, 83
Stitch's Great Escape 8
Stingray Lagoon 30
Stonewall 79
The Storm 34
Storm Force Accelatron 22
stroller rental 139
studio tours
    Disney Hollywood
    Studios® 6, 16–17, 89
    Universal Studios®
    Florida 7, 24–7, 97
Der Stuka 34
Summer Bay Resort 148

Summerfield Suites Lake
    Buena Vista 143
Summit Plummet 43
sunburn 135
SunTrust 130
surfing 57
Swan Boats in Lake Eola 47
swimming 56

T
Tarantino's Italian
    Restaurant 111
Taste of Punjab 111
taxes
    bed tax 141
    sales tax 132, 136, 141
taxis 127
telephones 136, 141
television 128
tennis 56
Terminator 2: 3-D 24
Test Track 12
Theatre Downtown 62
theft 137
Theme Park Insider 130
theme parks
    beating the crowds 126
    Busch Gardens 82
    DisneyQuest 90, 93
    Disney's Animal
    Kingdom® Park 6, 18–19,
    89
    Epcot® 6, 12–15, 89
    Gatorland 107, 109
    The Holy Land
    Experience 98
    Islands of Adventure®
    6, 20–3, 97
    Magic Kingdom® Park
    6, 8–11, 89, 129
    restaurants 95, 140
    SeaWorld® Orlando 7,
    28–31, 97, 129
    things to avoid 140
    tickets 132
    tips for families 139
    Universal Studios®
    Florida 7, 24–7, 97
    Wet 'n Wild 7, 34–5, 97
Thompson Aire 110
Thrifty 130
thrill rides 42–3
Thurston House 145
Tiffany, Louis Comfort 60
timeshare rentals 148
tipping 134
Titan Centaur rocket 40
Titan II rocket 40

Titanic – The Experience 44, 99, 100
Titanic Dinner Event 81
Todd English's bluezoo 69
Tomorrowland's Lunching Pad 8
Tosohatchee State Reserve 53
tourist information 128, 130
Tourist Information Center 130
trains 126
Transformers: The Ride 3D 25
travel 126–7
traveler's checks 136
Treasure Tavern 81
Tree of Life 19
TrenD 92
Tri-Circle-D Ranch 56
Turtle Point 30
Turtle Trek 30
Twain, Mark 14
Twilight Zone Tower of Terror 16, 42
Twister – Ride It Out 24
Typhoon Lagoon 48, 89

U

United Kingdom
Consulate 131
World Showcase Pavilion 15
Universal
CityWalk® & Portofino Bay Ride 47
dining with Universal characters 71
disabled guests 138
Islands of Adventure® 6, 20–3, 97
resorts 142
restaurants 139
Universal Studios® Florida 7, 24–7, 97
Uptown Art Expo 64
US entry requirements 126

V

vegetarian food 134
Via Napoli 95
Victoria & Albert's 68, 94
Vietnamese District 114
Villas at Disney Institute 149
Villas of Grand Cypress 143

VIP Tours 129
visas 126
Visit Florida 135
von Braun, Wernher 40
Voyage of the Little Mermaid 17

W

Waldorf Astoria Golf Club 54
Walgreens 131
walk-in clinics 131, 135
Walker Medical & Mobility Products 138
walking 127
Walt Disney World Dolphin 142
Walt Disney World Marathon 57
Walt Disney World Railroad 10
Walt Disney World® Resort and Lake Buena Vista 88–95
map 88
nighttime attractions 93
restaurants 94–5
shopping 92
Walt Disney World Swan 142
Warbird Adventures 110
Washington Mutual 130
water, drinking 133, 135
water parks 48–9, 89
Blizzard Beach 48, 89
clothing for 139, 140
Discovery Cove 48, 97
Kissimmee Family Aquatic Center 49
River Country 48–9, 89
Typhoon Lagoon 48, 89
Water Mania 48, 108
Wet 'n Wild® 7, 34–5, 48, 97
Waterhouse, William H. 120
Waterhouse Residence & Carpentry Museum 120
Watermark 128
watersports 56
Wekiwa Springs State Park 52
Wells Fargo 130
Western Union 136
Wet 'n Wild® 7, 34–5, 48, 97
Wheatley Park 53
White, Edward H. 41
White Wolf Café 117
Wild Arctic 28

Wings of Wonder 36
Winnie the Pooh 9
Winter Park Family Practice 131
Winter Park Farmers' Market 121
Winter Park, Maitland and Eatonville 118–23
bars and nightspots 122
cafés and restaurants 123
map 118
Winter Park Memorial Hospital 131
Winter Park Police 131
Winter Park Scenic Boat Tour 45, 119, 121
Winter Park Sidewalk Arts Festival 64
Winter Summerland Miniature Golf 90–91
Wishes Nighttime Spectacular 10
WMFE 90.7-FM 128
Wolfgang Puck's Café 94
Wonderland Tea Party 71
WonderWorks 45, 99, 100
Woody Woodpecker's Nuthouse Coaster 26, 43
World Gate Resort 145
World of Disney 92
World Showcase Pavilions 14–15
Wright, Frank Lloyd 83
WTKS 104.1-FM 128

X

X-15 rocket 40
X-43A Launch Vehicle 40

Y

Ybor City 82
Yuletide Fantasy 129

Z

Zellwood Sweetcorn Festival 64–5
Zip Orlando 45 107
zoos
Central Florida Zoo & Botanical Gardens 85
Jungleland Zoo 45
Lowry Park Zoo 82
Zora Neale Hurston National Museum of Fine Arts 61, 120

Acknowledgments

The Authors
Richard Grula lives in Orlando and specializes in writing about the downtown and cultural scenes. He's contributed to the *Orlando Weekly*, *Orlando Magazine*, *Sidewalk.com*, and *Time Out's Guide to Miami and Orlando*.

Jim and Cynthia Tunstall are Central Florida natives who have written five other Florida guides, including Frommer's *Walt Disney World & Orlando*.

Produced by Departure Lounge, London
Editorial Director Naomi Peck
Art Editor Lee Redmond
Editor Clare Tomlinson
Designer Lisa Kosky, Rachel Symons
DTP Designer Ingrid Vienings
Picture Researcher Monica Allende, Ellen Root
Research Assistance Amaia Allende, Ana Virginia Aranha, Diveen Henry, Faiyaz Kara
Proofreader Stephanie Driver
Indexer Hilary Bird
Fact Checkers Phyllis and Arvin Steinberg
Photographers Gregory Matthews, Magnus Rew
Additional Photography Dan Bannister, Demetrio Carrasco, Stephen Whitehorn, Linda Whitwham,
Illustrator Lee Redmond
Maps John Plumer

AT DORLING KINDERSLEY
Publishing Manager Kate Poole
Senior Art Editor Marisa Renzullo
Director of Publishing Gillian Allan
Publisher Douglas Amrine
Revisions Team Ashwin Adimari, Emma Anacootee, Claire Baranowski, Sherry Collins, Joseph Hayes, Christine Heilman, Laura Jones, Bharti Karakoti, Sumita Khatwani, Esther Labi, Kathryn Lane, Anwesha Madhukalya, Sonal Modha, Mary Ormandy, Rada Radojicic, Mani Ramaswamy, Beverly Smart, Susana Smith Bos Walford, Ajay Verma, Marian Virginia Warder
Cartography Co-ordinator Casper Morris
DTP Jason Little, Conrad van Dyk
Production Sarah Dodd

Picture Credits
Key: a-above; b-below/bottom; c-center; f-far; l-left; r-right; t-top.

This book makes reference to various Disney copyrighted characters, trademarks, marks and registered marks owned by The Walt Disney Company and Disney Enterprises, Inc.

The publishers would like to thank the following individuals, companies and picture libraries for permission to reproduce their photographs:

ALAMY IMAGES: Gerrit de Heus 27cl; Kelly Shannon Kelly 92tl; Ilene MacDonald 66tl; ARABIAN NIGHTS: 80b; BLUE MARTINI 74tl; BOGGY CREEK AIRBOAT RIDES: 110tl

CHOICE HOTELS INTERNATIONAL, INC.: 146tl; CHRIS CASLER: 77ca, 78b; 2000 CORNELL FINE ARTS MUSEUM: 118tr

CORBIS /Phelan Ebenhack/ZUMA Press 107tl; /Kevin Morris 64tr; /David Muench 36-7; /Michael T. Sedam 64tr; /Patrick Ward 109bl; COWBOYS ORLANDO: 116tr
DEPARTURE LOUNGE: 136tr, 137tl; DISCOVERY COVE: 48tr, 50-51, 97c;

© DISNEY 8-9, 10, 12-13, 14, 16-17, 18-19, 56cl, *La Nouba* by Cirque du Soleil, 89, 91, 93, 94, 95, DOUBLETREE GUEST SUITES: 144tl; FIRESTONE LIVE: 76tl, 78tl; FLORIDA ECO_SAFARIS: 108bl, FLORIDA FILM FESTIVAL 64c, 65br; GAY DAYS: 65bl; GAYLORD PALMS RESORT & CONVENTION CENTER: 58c; GENESIS SPACE PHOTO LIBRARY: 40tc, 40c; GUESTCOUNTS HOSPITALITY: 105tl; HARD ROCK Orlando: 76cl; © HEIDI TARGEE: 46tl, 99c, 114b, HOLIDAY INN: 141tl; HOLIDAY INN WALT DISNEY: 144tr; ICEBAR Orlando: 100tl.

KENNEDY SPACE CENTER: 3br, 7b, 38-39c, 38c, 38b, 39t, 39c, 39b, 40tl; KISSIMMEE-ST CLOUD CONVENTION & VISITORS' BUREAU, 48c, 108tc, 110tr; Doug Dukane: 47, 56tl, 56tr, 57tr, 106tl, 109tl, 110tc

MAD COW THEATRE Tom Hurst 63ca; © MEDIEVAL TIMES: 80tl; MERRITT ISLAND NATIONAL WILDLIFE REFUGE: 7cr, 36c, 36, 37b

© NASA: 40tr, 41c, 41b; ORLANDO TOURISM BUREAU, London: 53, 57cl, 57cr, 00tl, 00tr

ORLANDO & ORANGE COUNTY CONVENTION & VISITORS' BUREAU, INC: 3tr, 44tl, 54b, 55, 62tl, 62tr, 62b, 67tl, 75tr, 76cl, 101tr, 106tr, 109tr, 109br, 112c, 115cr, 119t, 127tl; ORLANDO INTERNATIONAL FRINGE FESTIVAL: 64tl; PARK PLAZA GARDENS: 68tr; PARLIAMENT HOUSE. 79, RIVERSHIP ROMANCE: Jeff Drake 84cr; ROMANO'S MACARONI GRILL: 70cl; ROSEN INN INTERNATIONAL: 146tl

SEAWORLD PARKS AND ENTERTAINMENT All rights reserved: 3bl, 3tl, 7tr, 28-29cs, 28t, 28c, 29t, 29clb; 30tl, 30tr, 30b, 31c, 31b, 32-33, 42-43b, 43tl, 43c, 129, 139tl, Jason Collier 29clb; SKYVENTURE LLC, ORLANDO: 45tc; THE SOCIAL CLUB: 116tl; SPA AT THE WYNDHAM PALACE RESORT: 59; STARWOOD 148tl

© UNIVERSAL ORLANDO RESORT All rights reserved: 3tc, 4-5, 6tr, 6bl, 20-21c, 20t, 20b, 21t, 22tl, 22tc, 22tr, 22c, 23c, 23b, 24-25, 24t, 24c, 24b, 25t, 26t, 26tr, 42tl, 42tr, 42c, 43b, 46tr, 65cr, 68b, 86-87, 96tr, 97t, 104tl, 104tc, 126tr, 142; US FISH AND WILDLIFE SERVICE: Gary M. Stolz 37t; VILLAS OF GRAND CYPRESS: 56tl, 57br, 88tr, 143; WALT DISNEY WORLD DOLPHIN RESORT: 69tl; WET 'N WILD: 7cl, 34-35cs, 34t, 34cl, 34b, 35t, 35cr, 35b, 48tl, 96tl; WONDERWORKS: 100tr

THE ZIMMERMAN AGENCY: The Kessler Collection: 72tl, 117tl; © ZORA NEALE HURSTON NATIONAL MUSEUM OF FINE ARTS *Festival Girl*, Jane Turner 121cl

Front Flap: SEAWORLD PHOTO/VIDEO SERVICES, FLORIDA: bcl

All other images are © Dorling Kindersley. For further information see www.dkimages.com.

Index of Main Streets

Street	Grid
Adventure Way	T2
Airport Boulevard	F6
Aloma Avenue	L5
Altamonte Avenue	B4
Amelia Street	P4
Americana Boulevard	E4
Apopka Boulevard	B3
Apopka Vineland Road	E2
Atlanta Avenue	Q2
Bear Lake Road	B3
Beachline Expressway	U5
Bennet Road	N5
Bermuda Avenue	G4
Boggy Creek Road	F5
Bonnet Creek Road	F2
Brack Street	G4
Briercliff Drive	Q3
Buena Vista Drive	G2
Bumby Avenue	N4
Canada Avenue	T3
Canton Avenue	L4
Carrier Drive	T2
Central Boulevard	P2
Central Florida Greeneway	G3
Central Florida Parkway	T6
Chase Road	E2
Church Street	P2
Clarcona-Ocoee Road	C2
Clay Street	M3
Concord Street	N4
Conroy Road	E3
Conway Gardens Road	R5
Conway Road	Q5
Corrine Drive	N4
Crystal Lake Drive	P4
Curry Ford Road	Q4
Del Verde Way	U2
Denning Drive	L4
Division Avenue	Q2
Dixie Belle Drive	Q6
Dr Phillips Boulevard	S2
East Colonial Drive	N4
East–West Expressway	P4
Edgewater Drive	N2
Epcot Center Drive	F2
Fairbanks Avenue	L3
Ferncreek Avenue	N4
Ficquette Road	E1
Florida's Turnpike	U1
Floridian Way	F1
Forest City Road	K1
Formosa Avenue	M3
Gaston Foster Road	Q5
General Rees Road	M5
Glenridge Way	M4
Golden Rod Road	C6
Gore Street	P2
Grand Avenue	M1
Grant Street	Q3
Greenbriar Parkway	U2
Hampton Avenue	N4
Hiawassee Road	C3
Hoagland Boulevard	H3
Hollywood Way	T2
Horatio Avenue	J4
Howell Branch Road	J5
International Drive	T3
Irlo Bronson Memorial Parkway	G2
John Young Parkway	Q1
Kaley Street	Q3
Keller Road	K2
Kennedy Boulevard	K1
Kirkman Road	U2
Lake Avenue	K3
Lake Howell Road	J5
Lake Margaret Drive	R4
Lake Street	A5
Lake Sue Avenue	M4
Lake Underhill Road	P5
Lakehurst Drive	T3
Lakemont Avenue	L5
Lakeview Drive	M6
Lakeview Street	N2
Lakeville Road	B3
Langley Street	N5
Lee Road	K3
Livingston Street	P3
Magnolia Avenue	P3
Maguire Boulevard	N4
Maitland Avenue	J3
Maitland Boulevard	J3
Major Boulevard	U1
Marks Street	N3
Maury Road	M2
Michigan Street	Q3
Mills Avenue	P3
Minnesota Avenue	L3
Morse Boulevard	L4
Municipal Drive	U2
Neptune Road	H4
New York Avenue	L4
Oak Ridge Road	E4
Ocoee-Apopka Road	C2
Old Lake Wilson Drive	H1
Old Winter Garden Road	D2
Orange Avenue	P3
Orange Blossom Trail	Q2
Orange Center Boulevard	P1
Orlando Avenue	L3
Osceola Avenue	L4
Osceola Parkway	G3
Palmer Avenue	K5
Paramore Avenue	Q2
Par Street	M2
Park Avenue	A2
Pembrook Drive	J1
Pennsylvania Avenue	L4
Perimeter Road	T3
Pershing Avenue	R4
Pine Hills Road	C3
Poinciana Road	G3
Primrose Drive	P4
Princeton Street	M2
Reams Road	E1
Red Bug Lake Road	B6
Republic Drive	T4
Rio Grande Avenue	Q1
Robinson Street	P3
Sand Lake Road	S3
Sandspur Road	J3
Sanlando Springs Road	A5
Sea Harbour Drive	T5
Seaworld Drive	T5
Semoran Boulevard	N6
Silver Star Road	M1
South Street	P3
Summerlin Avenue	R3
Tampa Avenue	P1
Temple Drive	K5
Tilden Road	D1
Turkey Lake Road	T1
Universal Boulevard	T3
Via Mercado	T3
Vine Street	H4
Vineland Road	D4
Virginia Drive	N3
Vista Boulevard	F2
Wallace Road	S2
Washington Street	P2
Webster Avenue	L4
Wekwia Springs Road	A3
West Colonial Drive	N1
Westmoreland Drive	Q2
Westwood Boulevard	T5
Wetherbee Road	F5
Winter Garden-Vineland Road	E2
Winter Park Road	M4
World Drive	F2
Wymore Road	K2